the
STRATEGIC DESIGNER

the

STRATEGIC DESIGNER

tools and techniques for managing the design process

DAVID HOLSTON

CINCINNATI, OHIO
WWW.HOWDESIGN.COM

For more excellent books and resources for designers, visit www.howdesign.com.

15 14 13 12 11   5 4 3 2 1

Distributed in Canada by Fraser Direct, 100 Armstrong Avenue, Georgetown, Ontario, Canada L7G 5S4, Tel: (905) 877-4411. Distributed in the U.K and Europe by F+W Media International, Brunel House, Newton Abbot, Devon, TQ12 4PU, England, Tel: (+44) 1626-323200, Fax: (+44) 1626-323319, E-mail: postmaster@davidandcharles. co.uk. Distributed in Australia by Capricorn Link, P.O. Box 704, Windsor, NSW 2756 Australia, Tel: (02) 4577-3555.

Library of Congress Cataloging-in-Publication Data

Holston, David.
  The strategic designer / David Holston.
      p. cm.
  ISBN 978-1-60061-799-7 (pbk. : alk. paper)
  1. Design services. 2. Artistic collaboration. 3. Customer relations. I. Title.
  NK1173.H65 2011
  745.4--dc22

                        2010045530

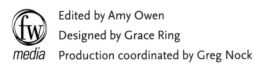
Edited by Amy Owen
Designed by Grace Ring
Production coordinated by Greg Nock

ABOUT THE AUTHOR

© Marsha Miller

With over 25 years experience, Dave Holston has worked in the fields of design management, advertising, marketing and public affairs for some of the world's largest organizations—helping them take a strategic design approach that integrates planning, research, implementation and evaluation.

As the Director of Strategic Design Management at The University of Texas at Austin, Dave is responsible for the development and management of the university's brand as well as leading a nationally recognized design team in the creation of print and web collateral, research, advertising and brand management.

Prior to working with the university, Dave served as lead designer for General Electric Services, Martin Marietta Services and Lockheed Martin Services companies. He has also held the position of Senior Art Director at the Philadelphia advertising firm Signature Communications, and later Creative Director for the European PC game developer Blue Byte Software. Throughout his career, Dave has focused on positioning design as key component of business success.

He lives in Austin, Texas, with his wife and two daughters.

TABLE OF CONTENTS

foreword
A SHARED LANGUAGE x
by Shawn M. McKinney

introduction
THE NEW DESIGNER I
New Skills for the Conceptual Economy

chapter 1
MAGIC FOOTSTEPS AND WICKED PROBLEMS 17
An Overview of the Design Process

chapter 2
A FRAMEWORK FOR GETTING THINGS DONE WELL 39
The Value of Process

chapter 3
THE COLLABORATIVE DESIGNER 65
Creating a Strong Client–Designer Relationship

chapter 4
DESIGNING IN CONTEXT 97
Empathic Design Through Research

chapter 5
UNDERSTANDING THE BUSINESS III
Linking Design and Business

chapter 6
UNDERSTANDING THE AUDIENCE 140
Designing for People

chapter 7
WHAT'S THE BIG IDEA? 176
Managing the Complexity of Concept Development

chapter 8
MAKING STRATEGY VISIBLE 206
Design Development

chapter 9
DESIGN ACCOUNTABILITY 230
Design in the Land of the Bottom Line

chapter 10
PLANNING IN A TURBULENT ENVIRONMENT 251
Managing the Design Process

chapter 11
REFINING YOUR PROCESS 273
Implementing Design Process

ACKNOWLEDGMENTS 284

INDEX 286

foreword
A SHARED LANGUAGE

BY SHAWN M. MCKINNEY

Several years ago, over dinner with a mentor, I brought up the perennially difficult question of explaining to someone what we designers do for a living. How does one possibly explain design to someone unfamiliar with the discipline, without getting bogged down in an exhaustive, self-referential exercise in futility?

He laughed and began moving his silverware around. He caused his knife to trade places with his fork, then after a moment's consideration, returned them to their original positions. He slid his fork a half-inch to his left, then a few nudges north. He straightened his spoon to run exactly parallel to his knife and fork. He moved his water glass a bit to his left, to left-align it precisely with his knife. This, he suggested, is what we do.

In essence, as designers, this IS what we do. We move things about. We consider new combinations, new possibilities. We align one thing with another. We create physical (and psychological, and metaphorical) relationships. We consider size, weight, space, proportion, materiality and so forth. We utilize, knowingly or not, design author Robin Williams's catchy list of principles: Contrast, Repetition, Alignment, Proximity. We constantly add to the world's landfills while struggling to improve our visual environments. We do much, in fact, to order, organize, reinterpret, shape and communicate ideas, information and space.

Yet, we continue to struggle to communicate what exactly we do, and why it is of value and significance. In particular, we struggle to communicate the value of design to the business community. Our professional organization, the American Institute of Graphic Arts, has devoted many hours and resources over the past several years to address just this. Yet too often, designers perceive business as fundamentally foreign to our way of thinking, while business leaders are often reluctant to credit the role design plays in their own success. We can hardly fail to acknowledge each other's presence, yet we often find ourselves without a clue as to how to join forces, how to find common ground and share notes. Business we tend to think of as a left-brain activity, while certainly design belongs to the right. Yet, we need both sides, working together, to function effectively. Designers stand to benefit immensely from strengthening their business acumen, while business people only increase their chances of success by thinking more like designers.

How then, to bring both sides together, to build bridges, to encourage a mutually beneficial dialogue and collaboration? It just so happens we share a language. That language is "process," as Dave Holston makes clear in the pages that follow. Both designers and business people have their own ways of doing things, particular processes and procedures for solving problems and achieving results. Yet, we share many principles in common.

In both the worlds of business and design, as in many other walks of life, repetition is a key element of success. What distinguishes the professional from the amateur, first and foremost, are degrees of skill, discipline, and experience that enable someone to repeat a process as a means of obtaining a desired result, again and again. In areas of practice such as business, medicine and food preparation, repetition and predictability are essential. Creativity and experimentation are perhaps emphasized more strongly and more often in the field of design, yet here, too, on closer inspection, we see the importance of repetition and process. Here, too, we can see the essential role that process and repetition play in producing success.

How, then, does one move from amateur to professional status? One route is several years of intensive on-the-job training, under the expert tutelage of seasoned veterans dealing with everyday challenges. Many design disciplines do not currently require professional certification, or even a college degree. A strong portfolio of work, solid references, and the ability to make a convincing presentation may still be enough to secure an entry-level position. Yet, such designers are often marked by a lack of critical perspective, an ignorance of design history and theory, a limited understanding of responsible practice.

Another path involves pursuing a formal design education. A key component sustaining the educational philosophy of the Savannah College of Art and Design, among the nation's largest such institutions, "process" is no ordinary design term. For example, as any graphic design professor at SCAD will verify, most projects in most courses require students to create and submit a process book, along with final work they submit for a project grade. A process book represents an organized journal or scrapbook that helps a student organize and articulate the journey that led him to solve a design problem or complete a design experiment.

SCAD students do not simply operate without restraint, or attempt to "reinvent the wheel" every time they sit down to a blank piece of paper or a glowing computer screen. Even ideation often takes place in a context of mutual observation, feedback, discipline, accountability and purpose. Students are asked not only to explain their ideas and solutions, but also, given specific guidelines and requirements, to document their process. While creativity is certainly emphasized, organization and focus are considered equally valuable. Every student is also required to complete a course in "The Business of Graphic Design," an integral part of the curriculum rapidly gaining favor in other institutions. As this book and current trends in global competitiveness should make clear, in the near future creativity alone will hardly guarantee success in a field as complex and essential as design.

Process is a concept—a way of doing design, a way of doing business—that neither professionals nor students can afford to ignore. Process is the language of business. Process is the language of design.

—SHAWN M. MCKINNEY
eLearning Professor,
Savannah College of Art and Design
December, 2010

introduction

THE NEW DESIGNER

NEW SKILLS FOR THE
CONCEPTUAL ECONOMY

A few years back I had the good fortune of having lunch with a notable head of a design research firm. Our conversation ran the gamut from ethnography to corporate leadership to design's importance in business. When I asked whether his company employed designers, he responded matter-of-factly that they did not, and that "design is a commodity."

You may or may not agree with that statement, but consider that today just about anyone with an Internet connection and $300 can get a logo, brochure, or web design, all from the comfort of their couch, without ever having to meet with a designer. Companies like crowdSPRING, LogoTournament, Logoworks, IdeaBounty.com, and iStock can provide design customers with a range of options, quickly and cheaply through a crowd-sourcing strategy. In this model, designers compete against each other, and the client pays only for the idea he selects. These services are targeted at small to midsize companies that see value in developing visual identities, but either do not have the means or desire to engage with design agencies. Most significantly, these design clients do not see a difference in the value provided from crowd-sourced options and professional designers. When customers see products as similar and make their selection based on price, this is called commoditization.

For the design community this is unnerving on several levels. Not only is it seen as devaluing the design profession by allowing nonprofessionals to compete, but some of these services are seen as unethical and in violation of professional standards, particularly the concept of working on spec. However, for clients with limited budgets and limited thresholds for risk, these services provide a real value. To them, the value of a professionally designed logo, website, or photo compared to one designed by an anonymous designer is negligible. Ultimately the market cares little for professional standards, and no amount of fist shaking and professional credos will stop the democratization of design that has been made possible by the availability of computers, accessible graphic design software and a desire on the part of people to participate in the creation of not only design, but the products, services, and experiences that touch their lives.

The question is: How do designers compete in this new environment?

GOOD NEWS FOR RIGHT-BRAINERS

The answer lies in the ability for designers to offer a unique value to their clients—specifically a value that rivals cannot easily copy. An area that provides opportunities for this distinction is design thinking. Whereas the craft of design is threatening to be commoditized, design thinking has gained in stature. In 2000, U.S. Federal Reserve Board Chairman Alan Greenspan said that technical know-how would be superseded by "the ability to create, analyze, and transform information and to interact effectively with others." This idea is echoed in Daniel Pink's book *A Whole New Mind*, in which Pink projects that the future economy will be driven by six key "senses": design, story, symphony, empathy, play, and meaning. For designers with a collaborative spirit and the ability to collect and synthesize information, this is good news.

As competition increases and client needs expand, it is becoming clear that designers in this new era must not only be experts in form, as they traditionally have been, but they must be equally skilled in solving more complex problems by calling on a broader range of skills in the social sciences, technology, and the organization of teams. The ability to collaborate, manage the increasing complexity of design problems, to design "in context" to their target audiences, and to be accountable for design decisions through measurement transforms designers from "makers of things" to "design strategists." Along with the ability to create form, these skills complete the designer of the conceptual economy.

Anne Burdick, chair of the graduate Media Design Program at Art Center College of Design, has projected how design education can best prepare designers to take on these responsibilities. Burdick writes in her article "Graduate Education: Preparing Designers for Jobs That Don't Exist (Yet)," that designers are moving beyond traditional roles to take on bigger, more expansive responsibilities. Burdick goes on to say, "As researchers and entrepreneurs, they must be prepared to generate self-defined areas of investigation and opportunity. This expansion places a new set of demands on design education. Designers need the tools and skills to conceptualize people's lives, to visualize and understand the circulation of capital, people and culture at a global scale, and to intelligently envision the future."

Paul Nini, associate professor in the department of design at the Ohio State University, has been aware of the need to properly prepare students with a broader range of studies like research, social sciences, and business. In his design program at Ohio State, Nini makes a point of exposing students to these areas, showing them how these activities fit into the design profession. Nini describes the curriculum as a combination of courses like business, management, planning, sociology, psychology and other areas outside of the traditional fine arts curriculum.

Frank Tyneski, executive director of the Industrial Design Society of America (IDSA), believes that when imbued with a broader perspective that includes research, students can take their design to a new level. In a *BusinessWeek* interview, Tyneski says, "When it comes to problem solving, [design students] are going deep. They are doing research, contextual inquiry. They have the Internet now, so the tools are available to get a deeper understanding, and they really understand the process of design thinking with greater depth than previous generations."

The New York Times's creative director Khoi Vinh has echoed these ideas, stating in a *BusinessWeek* interview with design educator and author Steven Heller, "The new designer is adaptable across multiple media and multiple disciplines. She can design in a way that's truly native to the web, to mobile devices, to print, to environmental projects. And she can think in terms of concept, execution, and the business equation as well. She's used to doing it all herself, but she can reach out to others when she needs to—and orchestrate those teams to achieve her goals."

In their book, *The Design Experience,* professors Mike Press and Rachel Cooper observe this trend as well, pointing out, "Designers are a combination of craft maker, cultural intermediary, and opportunistic entrepreneur. And of course they are other things as well. They are skilled researchers, lifelong learners, who understand that design—as a very process of change itself—must be informed by knowledge."

Clearly the design profession is starting to put more emphasis on a broader set of skills. However, the idea of a well-rounded design professional is hardly a new concept. In 1957, Henry Dreyfuss said, "A successful performer in this *new* field is a man of many hats. He does more than merely design things. He is a businessman as well as a person who makes drawings and models. He is a keen observer of public taste, and he has painstakingly cultivated his own taste. He has an understanding of merchandising, how things are made, packed, and distributed, and displayed. He accepts the responsibility of his position as liaison linking management, engineering, and the consumer and cooperates with all three."

THE FOUR PRINCIPALS OF THE NEW DESIGNER

The thought of orchestrating the diverse disciplines that make up business, research, social sciences, and design into the design process can seem daunting. However, we see that these areas can be captured in four basic principles.

PRINCIPAL 1: THE NEW DESIGNER EMBRACES COMPLEXITY

How do designers move from the realm of "makers of things" to that of strategists? The first step is to embrace the complexity of design problems. Design is not solely about creating good-looking artifacts, but requires multiple considerations when solving problems such as audience context and the client's business environment. The ability of designers to dive deeply into complex problems takes them from decorators to problem solvers.

PRINCIPAL 2: THE NEW DESIGNER IS COLLABORATIVE

How do designers bring expertise and insight to bear on design problems? Elizabeth Sanders, founder of the design research firm MakeTools, says that,

"The market-driven world has given way to the people-driven era." Sanders points out that a great deal of people without design backgrounds are actively participating in design, and that the distinction between the various aspects of design disciplines are blurring. These factors have put a great deal of emphasis on the collaborative nature of design, particularly on the front-end phases of the design process. Designers are now co-creators with people from other disciplines. Search engine optimization (SEO) specialists, shopper marketing consultants, design researchers, systems analysts, copywriters, and even other designers. In addition to these work teams, clients and audiences must also be engaged. As designers participate more collaboratively, they need to be able to explain their work processes and how they create value. By providing a framework for working together, designers elevate themselves in the hierarchy of teams and organizations, and become valued strategic partners. In the face of increased competition, collaboration is one advantage designers have when working with clients. Designer and author Ellen Shapiro points out that "even the least informed clients with the lowest budgets need to meet with and work personally with their designers." As Shapiro said, only through real human interaction and collaboration can design position itself to go beyond the realms of commodity.

PRINCIPAL 3: THE NEW DESIGNER DESIGNS IN CONTEXT

How do we ensure our design solutions are meaningful? The short answer: By providing a solution that embraces both the business needs of the client and the needs of the audience. Business and audiences are the foundation for design problem solving. Research provides valuable tools for gaining insight into the organizational needs of these two groups. Business tools, like competitive and situational analysis, help designers understand the business environment, allowing them to develop design solutions that are strategic. With audiences, designers can call upon visualization exercises, word games, prototyping and participatory design, actively engaging users in the development of ideas. Traditional tools like focus group, interviews, and ethnography can also provide valuable insights. To paraphrase communications guru Don Schultz, communication is about people, and when we lose sight of the individual, we lose sight of the objectives of communication.

PRINCIPAL 4: THE NEW DESIGNER IS ACCOUNTABLE

How do designers prove their value? The price of a seat at the decision-making table is accountability. For designers, this means being able to communicate the value of design in terms of a return that is meaningful to their clients. Whether tracking changing attitudes, behaviors, sales numbers, the return on investment of design activities, or customer satisfaction, designers elevate their work by establishing metrics for their projects. Although design does not exist in a vacuum and can be a challenge to measure, design metrics help clarify the value of design and provide a way to track the effectiveness of design activities. These four principles flow through the framework of design process. What follows is a typical design process.

1. **Project initiation:** This phase is focused on aligning stakeholders toward a common goal and requires collaborative planning to address complex design problems.

   Skills: Business, interpersonal, organizational, and communication planning skills.

2. **Design research:** This phase defines the context for making design decisions. Centered on the needs of business stakeholders and audiences, this phase relies heavily on collaboration as a means for gathering insights and understanding meaning.

   Skills: Social sciences, interpersonal, qualitative, quantitative, and analytical research skills.

3. **Concept development:** This phase synthesizes the research into an idea and requires divergent and collaborative thinking from multiple perspectives.

   Skills: Creative, ideation, and facilitation skills.

4. **Design development:** This phase is focused on convergence of ideas and developing an aesthetic that is relevant to the audience and the business goal.

   Skills: Design, production, and manufacturing skills.

5. Evaluation: This phase makes design accountable through the measurement of outcomes, whether they are financial, attitudinal, or behavioral.

Skills: Business, accounting and marketing skills.

By looking at design systemically, as a group of interacting skills brought together to create a whole, designers can think about their work in new ways and bring their inherent creativity to bear more broadly. Through process, designers can better orchestrate the needs of business and audiences, manage the complexity of design problems, and provide a framework for collaboration.

THE NEW DESIGNER IS A BUSINESS PARTNER

Darrel Rhea, CEO of Cheskin Added Value, has said that one of the biggest challenges designers face today is making themselves relevant to business. Unfortunately, designers are often brought in at the end of a project and asked to articulate a strategy without understanding what the strategy is or how it was devised. In these scenarios, design is seen as a support service. To break this pattern, the New Designer must exhibit an understanding of how business strategy is developed, and must provide tools to better understand audience need, and be fluent in the basics of business language. By spanning this gap between business and design disciplines, designers build credibility and trust with their clients.

The good news is that the business world is poised to embrace design. John Byrne, editor-in-chief of *Fast Company,* has observed that companies like Samsung and Target use design to achieve an advantage over their competitors. Byrne projects that in the next decade, design will offer a greater competitive advantage than technology has in the past because it is easy and quick, and offers the best chances for return on investment.

Consider how Starbucks and Walmart have both used visual design as part of their competitive strategy. Both companies faced business challenges that they addressed by employing a design solution. Starbucks, dealing with declining sales and closing stores, reverted to their original logo, with the goal of reminding patrons why they sipped their coffee there in the first place.

After an eight-year hiatus, CEO Howard Schultz brought back the old logo, which features a rustic Norse-inspired woodcut of a twin-tailed mermaid, developed by Seattle advertising and design agency Heckler & Associates. The company had phased out the original logo in 1987, when the more familiar modern style was introduced. Similarly, Walmart, in a bid to acknowledge its newfound greenness, updated its logo in the fall of 2008. The new logo is friendlier, softer, and features a flowerlike star, no doubt to put a kinder, gentler spin on a company that has faced concerns over its treatment of employees, environmental practices, and women's rights.

Beyond aesthetics, these updates were flags indicating significant change in the organizations' competitive strategy. What impact these updates will have remains to be seen; however, it represents a significant investment on the part of the companies, and illustrates both businesses' commitment to the power of design.

Roger Martin, dean of the Rotman School of Management at the University of Toronto, is reshaping his entire MBA program around the principle that "design skills and business skills are converging." Martin says, "It's time to embrace a new value proposition based on creating—indeed, often co-creating—new products and services with customers that fill their needs, make them happy, and make companies and shareholders rich." He also says that the design skills of "understanding, empathy, problem solving" are what businesses needs today.

On the design side of the coin, designers are reaching out to business. Dave Mason, principal of the Chicago/Vancouver design firm smbolic (formerly SamataMason), speaks of forging the link, with an emphasis on the value of design process. Mason says, "Businesspeople are a lot more aware of design now, and these businesspeople are process driven. And they believe, as they have been taught, that if they follow certain processes they will be successful." Mason points out that what business doesn't like is to work on instinct. "If you've taught all your life that process equals success, then you will naturally want to know that the people you are engaging with have a process that you can understand so you can make a rational judgment."

In addition to providing a transparent design process, it is also critical that designers are able to communicate the value of their work and include specific steps for measuring design. Rob Wallace, managing partner of the Manhattan-based brand and package design firm Wallace Church, believes that designers are still only speaking to themselves, and not to business. "Designers need to relate to businesspeople in the one measure of success that they have, which is the impact on sales and profit." Wallace says, "It's important that designers learn the language, learn the vernacular, and start speaking in terms of financial investment and design's impact." Process offers a shared language and methodology that businesspeople understand, and when it includes a measurement phase, designers step up and become accountable like other disciplines in the business world.

HOW DESIGN PROCESS PROVIDES VALUE TO THE CLIENT

Business is competitive. Firms jockey for advantage while navigating an ever-changing social, financial, and political environment, struggling to continually refine processes, products, and services; keep abreast of changing consumer demands; and work in emerging markets. To stay on top, firms try to capitalize in the areas of innovation, speed to market, risk management, and effective work processes. These areas are relevant to designers as well. Consider how the design team at Kraft must react to the constantly changing needs of over 220 brands, or how websites like Amazon must constantly monitor and modify their online presence to stay ahead of the curve. Process offers a framework for managing these important considerations.

THE NEED TO INNOVATE

New ideas drive business. The Council of Competitiveness, a group of CEOs, university presidents, and labor leaders, sees innovation as the basis of America's economic success. As companies compete to find the next great thing, they look for ways to move from concept to market as quickly as possible. To do this, they use structured ways of developing, testing, and moving ideas towards production.

Businesses, like designers, need to be in a constant state of ideation. Design gives firms a competitive advantage in overcrowded markets by identifying unique value and connecting audiences, as well as reacting quickly to social trends. By using a defined process that accommodates the development of new ideas, designers give themselves the tools to innovate and ensure that ideas get implemented within the organization. These processes are applicable to product design, communication design, and service design.

THE NEED FOR SPEED

From e-mail, instant messaging, Twitter, and Skype, the ability to quickly connect person-to-person is now commonplace. This speed is expected in business as well. The first to establish an offering usually dominates the market, making speed to market an important factor in competitive strategy. Design process offers designers and clients a framework for moving forward on projects quickly. Process cuts down on development time by offering a structure for coming up with meaningful concepts that are tied to business objectives. Process also keeps the project team aligned so that downtime is minimized and up time is used more efficiently.

THE NEED TO MANAGE RISK

By its very nature, design projects are ripe for risk. The content arrives late or is incomplete, or worse, incorrect. Schedules are jeopardized by late agreement on direction or sudden changes in content. Budgets are blown. Clients are unhappy. The final piece is ineffective. In short, design is a risky endeavor often centered around an uncertain outcome. Design process integrates controls like design briefs, change orders and sign-offs at critical phases to help manage the uncertainties.

THE NEED TO MANAGE PROJECTS EFFICIENTLY

Design projects often entail aligning people, building consensus, gathering information, and thinking creatively to produce an artifact or service that motivates the audience to act or think in a certain way. Project management skills are applicable in a variety of design-related disciplines, including architecture, new product development, and communications. Almost all of these disciplines impose some structure on the development of their product, whether it is a new building, a coffeepot, a brochure, a retail space, or a website.

THE NEED FOR COLLABORATION AND CO-CREATION

Consider how LEGO harnesses the power of consumers to help develop new products. In 2003, LEGO began gathering data from consumers over the Internet via online dialogs. Through these conversations, LEGO began to realize that their customers don't only want to be consumers; they want to be influencers of the brand. In similar fashion, Converse engaged its users to make ads for its 2005 campaign. As a result, web traffic increased a whopping 40 percent and sales went up 12 percent that quarter. Today, people who have passion and knowledge about music, art, design and video are now doing many of the things that used to be the sole property of design and marketing professionals. This is a result of the public being exposed to a broader range of educational experiences, as well as the accessibility of the tools needed to create new works. For designers, this means clients and audiences are savvy about communication and can offer intelligent opinions on how it's done. Additionally, there is an expectation from clients and audiences that they will be active members of the design process. Therefore, the design process should be transparent so that these creative minds can be active participants in solving their own design problems.

Today, co-creation and participatory design are fueling several successful business models. Companies are benefiting from the creativity that a willing public provides. Co-creation brings companies and audiences together, allowing audiences an opportunity to create ideas and designs while companies provide the manufacturing and distribution. The T-shirt design company Threadless typifies this idea. The company had its humble beginnings in Chicago when Jake Nickell and Jacob DeHart started the online company on a shoestring budget. Fans of the site contribute designs, and the company allows customers to vote on the T-shirts they like best. The winning designs are put into production and offered online. Eight years after its start, Threadless has revenues of $30 million.

As companies strive to connect to audiences, they find that engaging them in the front end of design decisions has many advantages. Audiences have typically had difficulty expressing their needs. This would explain the incredibly high rate of failure for new products. The traditional marketing methods of surveys, focus groups, and interviews are not always enough to truly understand what customers want. Only when audiences become active participants in the design process do companies gain true insight.

The designer's process has been until recently a closed door. Protective of their processes, afraid of exposing how the "magic" of design is done, designers have tightly guarded their methods. However, these attitudes are changing. In the new collaborative environment design is becoming open source, available to team members, clients, and audiences. Designers are now asked to co-create with people from other disciplines. Clients, once thought of as the spoilers of great design, are now seen as the source of creative ideas and an integral part of developing meaningful design concepts. Audiences are mixing into the equation as well, often providing the most influential insights toward solving design problems. By having a framework for working together, designers can harness the knowledge and insight of these groups, elevate themselves in the hierarchy of teams and organizations, and become valued strategic partners.

For many creatives, collaboration can be uncomfortable—multiple voices competing for dominance, toes being stepped on, and egos bruised come to mind. But consider the Orpheus Chamber Orchestra. Orpheus was founded by New York City cellist Julian Fifer, who started the Grammy Award–winning chamber music orchestra almost thirty years ago. Traditional orchestras are made up of multidisciplined musicians who must be sensitive to each other in order to produce complicated works. In most orchestras, conductors are the norm, acting as a stabilizing force, directing the musicians toward their own interpretation of the music. Orpheus, however, is unique among orchestras in that it has no conductor. In fact, the role of conductor is shared among its members. The group works on a collaborative democratic principle, with shared responsibilities and rotating participants. This collaborative spirit has won them several Grammy Awards and international collaboration from the likes of Yo-Yo Ma, Isaac Stern and Dawn Upshaw. The group has been so successful with their collaborative approach that businesses like Kraft Foods and Novartis have invited them to speak about their collaborative work process.

Designer-centric design has been a staple in the design industry for years. Often the designer's individual style is what brought him recognition and fame.

The industry, and the education programs that feed it, are now going through a sea change. The idea of authorship is eroding in the face of an increased need to reflect the audience's needs as opposed to an individual designer's style. Todd Wilkens of Adaptive Path refers to designer-centric design as "genius design," where the designer comes in with the perspective of "I am a genius. Give me the problem. I will sit in a room and solve your problem." Whereas there are some situations where this type of approach makes sense, for the most part, a more collaborative, socially constructive type of design, in which the designer is the facilitator, yields better results.

In the design program at the Ohio State University, professor Paul Nini acknowledges this evolution. "That is the key for students—creating something meaningful," he says. "I think that's the thing that students need to figure out, that they can create things for themselves, or they can create them for the people that will actually experience and use them in some way. They can actually do both, where the designer can achieve some satisfaction, and the user and audience can get something meaningful as well."

The goal of graphic design is to communicate messages by attracting and retaining viewers, with the intent of influencing their thinking and behavior. Design must consider numerous factors like perceptions, beliefs, visual language, trends, business, and culture. By including specific stages in the design process to address these factors, designers can make their work more meaningful to both clients and audiences.

THE NEED FOR TRANSPARENCY

Over the last two decades, process management has played an increasingly important role in business. From W. Edwards Deming and Total Quality Management in the 1980s to Six Sigma and Lean in the 2000s, businesses have looked to process as a way to improve quality and efficiency in their organizations. By understanding workflow, information, communication and controls, firms are able to address problems quicker, increase quality, and ultimately create value for the customer.

Design is an iterative process, requiring a series of explorations, a layering of ideas and constant refinement. Unlike the factory, which requires systematic processes to develop consistent products, design process is about going into the unknown and having the flexibility to react to any number of organizational or audience considerations.

Design processes are often tacit, and designers tend to work internally, developing concepts and ideas through idiosyncratic methods. These methods, though at times successful, frequently are difficult to share with others. As designers are asked to work in more collaborative environments, they must be able to communicate process clearly to co-workers and clients.

"Process is more important than outcome," says designer Bruce Mau. "When the outcome drives the process, we will only go to where we've already been. If process drives outcome, we may not know where we're going, but we will know we want to be there." By defining the process and going through all of the stages, the designer is able to reach his design solution via a structured thought process, arriving at an idea that meets the need of the client and addresses a specific goal. This process helps avoid the common design problem of sameness. In other words, much of design feels derivative as designers look to others' work for inspiration. Design process offers a clean approach, without assumptions or indulgences.

The process outlined in this book includes the phases of design research, concept development, design development, and measurement. These phases are common to most design projects and are used, whether consciously or not, by most designers. Granted, there are as many design processes as there are designers, each having their own approach and tools to achieve their ends. But with few exceptions design projects go through each of these phases.

IN CONCLUSION

According to the Bureau of Labor Statistics, the field of graphic design is expected to grow 13 percent through 2018. Demand for design professionals will increase, and competition for design positions will become tighter. As businesses look to hire design professionals, those who have the ability to collaborate and to manage the increasing complexity of design problems and to design "in context" to their target audiences, and to be accountable through measurement, will have greater opportunities in the marketplace. Design process provides a framework for integrating these activities, offering unique client value and differentiating their offerings in a crowded market.

chapter 1

MAGIC FOOTSTEPS
AND WICKED PROBLEMS

AN OVERVIEW OF THE DESIGN PROCESS

One hundred years ago, in a small damp basement below the streets of Seattle, teenagers Jim Casey and Claude Ryan started one of the most pervasive and successful companies in the world. United Parcel Service has emerged from its modest beginnings of a few bicycles and several well-trained family and friends to become the leader in package delivery. With over 90,000 vehicles, 300 large jets, 1,800 facilities, and more than 450,000 uniformed employees, UPS delivers more than 15 million packages to 6 million customers a day. On each of its vehicles, planes, and uniforms, the familiar UPS shield, sporting the UPS name and neatly bow-tied package, branded the service. The logo, developed by Paul Rand in 1961, became a familiar symbol across the world. But in 2003, UPS decided it was time for a change in its identity. With this kind of investment in one of their most valuable assets, why would a company the size of UPS want to make a change to their identity, and how would they go about considering all the factors that would influence and shape the new design?

BUSINESS IS EVOLVING

For UPS, the leader in air and ground shipping, the change represented not only a difference in the way they presented themselves, but a deeper change in who they were and how they would be understood by the public. The company that had made overnight package delivery a billion dollar business was growing. While package delivery would remain the core service of its business, UPS wanted to expand the range of services it provided its customers. UPS was acquiring complementary services, particularly in the area of supply chain solutions, allowing the company to expand into areas of heavy freight, ocean, and rail transport. The company also expanded into the retail business by purchasing Mail Boxes Etc., rebranding it as the The UPS Store after seeing a 70 percent increase in UPS branded stores.

Former UPS Chairman Mike Eskew understood that package delivery was the foundation of UPS's success, but that as the company responded to the expanding needs of its customers it would need to update its logo to reflect the evolution of the company. Seeing the value in communicating the right idea to the people he was serving, Eskew was willing to make a huge commitment to ensure that the perception created through its corporate identity was accurate, honest, and up-to-date.

THE UPS DESIGN PROCESS

The process UPS followed included a distinct set of phases. Each phase allowed the firm to consider factors that would influence the design, including trends, tradition, operations, stockholders, business, and customer need.

PROBLEM DEFINITION AND RESEARCH

The impetus for making a design change was based on the company's new goals and visions. But before making any design changes they hired FutureBrand, the international brand development firm, to conduct two years of design research that analyzed perceptions around the existing brand and provided insight into evolving their new identity.

CONCEPT DEVELOPMENT

Since their beginning in Seattle in 1907, UPS has had four versions of their mark. The mark has evolved over time, at first as a shield with an eagle; then a shield with "UPS" written on it, the lowercase type treatment setting the foundation for future versions; then Rand's popular shield and bow-tied package. UPS has maintained these core elements over time, reflecting an approach that favored a slow evolution of the brand. This conservative approach let shareholders, staff, stakeholders, and customers know that the redesign would be the next step in the company's evolution, but without losing its culture or tradition.

DESIGN DEVELOPMENT

With this goal in mind, designers went to work evolving the logo to its next incarnation. The famous bow-tied package was eliminated, because UPS no longer accepted tied parcels, and the company did not want to limit the perceptions to simply package delivery. The shield, which heralded back to the first logo in 1907, was made bolder and dimensional to give it more presence. Research showed that although the Rand mark was popular, audiences could not remember it and often confused it with other design elements, like the globe on the side of the delivery vehicles. Worse, audiences confused the mark with competitors' marks.

IMPLEMENTATION

Reinvigorating the mark would help in another way. With a company of UPS's scale, inconsistency in how it represented itself was always an issue. The best identity system will always have some holes in it, and this was true for UPS. Thus, the rebranding offered an opportunity for the company to rein in all of its units and get them back on the same page. In its forms, boxes, envelopes, websites and catalogs, signage, uniforms, and vehicles, UPS had not had a comprehensive design system in place. Through the new initiative, UPS would make a concerted effort to bring standards and guidance for the development of communications material, aligning its multiple units under one visual umbrella.

EVALUATION

The redesign of the UPS identity was created on the heels of the company's largest marketing campaign, "What Can Brown Do For You?" The campaign, launched in 2003, promoted the company's new capabilities and set the stage for rebranding. In 2003, UPS's revenue had increased over $2 billion. Much of this success is attributed to the rebranding initiative. UPS saw this endeavor as more than just a logo change: It was a strategic business initiative that would impact the way it was perceived by customers, employees, and stockholders. More than just a visual update, the logo would reflect a new way of working and signify a change in UPS's business strategy. Driving the redesign was a methodical process that considered business strategy, environment, and customer perceptions.

The UPS redesign offers us a look at the importance firms place on customer perceptions. UPS was willing to make a large investment in a risky change to its brand. However, with new design research emerging over the last ten years, organizations are becoming aware of the power behind their communication designs and are starting to see design as an important business asset that can be managed and structured.

As a business tool, design is coming into its own. Organizations are realizing the power of design as a tool for connecting, visually and emotionally, with audiences and customers. The effect of design can take many forms: the awareness of a new product or service, recognition of a trusted brand, or a new understanding of an old brand. The designer's role is critical to the success of these activities, and appropriate preparation and management of the design process is essential for success.

As corporate identity guru Wally Olins says, "Design is a business tool that makes a strategy visible." The visual language that designers develop is the trigger that sparks reactions in business audiences. Designers who consider a broad range of information about their audiences and work through a structured process take an important step toward elevating their discipline from a service to a strategic business tool.

THE EVOLUTION OF DESIGN PROCESS

Two and a half million years ago in the Olduvai Gorge in Tanzania, Paleolithic man developed some of the first stone tools. Rocks chipped to a fine edge allowed early man not only the ability to hunt, but also to fashion the world around him. These simple tools opened up a world of possibilities for the creation of useful objects, for both practical purposes as well as spiritual and aesthetic needs. Tracking the origins of design process back this far might seem a bit extreme, but it illustrates a point about the inherently creative nature of human beings, and our desire and need to make the world around us more livable.

Design process is born out of this need. At its core, design is about problem solving. Whether in engineering, architecture or communication, design process follows a similar methodology of problem definition, research, concept development, design and prototype development, and evaluation. Consider how software development processes parallel design process: Each requires the determination of requirements, specifications, prototyping, development, testing, and measuring of results. Unlike manufacturing process, software development requires the ability to make rapid changes throughout the process. These changes are not seen as mistakes, but as a vital part of the development process. What links design and software development is that neither have solutions that can be easily solved in linear ways. Most design and software projects have incomplete information, changing requirements, or unclear targets. These types of problems have been described as "wicked problems," or problems that are very complex and have numerous interdependencies. To address these types of problems it's required that the developer or the designer is able to "plan in a turbulent environment."

LINEAR PROCESS

When we talk of process we often envision a disciplined model, where specific phases occur in sequence, each with an assigned deliverable. Linear process is typified by its strict controls, and is used primarily to manage risk in the development process. Each phase must be fully completed before going onto the next phase, allowing designers to catch errors when they are the least expensive and time-consuming to fix. This method requires that specifications for each phase be clear and accurately described. Any error in the requirements will end up costing both time and money. This linear method is straightforward but requires discipline if it's to work effectively. It is most appropriate for projects that are "known entities," meaning there is little problem solving to be done.

In the early 1970s, the software engineer Winston Royce named this type of linear method the "waterfall" model. In general, it is useful when a specific requirement is asked for; however, when unknowns exist, as is typical in design projects, the methodology does not allow for time to "discover" and iterate through the course of the project. Royce ultimately rejected the waterfall model's effectiveness, noting that a designer needed to consider feedback between phases. Variations of the waterfall method that account for feedback and overlapping between phases, thereby allowing for the identification and correction of issues, were developed by others along the way. The spiral method, for example, combines concept development and design development phases, resulting in an iterative design approach. This method starts with information gathering, in which users are interviewed and the project scope is defined. Once this information is collected, an initial set of designs are developed, then critiqued based on how well they meet users' needs. From there, a series of prototypes are developed, each being reviewed, then evolved based on feedback. This process continues until an acceptable prototype has been developed.

AGILE METHODS: PLANNING IN A TURBULENT ENVIRONMENT

The ability to plan for the unknown is key to the design process. In their influential article, "The New New Product Development Game," Hirotaka Takeuchi and Ikujiro Nonaka describe linear and other development processes as a "relay race" where a specific phase is worked on by "specialists," and only when complete, is handed off to the next group. Takeuchi and Nonaka go on to describe a new method they call the "rugby approach," where a multidisciplinary team moves through the project together (like a rugby scrum). In stark contrast to the rigorous linear method, projects can be initiated at any phase, whether in design development, requirements or feasibility testing. The key behind this method is the interaction of the team members, whose multidisciplinary background allows the team to address the project from multiple perspectives at all its stages.

Out of this approach grew a cluster of similar flexible methods including Scrum, Extreme Programming, and Crystal Clear. All of these methods fell under the heading of "Agile" development. Agile was a response to the restrictive linear methods that seemed out of sync with the way design development actually happened, and came out of a now famous meeting of software developers in Snowbird, Utah, in 2001. The created an Agile manifesto that outlined several key points including a call for a close-knit team that communicates face-to-face, the ability to work quickly to produce a piece of working software, and the flexibility to make changes on the fly, even in the final stages of development.

The hallmark of the agile method is that it embraces change and circumstance, approaching the project knowing that it will require iteration as it progresses. This iterative model reflects the way most visual designers and design firms work, gathering data, building out quick comps (prototypes), going through several rounds of revisions, then creating a final design.

As we look at design process, it's important to realize that most design project scenarios will not be predictive but will require flexibility and the ability to react to new information and circumstances. Most importantly, the process is iterative and requires that directions, concepts, and designs be continuously refined until a final design is achieved. Though the agile approach is not as rigid as a linear process, it still requires a great deal of discipline and needs to be well managed as there are many opportunities for breakdowns, given its free-flowing nature.

Mainly design process allows designers to consider all of the critical facets of a design problem, and it provides transparency in the way that they work. The goal of using a process is not to make the "magic" creative moment scientific, or something that can be achieved by following a simple pattern. Rather, process offers opportunities to prepare the mind and provide tools to facilitate meaningful creative explorations.

Many great minds have contributed to the evolution of design process. From Moholy-Nagy and Gropius, who looked to create rational methods for design, to Herbert Simon, who applied the scientific method to design problems, experts in the disciplines of engineering, architecture, and product design have made great contributions to the advancement and understanding of design process, moving the focus of design from that of form to that of the needs of the people. One approach, developed by John Chris Jones, has been regarded as the basis for the commonly held understanding of design process. Though not the only approach, nor the most sophisticated, Jones provides a strong example of a model design process.

JOHN CHRIS JONES: DESIGN METHODS

Many consider John Chris Jones to be the godfather of modern design process. By exploring disciplines as diverse as engineering, architecture, and industrial design, Jones explored methodologies for design that considered users, aesthetics, and ergonomics, and spearheaded the "design methods" movement of the 1960s by organizing the Conference on Design Methods held in London in 1962. His goal was to bring some objectivity and rationality to the discipline of design. His thoughts were later captured in his 1970 *Design Methods* book, which outlines the stages and tools of the design process.

Jones saw that traditional methods of design were not adequate to meet the complexities of the times. Design problems were becoming more intricate and required the expertise of multiple people from various disciplines. Because solving design problems had become a collaborative process, design team members needed to externalize their thinking with the goal of making the process transparent so that design team members could see what's going on and, as Jones writes, "...contribute to it information and insights that are outside the designer's knowledge and experience."

Jones defines the new methods as having the following characteristics:

- Designing as the process of devising not individual products but whole systems or environments such as airports, transportation, hypermarkets, educational curricula, broadcasting schedules, welfare schemes, banking systems, and computer networks;

- Design as participation, the involvement of the public in the decision-making process;

- Design as creativity, which is believed to be present in everyone, potentially;

- Design as an educational discipline that unites arts and science, and perhaps can go further than either.

Jones divides design methods into three categories: creative, rational, and control methods. Creativity is described as a "black box" where the internal creative process happens. The rational methods are described as a "glass box," where all the externalized thinking occurs during a design project. Control methods provide project structure and risk management tools to keep projects working efficiently.

To manage these conflicting methods of black box and glass box, Jones describes a method of project control. These methods include risk management, defining roles and responsibilities of design team members, conducting design research, and understanding the relationship of the design and the environment in which it will exist. These project management methods are critical tools for managing cross-disciplined design teams.

In *Design Methods,* Jones looks at thirty-five new design methods that provide designers insights into user needs. Focusing as much on process as product, Jones outlines methods for a variety of situations, including techniques for design research, concept development, and evaluation methods.

Most notably, Jones breaks down the design process into three stages: divergence, transformation, and convergence—methods for creative thinking and evaluation.

DIVERGENCE

Jones describes divergence as the act of extending the boundaries of a design problem, providing more room for creative thought. In the divergent stage, the problem is explored to understand what constraints are "fixed" and which are "flexible." As in brainstorming, criticism is waived at this stage, as the goal is to look at the problem as broadly as possible.

Using the client brief as a jumping off point, problem exploration begins. The brief is seen as a flexible document, with the expectation that it will evolve as new insights and perspectives are discovered. Design research is conducted so that the problem can be placed in context. Designers should look to understand several dimensions of the problem, including risks associated with the project, what can actually be done, dependencies, and what value they can bring to the problem.

• Expand the problem boundaries
• Defer criticism
• Conduct research about the problem
• Identify risks
• Identify value

TRANSFORMATION

Transformation is when patterns are developed so that a single design can be selected. Pattern making, as Jones describes it, is "the creative act of turning a complicated problem into a simple one by changing its form and by deciding what to emphasize and what to overlook." To do this, the parameters of the project must be clearly established, including the problem boundaries, variables, and constraints. Jones suggests that problems can be broken into subgoals that can be addressed either concurrently or individually. In the visual design context, subgoals can be best understood as design features.

FIGURE 1.1
JOHN CHRIS JONES'S DESIGN METHODS

DIVERGENCE	TRANSFORMATION	CONVERGENCE
Extending the problem boundary	**Redefining the problem**	**Focusing on a solution**
This phase focuses on extending the problem boundaries and determining what aspects of the problem are fixed and which are flexible.	This is the stage when objectives and project boundaries are fixed, when critical variables are defined, constraints recognized, opportunities are taken and judgments made.	At this stage the problem has been defined, the variables identified and objectives agreed upon. The designer's aim is to reduce uncertainties until one possible design is identified.

COMPLEXITY ———————————————————→ CERTAINTY

CONVERGENCE

At this stage, the problem has been clearly defined, and several design options have been presented and tested for how well they solve the problem. Now the design options must be further tested until a single solution that best meets the design criteria is identified. The vagaries of the design ideation process are put aside, and now concrete decisions based on design specifications are to be made as quickly and cost-effectively as possible.

Although Jones was primarily thinking about large-scale projects, the design method and tools he presents can be used for any project that requires design thinking, including experience, environmental, communication, and product design.

THE DESIGN PROCESS

As designers look to become collaborators with businesses and audiences, a transparent design approach is needed. Design process offers an inclusive approach for arriving at innovative design ideas that can differentiate the client from their competition and connect at a deeper level with audiences. The design process considers key facets of business, audiences, competition, and other strategic factors that create the foundation for honest design solutions that are not driven by style or trends, but by business and audience need.

With multiple considerations to make on any given project, process helps designers stay focused on those that are most important. Process helps to manage the complexity of projects by providing a system for organizing information and people. Process provides a framework for collaboration by laying out a transparent plan that can be seen and followed by all involved. Process provides tools for understanding the context in which the design exists, including business requirement and audience needs. And finally, process helps make designers and clients accountable by identifying specific goals.

Again, the role of collaboration is important to note, since virtually every phase of the design process requires clients, audiences, and designers to work together, oftentimes as co-creators. This shared responsibility creates a sense of ownership and allows the designer to move beyond the role of design "vendor"—who simply responds to request—and toward the role of a design consultant who is able to serve in an advisory role, guiding the client through the design problem-solving process.

Design process generally consists of a client introductory phase, a research phase, a concept development phase, design development phase, and an evaluation phase. These stages can be adapted to just about any design project. The following is a concise overview of the design process. Stages, tools, and techniques are mentioned here, and described in detail in subsequent chapters.

PHASE ONE: ESTABLISHING THE CLIENT–DESIGNER RELATIONSHIP

For Emily Carr, director of project management and strategy at the international design, architectural, and planning firm Gensler, aligning clients and designers is the key to success or failure of design projects. "People skills are probably more important than anything else," says Carr. "If you are not able to persuade people to do what is necessary, or people don't like working with each other, then they are never going to accomplish what needs to be done."

When working with a client for the first time, the designer has the opportunity to set the stage for how the project will proceed. Strong interpersonal skills are needed, and an empathic approach is key to creating strong bonds. As Carr suggests, the client–designer relationship—and the success or failure of the project—has a foundation in people skills. As designers move away from project-based work and move toward a client-need focus, they must seriously consider the time and effort they put not only in the design work, but in the relationships they are creating. There are several key areas that designers can focus on when communicating with clients. These include managing the client relationship, setting client expectations, and explaining the value of design.

MANAGING CLIENT RELATIONSHIPS

Client interactions can be one of the most challenging aspects of the designer-client relationship. To mitigate this, designers can take an active role in preparing their clients for the design process. By doing so, they make the client part of the project, set expectations, and reassure them that a framework and rationale for moving forward exists. For many clients, design is a nebulous activity whose only value is to "make it pretty." Their nervousness is often illustrated in their controlling behavior: If you are unsure about something, then you do your best to control it.

The most important aspect of the relationship is trust. Trust is developed through strong interpersonal and communication skills. Designers that can have honest and open relationships with their clients go a long way in creating the proper environment for collaboration. Designers that gain a client's trust open doors for future work and elevate their role in the relationship.

SETTING EXPECTATIONS

Beyond design value, designers also need to set expectations with clients regarding roles and responsibilities, project logistics, and project processes. By making these activities transparent and systemized, designers assume a professional role, complete with professional practices and methods. Designers should review their work agreement with the client to ensure mutual expectations regarding billing, client alterations, assignment termination, project cancellation, and ownership of files. Once these areas are discussed and agreed upon by both parties, the project can move forward to the next phase.

EXPLAINING THE VALUE OF DESIGN

Clients often misunderstand the role design plays, and its value. Four important points can help clarify design's value:

- **Design affects consumer behavior:** Design motivates consumers by creating a perceptual value. It is often a consumer's first impression of a product or service, which establishes the relationship.

- **Design is a differentiator:** As a competitive strategy, design offers a way for firms to differentiate their products or services from their competitors'.

- **Design creates meaning:** Design communicates value and helps consumers comprehend the product or service.

- **Design as a process manages risks:** Design process offers a structure that takes into account the strategic purposes of the communication being developed. Process aligns the client and designer, offers opportunities for collaboration and innovation, and manages risk by creating a common understanding of goals, roles, and a structure for diagnosing problems.

PHASE TWO: PROJECT DEFINITION

An important tool for defining the project definition is the design brief. As a corporate design director for such firms as Gillette and Digital Equipment and as a consultant for Fortune 500 companies, Peter Philips is considered by many to be the guru of design briefs. Phillips has described the brief as "…a written document that thoroughly explains the problem that needs to be solved by a designer or designer team. It should primarily focus on results of design, outcomes of design, and the business objectives of the design project. It should not attempt to deal with the aesthetics of design. That is the responsibility of the designer."

Philips recalls, "Companies that I have worked with over the last seven or eight years, working through the brief process, report back that after about a year they are able to complete significant design projects about 15 to 18 percent faster." Phillips goes on to say, "Another major company has estimated that they have saved 50 percent, moving much faster and getting much better results."

Although it's sometimes overlooked by designers, the brief is one of the most important documents in the design process. The brief outlines information about the client organization, its audience, its business strategy, its competition, its objectives, and the scope of the project. The brief works as both a project management tool and a design directive. Possibly the most important function of the brief is that it aligns all the stakeholders, helping minimize the chances of going down dead ends.

The brief is created in collaboration with the client. By working together on the brief, the client and designer have an opportunity to work out issues and clarify any potential misunderstandings regarding direction.

The creative brief answers all the strategic questions a designer needs to know to do meaningful work. What is the objective of the client? Who is its target audience? Who is its competition? How does the firm perceive itself? How do others perceive it? What are the design parameters that define the firm? How will project success be measured? In addition, the brief outlines schedules, budgets, and the process involved in the project.

While there is no rule for how a brief should look or what information needs to be in it, the following list outlines some basic information that is considered standard.

Project Overview

What is the single purpose of the new communication? What are the long-term goals? How will we know if the project is successful? The project overview defines the project, stating what is to be done, why it is being done and the value that it brings to the client. The overview acts as an executive summary of the project.

Define the Problem

What is the problem we are tying to solve? It's very easy to begin a project with assumptions. Some clients might request a new website or a new brochure without considering the deeper problem that needs to be solved. So before making an assumption about the solution, the problem must be defined. This is the first step in establishing the direction of the project. By clarifying the problem and getting everyone to agree, designers are able to address the need, as opposed to jumping ahead to an off-the-shelf solution.

State Your Goals

What do we want to achieve through the new design? Once the problem is defined, the goal can be stated. The goal defines the outcome of the project. Goals should be clearly written and to the point.

Define Objectives

What are the steps toward reaching the goal? Objectives are the tasks that must be accomplished to achieve the goal. When defining the objectives and outcome, you will need to define a timeframe and metrics for how the objectives will be achieved.

Determine Success Criteria

How will we know if the design is successful? Measuring the success of design has always been considered a difficult task because design does not exist in a vacuum and is often just one part of a business strategy. By determining what metrics will be used and establishing criteria for project success at the beginning of a project, designers can focus their efforts toward client goals. There are a number of ways to measure design success. They include looking at the project from an accounting standpoint (did the investment in design provide a return?), or noting behavioral changes in audiences. You may even measure the success of a project based on whether the process went well.

Business Analysis

What are the business goals and what is the business environment? The design is being created to fulfill a business need. Through situational analysis, designers can answer questions such as: What is the client organization doing? What is the client's business strategy? What assumptions about the company's relative position, strengths and weaknesses, competitors, and industry trends must be made for the current strategy to make sense? What is happening in the business environment? What are the key factors for competitive success and threats? What are the capabilities and limitations of existing and potential competitors, and their probable future moves?

For designers to be effective business partners, they must understand the firms they are serving. Design without information is pointless. It does not serve the firm, and it marginalizes the role of the designer.

Audience Analysis

What are the needs of the audience? An audience's ability to accept messages depends on how well the message fits with their beliefs, attitudes, and values. With a thorough understanding of these traits, a designer can develop an effective solution that is appropriate to the audience.

Competition and Competitive Positioning

What unique value does the business offer its customers? Business is competitive, and without competition there can be no strategy. For firms to exist and prosper they must develop an explicit strategy that helps them navigate their business environment. Firms look at social, competitive, industry, and internal strengths and weaknesses to formulate strategy that moves them toward their business goals. For designers, competitive strategy boils down to one critical concept: differentiation. Differentiation answers the question, "What unique value do you provide your customers?"

Communication Strategy

How will we convince our audience to engage us? One of the first steps is understanding the overall message the client is trying to convey to the audience. For example, are audiences looking for cost-effective solutions, or are they looking for status? Communication strategy also considers how the overall message will be conveyed.

Perception and Tone

How the client will visually communicate our strategy. What are the parameters of style? How does the client want to project itself? How do their clients perceive them? What cues need to be made prominent? Is the client organization traditional or contemporary? Are they local or international? By addressing these questions, the designer can develop a visual style that is based on strategic direction, as opposed to styles or trends.

Schedule

What are the key project milestones? Setting the schedule requires an understanding of the steps needed to accomplish the project. The individual steps and the time it will take to complete them are the foundation of project planning. For clients who have to answer to bosses and hit drop-dead dates, the schedule is their lifeline to the project and a key factor for success. Designers tend to focus on the quality of the design but not necessarily the timeliness of their deliverable. However, a great design delivered late misses the mark.

To be effective, schedules also need to be shared in a transparent way so that both designer and client can see what's happening and when. Several online tools allow for public display of schedules and other project-critical information.

Client Sign-Off

What are the key points in the project that require sign-off? One of the most valuable controls in the design process is the client sign-off. The sign-off is a checkpoint in the process and thus helps manage the inherent risks involved with developing a new idea. Sign-off usually occurs at the close of concept development and design development phases. It is a point at which client and designer confirm the direction of the project before moving to the next phase. Getting sign-off in these critical junctures ensures that the project is on target and that all parties are in agreement before going further. Sign-off brings structure to a potentially confusing process and ensures that all steps are completed along the way.

PHASE THREE: DESIGN RESEARCH

When Four Seasons Hotels and Resorts needed a competitive edge, they did not just crunch the numbers like most businesses. They looked to their customers as a source for innovation and differentiation. When CEO Isadore Sharp asked, "What do our customers consider their top value?" customer research told him it was luxury. But Sharp did not stop there. As easy as it would be to invest in top chefs and opulent décor, Sharp looked deeper and tried to understand what luxury meant to his customers. In the end, it was *time* that the customers really wanted. To satisfy this need, Four Seasons is relentless in its pursuit of designing first-class customer experiences that maximize their customers' time, providing around the clock services including twenty-four-hour dining, one-hour pressing and after-hours retail stores.

Effective design starts with understanding the context of the client's business and their respective customer needs. Where the client and customers cannot express these needs directly, the designer must conduct research to create a better understanding upon which to base their design direction. Design research uses tools and techniques for collecting secondary, quantitative, and experience data, including ethnography, interviews, behavioral, segmentation, and demographic and human factor studies.

BALANCING INTUITION AND INFORMATION

Understanding and context are the keys to any good design. However, many designers forgo research and rely on intuitive processes for developing ideas. Designers who can think laterally and make connections between seemingly unrelated ideas can develop new and creative concepts and approaches.

Intuitive approaches are critical to developing creative solutions, but before designers can develop concepts, they must be armed with information. This stage is the most critical in the process, for information will drive the direction of the project.

BUSINESS GOALS AND AUDIENCE NEEDS

Designers need to focus on two areas: the business goals of the client and the needs of their audiences. Important considerations include the internal and external environment of the client organization, an understanding of their audience, competitor analysis, and the environment. This is balanced with information about audience needs, including how peer organizations are already talking to them, their perceptions of the client organization, and the context in which the client organization plays a part in their lives.

Several time-tested tools for gathering data exist. Although most research techniques have their foundation in marketing and the social sciences, the following work well in a design context.

Situational Analysis

A solid knowledge of the business is critical to making good design decisions. Situational analysis provides designers with a framework for looking at internal and external forces within the client organization. This information forms the basis of any competitive strategy the client organization might have. Situational analysis looks at three key areas of business: what the organization is currently doing, what is happening in the business environment, and what the business should be doing. The most common tool for viewing the big picture is the SWOT chart, a simple matrix that compares strengths, weaknesses, opportunities, and threats.

Interviews and Focus Groups

Talking directly with audiences provides designers with a level of understanding that they would otherwise miss. Focus groups allow you to brainstorm with audiences for the purpose of developing deeper understanding. Focus groups come in a range of styles, from small groups of six to dyads and triads, where two to three persons (often friends) are gathered to answer questions based on a script. Personal interviews are one-on-one discussions with constituents. Interviews allow participants to answer questions without the influence of other individuals.

Ethnography

Ethnography is a research method that studies audiences in the context of their lives. Christopher Ireland, the former principal and CEO of Cheskin, defines ethnography as "...a research approach that produces a detailed in-depth observation of people's behavior, beliefs, and preferences by observing and interacting with them in a natural environment." Ethnography can give designers a better idea of who they are designing for and what is meaningful to them. Ethnographic methods include note taking, recording, photography, and video.

These tools help the designer prepare for the creative stages to come by giving them insight into the client's business and audience. Additionally, by educating himself, a designer can speak intelligently about the client organization's objectives and goals and drive the conversation in a strategic direction, thereby positioning himself as a valuable partner.

PHASE FOUR: CONCEPT DEVELOPMENT

Developing concepts has always been regarded as the "magic" moment in the design process. By using tools like brainstorming, analogies, mind maps, visual triggers, and other creative ideation tools, designers can expand their creative thinking and move beyond obvious solutions. This phase offers methods for understanding the problem to be solved, deconstructing the problem, and collecting and interpreting design research.

The primary methods in concept development involve open and uninhibited discussion about a well-defined problem. An atmosphere of uncritical and open discussion is key to the success of concept development sessions, as the focus is on the quantity of ideas generated and not necessarily the quality. By generating more ideas, the problem can be seen in ways that, at first, may seem unconventional. Conventional brainstorming, ideation techniques, and random imagery can help break participants out of their creative assumptions. Images, words, and projective exercises can be used to help clients free-associate, allowing them to make connections that they might not have made in more conventional ways. Other techniques like drawing and collage are useful for extracting hidden ideas.

PHASE FIVE: DESIGN DEVELOPMENT

Design development is the culmination of the research and ideation phases. At this stage, visualization and creative talent play the biggest role. Most of the skills involved are those typically associated with design professionals—that is, the visual articulation of the communication strategy. Color, typography, form, and style are all used to convey a message. Much of the development process revolves around the creation of a prototype, which acts as a model for the finished piece. Prototyping helps the concept come to life, allowing for further refinement and alignment of stakeholders. Prototypes help clients envision the final design and mitigate the risk of designing pieces that are off target. Prototypes evolve incrementally, providing places for checks to occur throughout the development process.

On the management side of the process, design development is the time for feedback and critiques that are constructive in their intent. Such tools ensure a high level of quality and keep the process moving forward at a reasonable rate. Feedback loops act as controls to manage success.

PHASE SIX: DESIGN EVALUATION

It is understood that design plays a big role in brand success, but assigning a business return to design has always been a struggle. Only recently have firms like Interbrand and Millward Brown begun to analyze and rate consumer relationships and brand equity, bringing to light design's role in fostering these important connections. For most designers, calculating design ROI (return on investment) has been not been a priority. But as designers seek credibility in the business world, ROI becomes increasingly important.

As design becomes a strategic business asset, it will be held accountable for its contribution to the goals of the organization. This is a challenge, as it is difficult to single out design among all the factors that contribute to business outcomes. In the last decade, there have been several studies on how design impacts business. Each study has approached the problem using different measures, from Robin Roy's 1987 initial research into design impact in Britain; to Hertenstein and Platt's work showing the positive effects of design investment on the bottom line; to the accounting methodology employed by design ROI evangelist Rob Wallace.

IN CONCLUSION

Design process is an inclusive endeavor that acts as a unifier, bringing clients and audiences together to develop new and meaningful communications. The process is rife with opportunities for miscommunication, dead ends, and divergent tracks, as well as amazing outcomes. By managing the activity as well as the artifact, designers are better able to satisfy client needs and arrive at new and innovative solutions.

Design is a valuable business tool and needs to be thoughtful and transparent in its approach. By integrating time-tested steps into the creative process and focusing on the areas of managing design complexity, audience, and business context, collaboration and accountability, designers change their perceived value from one of "mysterious creative" to a disciplined business partner.

chapter 2

A FRAMEWORK FOR GETTING THINGS DONE WELL

THE VALUE OF PROCESS

At the largest food and beverage company in North America, Kraft Foods, effective design management of over 220 brands is a critical component of success. The one-hundred-year-old company builds superior brand value by consistently delivering products that meet consumer's needs at a competitive price. Much of the brand value is reinforced through the packaging of long-established products including Maxwell House, Kool-Aid, Oscar Mayer, Velveeta, Jell-O and Oreo. Such products have been carefully designed and packaged to break through store shelf clutter and speak directly to the consumer. Many have reached iconic status. Kraft employs succinct visual cues in order to mirror consumer values. They also seek to connect with consumers on an emotional level.

Responsibility for managing these highly visible brand identities fell to Pamela DeCesare, former director for global packaging resources at Kraft Foods. In her tenure at Kraft, her goal was to create a design department modeled on the behaviors of design thinking and added value. With her thirteen-person in-house team designing packaging for more than sixty Kraft Foods brands, DeCesare was expected to meet the demand for shorter times to market, coordinate with both in-house and consultant teams, and maintain the quality and consistency of Kraft's brand message. The clear communication of design requirements and project logistics required that Kraft establish a design process that ensured designs were strategically driven, well-crafted, and on message.

Kraft looked to design process as a way to ensure quicker turnarounds and a more efficient workflow. Through a process that considers design standards, documented design briefs, and a system for quick design approvals, the Kraft design team was able to efficiently manage up to 175 projects at a time. Even with such a daunting workload, the process allowed adequate time for creative development and review cycles. Kraft's design process allowed for both efficiency and flexibility in supporting the requirements of multiple brands, and allowed the designers to focus on producing strategic design, as opposed to managing the process.

PROCESS MANAGEMENT

Process management is a discipline that had its beginnings in the manufacturing and service industries. In its earliest form, process management was used to streamline industries such as steel and textiles. An early proponent was Fredrick Winslow Taylor, who is credited with introducing the "efficiency movement." Taylor, noted for his time studies, broke jobs into component parts, similar to work breakdown structures found in modern project management. Taylor's "scientific management" approach maintained that employees needed to be trained to do their jobs by management, and that most workers did not have the ability to understand the nuances of their jobs.

The work of Frank and Lillian Gilbreth complemented Taylor's work. Whereas Taylor was more interested in the time it took to complete tasks, the Gilbreths focused on how to make the process more efficient. Frank, a bricklayer and contractor by trade, had a deep understanding of how people worked. Lillian, an organizational psychologist, provided a methodology for studying how the work was done. A typical example of their experiments involves, not surprisingly, bricklaying. By documenting the bricklayers' individual movements, and calculating the time required to complete each task, the Gilbreths were able to maximize the movement of the bricklayers, allowing them to both increase their efficiency and decrease the amount of energy needed to do the job. The Gilbreths' work also represented a new perspective in process improvement, in which the worker played a critical part in determining where improvements could be made. It should be mentioned that Frank and Lillian wrote the autobiographical book, *Cheaper by the Dozen*, which tells the story of their life with their twelve children. No doubt, their expertise in organizational psychology came in handy.

The popularity of process improvement in business circles continues today. As firms have tried to streamline the path from concept to market, measures-based strategies that look at quality improvement and variation reduction like Six Sigma, Total Quality Management Lean and Kaizen, have been implemented. Each of these methods strives to ensure the quality of products and services, with the ultimate goal of providing increased customer satisfaction. Many of these strategies include the participation of workers to find and offer suggestions on process improvements.

As companies like Kraft demonstrate, a managed process is a critical element of design activity. Yet, to many outside the discipline, design is perceived as a mostly intuitive activity that refuses definition or structure. The common belief that there are as many creative approaches as there are designers leads to the conclusion that no single design process is applicable or transferable. Thus, each project, the thinking goes, requires a unique approach to account for variables in specifications, scope, culture, and other unique factors. Nevertheless, the basic steps involved in any design project, whether it involves communications, architectural design, engineering, product design, or software, are, in fact, generally definable and repeatable. Any design process inevitably requires information gathering, concept development, design development, production, implementation and analysis. Variation is possible within this structure, to be sure, but the process remains notably consistent.

With more organizations embracing design as a means to achieve competitive advantage, design will come to be understood as a manageable component of business activity. A clearly defined process can provide many organizations with a tool to manage problem solving and improve interdepartmental communication. It is a tool for stimulating creativity and fostering innovation, for managing risk and increasing product/service success rates. As such, a design process can do much to ensure that projects run smoothly and produce measurable outcomes, on time and on budget.

THE PROCESS ADVANTAGE

- Strengthens alignment between users and clients
- Quickens development of innovative concepts
- Tightens management of production work flow
- Facilitates resolution of interdepartmental conflicts
- Increases understanding of measurable results

STRENGTHENING ALIGNMENT BETWEEN USERS AND CLIENTS

The design process constitutes a framework for collaboration, increasing opportunities for aligning clients and designers. Collaborative processes and environments have been hailed as a key to innovation and creativity. Design problems call for an understanding of not only aesthetic elements, but also technological, economical, environmental, cultural, and strategic factors. Each stands to benefit from insights provided by specialists working across the entire process. Working with specialists does present a few challenges, including the lack of a shared vocabulary combined with potentially conflicting priorities. The ability to align project team members is thus critical to achieve project team success.

COLLABORATION CREATES TRUST

The design process can baffle clients and nondesigners alike. Sometimes designers don't make things much easier. Frequently resorting to design jargon, disguising ulterior objectives, and neglecting to define or accept individual roles, designers may exacerbate points of conflict that arise over the course of most design projects. Such projects require that a level of trust be established between all interested parties. By including stakeholders in the process and explaining it up front, as well as reviewing it periodically, designers can gain the trust essential to achieve success. Given a means of understanding and appreciating their role in the process, stakeholders gain a sense of control. As a result, they are more likely to act as collaborators and are open to new ideas and directions.

THE COLLABORATIVE ADVANTAGE

- Increases participant motivation
- Lessens resistance to change
- Widens the knowledge pool
- Fosters trust
- Manages risk
- Offers multiple solutions

END OF THE SOLO ACT

In Ayn Rand's 1943 novel *The Fountainhead*, the young idealistic hero Howard Roark battles the philistines around him who constantly try to marginalize his heroic architectural vision. Roark refuses to meet the demands of clients and employers, and ends up banished to the lowest rank of the architectural spectrum. Roark ultimately blows up his own building after its design has been marginalized by others' interests. At his trial, in an impassioned speech, Roark praises the individual and claims that all of civilization's progress can be attributed to the work of individuals, who in the face of criticism from the mob, manage to chart advances. Roark declares the power of the indi-vidual. "The creators were not selfless," he says. "It is the whole secret of their power—that it was self-sufficient, self-motivated, self-generated. A first cause, a fount of energy, a life force, a prime mover. The creator served nothing and no one. He lived for himself."

Subsequently, Roark emerges triumphant and fulfills his architectural vision. Roark's perspective makes sense in the context of mid-century history, where nationalism and communism reigned, and ultimately threw the world into a series of devastating wars.

In the late 1920s, Ayn Rand worked in Hollywood as a screenwriter. Surely it was there she learned that her particular vision was fodder for producers and directors alike. Yet ironically, Rand's own philosophy contradicts itself. The 'Objectivists' praise laissez-faire capitalism, which is driven by consumer demand, but Roark's ideals generally suppress or ignore the clients' needs in favor of personal vision. On a side note, Rand wrote the entire speech Roark gives in the movie and demanded it be read exactly as she wrote it.

Today, we understand that design is less likely to represent the vision of a single individual who knows "what's good for people." More often, design represents a collaborative effort that considers multiple perspectives. Collaboration offers an opportunity for reflection and access to specialized knowledge from diverse disciplines. Organizational expert Warren Bennis defined collaboration as a voluntary joint effort that is based on a common goal, backed by data that is shared in an open and transparent environment. The relationship is based on sharing power between collaborating partners.

THE ARCHITECT'S COLLABORATIVE

In 1945, architect and educator Walter Gropius established a partnership with several other architects committed to a collaborative philosophy. Each project was assigned to a team lead by a partner-in-charge who would direct the other architects during the course of the project. Each architect had a say in every aspect of the project. This was a departure from traditional working methods, which gave ownership to one individual. An absence of ego defined the partnership. The concept is echoed in Gropius's statement that "...a team can raise its integrated work to higher potentials than the sum of the work of just so many individuals." The Architect's Collaborative tackled several large-scale projects, producing a rich variety of design solutions including the University of Baghdad, Pan American World Airways (now the MetLife building), and the CIGNA corporate headquarters. This collaborative spirit spilled over into their personal lives as well: The partners went as far as creating their own subdivision in Cambridge, Massachusetts, named Six Moon Hill. Here the architects lived together in small modernist homes featuring large glass windows and cantilever roofs. Each home was priced affordably ($15,000 in 1945) and built on equal-size lots with shared community amenities such as a swimming pool and park areas.

COLLABORATION: CO-CREATION WITH THE CLIENT

It is widely agreed that collaboration between an organization and its audiences is a useful tool for innovation. It also marks a change in thinking in how organizations concept, produce, and distribute products and services. Born out of the open source programming movement that developed such standouts as the Linux operating system, co-creation has now taken root in business circles. As C.K. Prahalad, former professor of corporate strategy at the University of Michigan Stephen M. Ross School of Business, says in his book *The Future of Competition*, "The emerging reality is forcing us to reexamine the traditional system of company-centric value creation... We now need a new frame of reference for value creation. The answer, we believe, lies in a different premise centered on co-creation of value." Prahalad and others believe that true value creation can be done only through co-creation experiences in which "individual-centered co-creation of value between consumers and companies" occurs.

Organizations are marshalling their customers to help promote products and services they are passionate about. L'Oreal Paris, the international beauty care company, working with Varsity Media Group, an entertainment media company that harnesses the creative power of teenagers, offered high school students the opportunity to create their own thirty-second commercials for their Colour Juice brand in a "You make the commercial" contest. With over one hundred entries from across the nation, the contest drew over a quarter of a million voters.

Converse, the maker of geek chic Chuck Taylor sneakers, has taken a similar approach, asking their fans to make a twenty-four-second film telling what Converse means to them. Winners were posted on the "Converse Gallery," which featured both amateur and professional films. The films are testimony to Converse's authenticity and unique connection to their customers.

Some dangers come with this approach as well. Consider the Chevy Tahoe debacle. Chevrolet provided some basic brand assets, including logos, music, and images on a website, and encouraged would-be TV commercial directors to develop their own ads for the Chevy Tahoe SUV. The results were unexpected. Instead of getting ringing endorsements from happy Tahoe owners, the blogosphere filled up with videos that bashed the Tahoe as a gas-guzzling, environmentally unfriendly vehicle.

BrandImage: Collaboration Within Internal and External Teams

Rob Swan, vice president, executive creative director at BrandImage Desgrippes & Laga, places a great value on creative culture. Swan has managed office staffs ranging in size from eight to eighty, in organizations from small private design firms to large global design firms. Along the way he has discovered some universal truths that he has identified regarding working in a creative environment. "To create a creative culture," he says, "it's critical to make sure there is an understanding that everyone has a vital role to play, and that every single role is just as important as the next, regardless of title."

For Swan, understanding his clients' brands, their business goals, and their consumers (both shoppers and users) is key to developing meaningful design. "I'm a big believer in measuring twice and cutting once," says Swan. "You can't just take a scattered, shotgun approach to solving design problems. I think if you do this, you have a high chance of not hitting the mark and having to start over again." Swan works closely with a range of creative staff to develop a design strategy that considers business and consumer perspectives.

At the outset of the project, Swan works with a design strategy director, tasked with bringing the design team and client together to work collaboratively on developing an actionable strategy. Swan takes the design team and clients through a successive series of distillation exercises to get at how to focus the development of design, starting with core consumer needs and insight, then looking at the relevant brand landscape, and finally filtering implications through the brand imperatives, building an understanding of the whys, whats, and hows of how design can best address the opportunity for the brand.

The result is identifying resonant opportunities for the brand to create authentic and meaningful solutions. At this stage, Swan and his team work to understand how the design is manifested through great ideas paired with culturally resonant visual cues, creating positive emotional responses and experiences for customers. "That is the magic of design," says Swan, "getting at really resonant ideas that help achieve this very specific goal." The idea behind design strategy is to proactively identify real opportunities so that you can more effectively target and execute the often time-consuming, and potentially expensive, power of design.

Swan says, "The most important facet of developing design strategy is collaboration." Often, BrandImage facilitates a strategy development session with clients and other agency stakeholders in a big session, covering conference room walls with stimulus, allowing participants to freely capture and discuss ideas. Far from a formal business meeting, the sessions are immersive, fun, and engaging, with the express goal of investing the designers as well as key stakeholders in the strategy, so they don't feel like they are just being handed an idea cold, from a "black box." By having the client actively participate in the development of the strategy, early alignment is created between the design team and the client and other partners. This "if they create it, they will support it" approach helps with clients returning later in the process and understanding and supporting the design direction. The results are often "platforms of expression." These might be a movie, a board, a book, or whatever seems to capture the essence of the brand. Such platforms act as a visual brief for how Swan's team would approach the design solution.

Once out of the meeting, Swan's team immediately starts ideating so that they maintain the energy level and understanding of the task at hand. No more than a day is given to "bottle up the lightning" from the immersion session. From here, the creative director takes the lead and the strategy director becomes a consultant. In a three- to four-hour meeting, concepts are developed with the core group, with the goal of getting everyone aligned and excited about the direction.

Whereas the concept phase is an open exchange of ideas and is collaborative, the design development and execution stage requires designers to work alone, digesting and internalizing the information gathered in the immersion session. The rule of thumb in design development is to meet "early and often," focusing on developing ideas first in broad strokes, and then refining and tightening as they go. More often than not, exposing ideas to clients in sketch form as a work in progress is also employed to retain alignment and not waste any effort. It's all about being proactive and collaborative.

Fossil: A Collaborative Open Environment

For the "American vintage inspired" watch company Fossil, working collaboratively is a key to its success. Since 1987, the once-small design firm has grown by leaps and bounds, offering over three hundred varieties of watches (each of which comes in a tin case) and over sixty outlet and apparel stores internationally. Tim Hale, senior vice president at Fossil Design, describes the company's core philosophy as teaming and collaboration. This spirit of teamwork comes from Hale's belief in the value of people and the unique skills that each person brings to the problem-solving equation. With over seventy team members that range from digital photographers, web designers, and video and motion graphics designers, Fossil is able to pull from a broad talent pool. Each team member is instilled with the value that they bring to the group. As Hale says, "Value begets ownership, ownership begets accountability, and accountability begets a passion to produce the best work that creates results for the company." When a new team member comes on board, she is indoctrinated in the Fossil brand, then asked to show her interpretation of it with the intent that her perspective could become part of the Fossil visual language. Hale has created an "open and collaborative environment" where team members are valued and given an opportunity to contribute and grow, each in their own unique way.

Fossil provides an example of how collaborative process helps designers work with cross-disciplinary teams. As design becomes integrated into the business culture, designers will be required to work in cross-disciplinary teams and be able to communicate effectively, problem solve, build commitment from the team, and manage multiple stakeholders. Additionally, they will need to be able to navigate various organizational environments. This new challenge requires that designers align with the stakeholders and, acting as a problem-solving partner, create the proper atmosphere for addressing needs. Stakeholders hold much of the information needed to develop meaningful solutions, so by working collaboratively designers can gain a deeper understanding of the stakeholders' position and environment, allowing them to make better design decisions. Organizations that are inclusive in their decision making are more likely to have support for new ideas from team members and likely to work more creatively and efficiently.

TIGHTEN MANAGEMENT OF PRODUCTION WORK FLOW

In her article, "The Need for Speed: Synchronization Ensures Brand Success," Janice Jaworski, managing director and strategist for the global strategic design firm Anthem!, says, "The need for speed, efficiency, and predictability from initial conception through production requires the development of a work-flow system that ensures the delivery of the right package, with the right message, for the right product, to the right consumer, to the shelf at the right time." Speed is a critical success factor for businesses. The ability to respond to the marketplace can mean the difference between success and failure. Companies that can react faster to changes in the market have a better chance of staying competitive. In the business of design, speed is seen as essential. Getting products from idea to completion in the quickest way possible so that costs can be paid and profits taken is paramount. Prolonged projects cost more than quicker projects; however, projects that skimp on process can end up costing in a lack of quality. This is especially dangerous when the critical front end of a project is shortened, thereby creating misaligned goals and off target deliverables.

Design process increases speed to market by establishing controlled phases that are built around success criteria. Processes also mitigate many of the time-consuming problems, like client alignment and concept development. Without a process, you're reinventing each activity, adding time to the process and possibly making repeated mistakes.

Lucent: Managing Tight Turns With Process

When the telecommunications giant AT&T spun off its communications equipment manufacturing arm and formed Lucent Technologies, there was little time to develop an understanding among customers as to its purpose and unique offerings. With an impending initial public offering date approaching, Lucent's first step toward clarifying who it was and what it offered was to enlist the skills of San Francisco brand consultancy firm Landor & Associates.

In order for Lucent to meet its upcoming initial public offering of stock, the entire project had to be delivered in a twelve-week timeframe. But even with this compressed deadline, Landor did not jump into the design phase. Instead, they enlisted a methodical process that included conducting up-front research. As Patrice Kavanaugh, executive director of Landor Associates, recalls in her Design Management Institute article "Creating the Identity for a $20 Billion Start-Up," Landor initiated the project by gathering information to better understand how Lucent would differentiate itself from its competitors. She had managers, staff, customers, and suppliers interviewed so that ideas concerning perceptions, personality, strengths, and weaknesses could be collected. A competitive analysis provided information to help the Lucent brand stand out from the crowded technology arena. On review of the marketplace, most competitors' brands used a common corporate visual approach. Stately blues and grays dominated their pallets, and names all integrated themes of technology by adding *tel*, *syst*, or *com* as prefixes or suffixes. Landor wanted to make a departure from these conventions.

With the help of Lucent's management team, Landor whittled down multiple naming options based on ideas of connection, systems, creativity, and light. The latter option, light, with its connotations of innovation and vision, ultimately won the day, and the Lucent name was founded. In addition, Bell Labs endorsed the name, leveraging the weight and respect that it bore in the industry. The name was screened for any translation problems that might carry over.

At this point, Landor was ready to move onto the design development phase. The now-famous red brushstroke logo was chosen out of hundreds of options. With its hand-drawn motif, the logo was decidedly different from its competitors, and would help Lucent proclaim its uniqueness in the market.

Lucent's IPO ended up being the largest in U.S. history, raising roughly $2.9 billion. "It isn't often you spin off as a market leader. We literally formed a company, got a name, established a brand, separated from our parent, had an IPO, and didn't miss a beat," says Patricia Russo, executive vice president of Lucent.

Even though Landor faced a tight deadline, they did not stray from their process by cutting out critical phases like information gathering. Without the research to base the new identity on, Landor knew they would not be able to develop a meaningful, defensible solution that would differentiate Lucent from its competition and reflect the vision of the organization.

FACILITATE RESOLUTION OF PROJECT CONFLICTS

Every designer has worked on a project that has had moments of frustration. Some frustrations are common and have become part of design lore. The client who changes the direction of the project late in the game; the client who can't leave the content alone and makes multiple revisions right up to the deadline; the new stakeholder who's brought in late in the game and changes the direction at the last minute. For designers, these are more than just bumps in the road. They represent wasted time, money and effort. Common frustrations include:

- Running off in the wrong direction
- Rework/constant updates
- Changing direction midstream
- A new stakeholder signing onto the project late
- Clients playing designer

These frustrations are not only irritating, but in some cases they are the difference between doing average work and doing great work. Although frustrations like these cannot be eliminated, they can be managed. Identify potential areas of frustration and prioritizing the ones that are the most costly and have the highest probability of happening can help designers focus on what needs to be addressed first.

Design by its nature is a risky endeavor. Designers make things and express complicated ideas in ways that have never been seen before. So how do designers manage risk while developing new and exciting works?

Design process uses several controls in the project so that designer and client can check their alignment. Design briefs are created at the beginning of the process and act as a scope-of-work document, including basic project specifications, information about voice and tone, and positioning. Along with the brief, sign-offs placed at critical junctures help preserve alignment and minimize frustration. Along with these tools, there are methods of working that promote alignment from stakeholders.

Design process offers several tools for managing project frustrations.

The Design Brief

By developing the brief with the client's help, the designer creates a guide for how to proceed that can be shared with all stakeholders. As an alignment tool, the brief documents direction—taking some of the subjectivity out of the design process.

The design brief is a very important control tool. By outlining the direction with stakeholders and documenting it, designers create accountability for all involved in the project. By having the brief in writing and accessible to all, clients are less likely to make costly and time-consuming changes later in the design process.

The Sign-Off

Along with the design brief, sign-offs at specific times during the process help check progress so that designer and client are in sync on status before committing time and effort toward a particular direction. Sign-offs are usually done before and after the concept phases, so designers can confirm a general direction before executing the concept.

"I have the client sign off on the project brief before I get started with the design process," says Jose Nieto, principal and creative director of the design firm square zero. "That allows us to deal with any misconceptions that I might have with the project from the beginning. So if there's any problem in what I interpreted, it's dealt with before the project starts."

QUICKEN DEVELOPMENT OF INNOVATIVE CONCEPTS

An additional advantage of working closely with stakeholders is that designers position themselves to push their client's thinking about their work. Clients can approach design as humdrum (just get it done) and full of assumptions (we know what we want). Designers can help their clients break out of this kind of thinking by asking them questions that lead to deeper meaning and insight into a client's objectives. Conversely, designers benefit from stakeholders as a source for creative ideas and directions.

New ideas are what drive firms in the marketplace. By continually developing new products or services, companies are able to meet the constantly changing needs of consumers and maintain their presence in the marketplace.

Since most markets are in a constant state of flux, firms no longer look to maintain a status quo, but instead are thinking about what's new. Through a defined concept-development process, most firms are looking to users and clients to develop new and innovative products. In the same way that new product development looks to users for insight, communications designers mine their clients and their audiences for creative ideas.

A process that accounts for client input gives designers the raw material they need to develop communications that will connect with audiences. Process allows for increased creativity by providing a methodology for new thinking based on information. The process helps define the fuzzy front-end of projects by gathering data through market and design research, which promotes divergent thinking.

By preparing the mind with information and letting the facts act as a guide, designers can be led in many new, exciting, and unanticipated directions. Because the information for each client and audience is exclusive, a unique design solution is almost guaranteed. This approach helps control a tendency to rely on randomly chosen styles or trends, or the designer's idiosyncratic preferences. Design process provides methods for gaining user insights.

John Bielenberg, principal of the San Francisco design firm C2, addresses this tendency in design: "Just like an addict creates a lust for drugs or alcohol, the designer develops a craving for the new, the visually compelling, and the beautiful. The image becomes an end in itself. The graphic language sometimes takes a dominant role over the message being communicated... graphic designers have developed a hyperliterate visual sense and a highly refined appreciation for the craft of graphic design. I call it the intoxication of craft. ... Conflict often exists when you combine the intoxication of craft, exposure to and interest in cutting-edge design with the engineering of a client-driven message to a client-defined audience." To break this cycle, designers can use information to influence design decisions.

AUDIENCE PERSPECTIVES

When audiences are included at the earliest stages of the design process, they can offer important insights. In Eric von Hippel's book *Democratizing*

Innovation, he says, "Users that innovate can develop exactly what they want, rather (than) relying on manufacturers to act as their agents." Von Hippel is a leading researcher in the area of end-user innovation, a method in which users of products or services develop modifications to meet their unique needs. These user modifications are then given back to the company or offered as an open source for the general public, often becoming the leading source of innovation for the company. By prompting lead users to freely experiment with modifications to products or services, designers open the door for even more valuable insights.

Including user perspectives as part of your process gives you an opportunity to hear directly from the people you are designing for. New products are smartly tested with consumers to keep failure rates down and make certain the "voice of the customer" is built into the design.

THE DIFFERENCE BETWEEN LEARNING AND TESTING

Co-creation and collaborative design requires users and audiences to be active participants in the process. Users take on two distinct roles. In the initial "learning" stages of the project, users provide insights through "generative" activities where they participate in visual and written exercises. In contrast, design testing happens at the end of the process during the prototyping stage, or even after the launch, where users can provide feedback on how well design ideas resonate.

Some visual designers are reluctant to test design ideas with clients or audiences because they fear that those clients or audiences will take on an art director role, and attempt to make design decisions. But as design becomes a part of business culture, and a strategic business tool, the idea of design testing with audiences is growing in acceptance.

Testing Design With Audiences

By using a disciplined testing approach that subjects their work to rigorous review, designers gain respect as professionals. If the goal of design is to connect people and affect their behavior, then testing offers some assurance that the designs being created resonate with audiences.

With over thirty years experience in consumer research, Perception Research Services (PRS) works with industry giants Procter & Gamble,

General Mills, Microsoft, Staples and CVS to ensure that their packaging and print advertising resonates with consumers. Conducting over six hundred consumer research programs a year, PRS's most recent successes have included helping Slim-Fast brand increase sales by 20 percent to developing award-winning advertising campaigns for IBM.

In his article "A Designer's Guide to Consumer Research," Scott Young, president of Perception Research Services, observes that many designers see audience research as too analytical, or worse, that it turns the design over to "housewives turned art directors." These fears aside, the reality is that research can only enhance the effectiveness of design. Designers are designing for people and must balance audience likes and dislikes while moving them in unexpected ways.

Young offers some solid suggestions to designers for using research in their design processes, including conducting research at the beginning of the design process to help establish design parameters and making sure that research is actionable for the design team. When presenting ideas, Young suggests that showing incomplete ideas of roughs should be avoided, and that ideas should be as fully formed as possible to get the most honest reaction from consumers.

As business calls for actionable feedback, designers are left to decide on the proper tools for working with users to gain insight. Each project requires special consideration, oftentimes making the selection of a research approach difficult. Following are some helpful approaches.

Monadic testing. The monadic method of testing design ideas is considered the most reliable. By testing a design on its own, designers are able to get an unbiased opinion from audiences about their likes and dislikes. Individual designs are shown to audiences for a period of time. Audiences are then asked to rate the designs based on a set of criteria. By eliminating competing designs, the testing takes on a real-life scenario and helps the audiences focus on the individual design solution. Concurrently, other designs are tested with different groups. After all the tests are concluded, the individual design solutions and their relative test responses are compared to see which met the criteria most successfully.

Sequential monadic. Sequential monadic methods also are used as a cost-effective approach to design testing. Two options are shown to audiences, one after the other. This method tends to cause some variance in the scores, especially if one of the options is particularly strong. Audiences then rate the second option significantly lower than if they had scored each option on its own.

Sensation transference. In the late 1930s, Louis Cheskin, founder of Cheskin design research firm, studied how customers' perceptions of products influence their buying decisions. Through his research he developed the idea of sensation transference. Cheskin understood the relationships that people had with the visual expressions of products and packaging.

Cheskin learned that by testing individuals' responses to a product, he inadvertently had them rate the design. Without asking people about the specifics of the designs, he asked them about the quality of the product. People told him that cheap brandy tasted better served from a beautiful bottle and lime soda tastes "too much like lime" if the can is too green.

Conjoint analysis. Conjoint analysis helps designers isolate and identify design strengths and weaknesses. By looking at combinations of design features, the individual value of design elements can be measured. Audiences are asked to rate combinations of design attributes in order of preference. Conjoint analysis helps predict what choice audiences will make among various design options.

After the mock-ups and prototypes to be tested have been selected, audiences are shown combinations of features. Audiences are then asked to rate which combinations work best for them. The most preferred combinations of features are then determined. This process is sometimes called discrete choice analysis.

Design review. A design review is a set of activities whose purpose is to evaluate how well the results of a design will meet all quality requirements. During the course of this review, problems must be identified and necessary actions proposed.

Exploratory Tests

Once an understanding of audience needs has been established, exploratory testing can be conducted. Initial design concepts are critiqued to see how they resonate with audiences. Questions are directed at audiences to see what they think about the concept, whether the design is appropriate, and if the design meets user needs. Testing early in the process helps designers challenge assumptions they might have made about the audience's needs or perceptions.

UNDERSTANDING CONTEXT

To communicate effectively, designers must be aware of several contextual issues, including the cultural environments of the audience, the environment in which the message will appear, competitive messages, the medium to convey the message, the language used, and the visual cues used in the imagery. To communicate value, designers need to have a deep understanding of the audience they are addressing and the organization they are representing. Information is the most important creative tool a designer can have when tackling a design issue.

Information gathering has traditionally been the responsibility of marketing, but often the information obtained is not useful or deep enough to develop a meaningful communication approach. Designers need to be responsible for making sure the information they receive is actionable, and they must have an understanding of what type of information they need to develop designs that work well.

Beyond marketing research, design research is a discipline that looks at how users can help designers create a more meaningful experience. Market research asks this question: "How do we connect the product to the user?" Design research asks, "What needs do consumers have and how do we build to suit them?" Marketing offers numerous tools for graphic designers to extract the proper information needed from users. By asking the right questions, clients can be a source of valuable design information. By collecting information in the early stages of the project, the designer is able to make better design decisions and mitigate a perception of subjectivity. Design research allows designers to better understand the people they are serving, and gives them an opportunity to grasp the meaning and values users attribute to the product or service being communicated.

MARKET RESEARCH AND DESIGN

Market research has been a staple of modern business since the early 1930s. In the early days, marketers looked to the social sciences to find out what would motivate consumers to buy. Marketing originally offered insight for firms that would allow them to simply sell more products or services. Most marketing did not consider what customers wanted, only what firms could produce.

As America came out of World War II, its industrial capability for mass production was at a peak, developed to meet the demands of the war. With soldiers returning home and an economy that was on the rise, firms looked to market products and tap into the psyche of the American people.

By the 1960s, firms started to define benefits and features in order to better sell products. Companies jockeyed for position while developing new features for existing products. By this time, however, the advances in manufacturing and technology had leveled the competitive field and products were becoming commodities. You could buy a radio from GE or Panasonic and it was essentially the same. This commoditization left many firms to compete only on cost.

However, competing on cost was not a good strategy for many organizations, and they looked to capture market share in a new way. By the 1980s more consumer psychology data became available, and technology was beginning to ramp up. About this time, firms found a new way to compete.

Differentiation became one of the generic competitive tactics enabling firms to compete. But differentiation needed to be more than just a new look and a new logo to work. Companies like Starbucks, the Body Shop, and Apple conducted deep research and found that by connecting to markets on a shared-values basis, they could penetrate more markets and create loyalty through a shared philosophy. As if increasing market share was not enough, these firms discovered that their customers were also willing to pay more for their products.

DESIGN RESEARCH

Up to this point, organizations relied on traditional market research to direct their strategies. Market research consisted of telephone surveys, focus groups, and interviews. But even with research, new products failed in the market a staggering 80 percent of the time. A new approach was needed.

Design research used many of the same methodologies as market research, and, in fact, there is some overlap in the approaches. Yet the key difference between the two is significant: Market research is about aligning products with consumers, and design research is about using consumers as a starting point for new products and communications.

Design research looks for context by means of in-depth interviews and observations. In some cases, researchers use ethnographic approaches to better understand audience's experiences and the context in which the product or service is part of their lifestyle.

BEYOND EXPERIENCES

Meaning, as described by Nathan Shedroff, coauthor of the book *Making Meaning*, is "the most powerful communication, learning, and development tool we can use to relate to people—especially potential customers." Meaning represents the next rung on the ladder of consumer needs. From mere function to basic benefits to experiences, meaning represents "how we understand the world around us." Shedroff suggests that organizations that want to take the next step in connecting with audiences need to address audience meaning at the strategic level. By identifying what is meaningful to audiences via the use of indirect processes, such as research techniques like interviews and ethnography, organizations can identify what cues create meaning. In this way, they can forge deeper relationships with their audiences, connecting their offerings to the higher motivations in their audience's lives.

By including design research at the onset of communication design projects, designers take a step toward better understanding people and the values that are meaningful to them. Without this insight, designers perpetuate the "window dressing" stigma that has haunted them. This part of the design process is probably the most critical and most overlooked by communications designers.

MANAGING WORK FLOW

Any given design project entails aligning people, building consensus, gathering information, and thinking creatively to produce communications that motivate the viewer to act or think in a certain way. Project management skills are applicable to a variety of design-related disciplines, including architecture, new product development, and communications. These disciplines use project management to bring structure to the development of their product, whether it is a new building, a new coffeepot, or a new communication.

Tasks ranging from defining design deliverables, setting up approvals, critiquing design concepts, and developing the design brief to acting as project coordinator often fall to the designer. Design process offers a framework for managing these activities.

As designers initiate projects, their first task is to define what will be done. Meeting with the client, the designer and client agree on the scope of the project by answering questions about the problem to be solved, the primary goal to be achieved, the roles and responsibilities of participants, the success criteria, and plans for dealing with risks.

The next step is to develop the project plan, which usually takes the form of a design brief. Project scope information is collected, schedules are defined, budgets are agreed upon, and staff is assigned. Planning is critical since it outlines the activities and tasks needed to complete the project. Additionally, it creates a shared reference for what will happen, thereby reducing uncertainty among project participants. Once the goals of the project have been defined and a plan established, the major phases of the design process can begin.

Finally, the designer brings the project to an end and evaluates the success of the efforts using these metrics: meeting design requirements and schedules, staying on budget, and using efficient processes. This is also the time for reviewing what worked and what didn't so that future projects can benefit from the lessons learned.

GAINING RESPECT

"Designers talk about creating a body of work, but they seldom talk about acquiring a body of knowledge," says William Drenttel, co-founder of the influential design blog Design Observer, and principal of the design consultancy Winterhouse. "They take pride in being makers, but seldom identify themselves as thinkers. They claim to be emissaries of communication—to give form to ideas. And while we would like to believe this is true, it seems to us that all too often, we, as designers, are called upon merely to make things look good—rather than contributing to the evolution and articulation of ideas themselves."

Jose Nieto of the Salem, Massachusetts-based design firm square zero, echoes this statement, saying, "Designers are not taken seriously in their role as communications experts. We are seen more as a pair of hands that can manufacture something that a client cannot do on their own. Letting clients know that this is a process, and we're not just sitting around asking random questions... that there is a goal to be achieved. I think designers tend to get a bit more respect for the thinking part of the process."

Designers have long decried the lack of respect they receive in business circles. Much of this comes from perceptions about what designers actually do. Often regarded as decorators, designers have historically been underutilized. Marketing guru Philip Kotler once said, "Design is a potent strategy tool that companies can use to gain a substantial competitive advantage. Yet most companies neglect design as a strategy tool. What they don't realize is that design can enhance products, environments, communications and corporate identity." The causes for this are manifold. Some typical issues that erode design's standing in the organization follow.

No Shared Vocabulary

Language can be a unifier or a divider. Some professions use language as a way of asserting control. By using jargon or overly technical language, designers and businesspeople shut down the dialogue, leaving both parties to interpret what the other means. This is not to say that designers should adopt business speak. Taking on the language of business can be a slippery slope. Designers (or anyone for that matter) who throw out the latest business platitude or buzzword run the risk of sounding superficial or sophomoric. A better approach is to speak plainly, precisely, and in terms they understand. More important than using the language of business is understanding the thinking of business.

Talking about design can be equally difficult. A better way for designers to break through communications issues with clients is to use visuals as references. You can show someone what you mean by *contemporary* faster than you can explain it. Visual benchmarking is direct, as designers can point to existing designs as reference for clients' likes and dislikes. Building totems (see chapter 7) and other visual exercises help close the gap on understanding what visual cues resonate with clients.

Beyond language, design process offers a common framework for working together. Much of design process uses methods that are familiar to businesspeople. In fact, many of the phases of design process are similar to that of building a business plan. Design process offers a common language for both designers and businesspeople, and keeps the focus on business goals and project logistics and away from subjective design discussions like "I like red."

Management Focus on What They Know: Business

We all speak the language we know best. Businesspeople focus on business problems and not on how to integrate design into their strategy. Design management pioneer Brigitte Borja de Mozota believes that design thinking and business thinking are so different the integration of the two is unlikely to happen without strong motivating forces. Because of this, designers need to be prepared to talk about design in the context of a business problem-solving tool.

Management Unsure of Design Value

Over the last decade, there's been several significant research studies conducted that prove the old adage, "Good design is good business." Yet few of these studies have made their way to the head offices in organizations. A recent survey conducted by Britain's Design Council proved design increased market shares, developed new markets, increased profit, and made the organization more competitive.

With evidence like this, designers should have an easy time selling design as a strategic business tool. But far too few designers know of this data and prefer to focus on design awards. As long as designers don't promote their work based on business success factors, clients will continue to marginalize them.

Design process considers success factors at the outset of each project. The business goals that design can actively play a part in influencing are identified.

Simply by asking questions like "What is the goal of the project?" or "What do we want audiences to do when they come in contact with this communication?" the designer begins to move design beyond the aesthetic and toward the strategic.

Designers Not Working in Transparent Ways

Because many design departments are not directly connected to company leadership, they tend to work under the wire, rarely getting much face time with the primary players. This exacerbates the problem of designers working in insulated environments. Collaboration from other parts of the organization should be the goal. On top of this, many designers work in idiosyncratic ways that make it difficult for others to participate in the design process.

By adopting a transparent process that can be shared with stakeholders, designers take a step in allowing others to collaborate in the process. This is a key step in making design an integral part of the organization. Once the organization is able to participate, its members become vested in the outcome of the project, and having been active participants in the project, they have a feeling of ownership, as well as an understanding of what value design can bring to the organization. Without a defined process, collaboration is nearly impossible.

Process helps designers take clients in new directions by giving the client a sense of control over the project. As opposed to handing off the work to the designer, the client remains an active participant with a defined role, working alongside the designer. Including the client in this process and explaining the process to the client can gain that trust. When clients are given some control in this way, they are more collaborative and less afraid of new directions.

IN CONCLUSION

Design process provides a structure for moving design projects forward. The designer's articulation of clear steps makes it possible for team members, stakeholders, and clients to become active participants who contribute to a design solution beyond what an individual could produce alone.

Once a clear understanding of the value of design is achieved, the next step is to explain its value to clients and other nondesign team members. The benefits of having a defined process are many:

- Aligning project stakeholders and clients
- Quicker design turnaround
- Managing common design frustrations
- Developing new ideas
- Managing work flow
- Gaining respect

chapter 3

THE COLLABORATIVE DESIGNER

CREATING A STRONG
CLIENT—DESIGNER RELATIONSHIP

"There are only two ways to secure design's opportunities: reputation and personal relationships," says Rick Valicenti, founder of Thirst, the internationally recognized design firm dedicated to taking their clients to the edge of the "Discomfort Zone." As Valicenti notes, graphic design, like most professions, is about the quality of the relationships we form with clients. Design is collaborative work and requires that both designers and clients pull together. Clients hire designers to help them solve business problems; designers push clients to communicate their unique value in fresh and unexpected ways. The resulting tension can develop ideas that are balanced and that consider multiple sides of a problem. Gaute Godage, founder of the world's leading independent computer game developer, Funcom, notes that managing this tension can be achieved only through trust.

Designers are meticulous craftspeople. They are experts in the subtle nuances of typography. They tweak colors by percentage points on press and refine their work over and over, seeking perfection. For many designers their work is more than a job; it is a reflection of who they are. Designers must master a plethora of software applications and work in multiple mediums. They are paid to write, draw, and invent. But technical skill is only one dimension of what clients expect. Design is also about relationships, and the ability to create strong relationships with clients plays as much a role in successful design outcomes as technical proficiency.

In-house design management guru Andy Epstein has a caveat for designers: "As irrelevant as it might seem to designers to form strong personal relationships with their clients, because they are thinking about the work, they must understand one thing—it's not just about the work." Designers must consider the ad hoc nature of the design profession. Most designers work on a project basis and need to have a consistent flow of projects to stay solvent. Relationship management is key for continuing the flow of work from clients. Designers that form solid relationships, developing a deep understanding of the client's need, their audiences, and the environment in which they operate, are more likely to maintain long-term relationships.

IT'S NOT JUST ABOUT THE WORK

How do you form good working relationships with your clients? Coca-Cola design director Moira Cullen has this advice: "Take them out to lunch… a lot." Cullen's point being that there is an emotional factor to creating strong client–designer relationships. Epstein echoes this sentiment: "The designer might want to be judged solely on the merits of his work, and feel that *that* is his sole goal in client relationships, but it's really not. The ability to form strong personal relationships is equally important. There has to be some empathy, and out of that empathy you end up with trust, and hopefully more creative freedom."

Trust develops over time, through the personal experiences people share. At its most basic, trust is doing what you say and saying what you do. By communicating openly about your intentions and following through with them, you establish trust. But trust is fragile and easily eroded. If trust is weak, a common mishap such as a missed deadline, a typo, or an unexpected expense can prove to be a deal breaker. Inevitably, these things will happen, producing anxiety and encouraging the question, "Will it happen again?" When trust is strong, a client can forgive a designer for errors or indiscretions.

Alternatively, if a client lets us down, we are more likely to let them down. Once trust is lost, it's hard to recover and can be regained only if both parties are willing to put past transgressions behind them and move forward. Most designers can recall times when they broke a client's trust, either through unavoidable circumstances or a breakdown in the design process, or when a client made trust impossible by missing or continually rescheduling deadlines or making unrealistic demands. When such breakdowns occur, both client and designer need to review their actions at once and ask themselves: "Am I doing anything that might jeopardize this relationship?"

THE BUILDING BLOCKS OF TRUST

- Effective communication
- Active listening
- Honest interaction
- Transparent procedures
- Consistent follow-through

POSITIONING DESIGN IN THE CLIENT'S MIND

Before we can discuss relationship building, we need to define the role of the designer. The term "professional designer" can apply to anything from a service provider to a strategic partner, depending on the designer's individual experience, her approach to problem solving, and her relationship with a client.

At the low end of the scale you find the design vendor. This person simply responds to a specific request made by a client, providing the client with a pre-described outcome. The design vendor performs mainly tasks that can be easily replicated by others. Competition for this type of service is based primarily on cost. It is at this stage in a client relationship that the designer's technical skills and/or reputation get him in the door. The designer has little input concerning the outcome of the project because his credibility has yet to be established or confirmed. If all goes well, and the client values the final product and enjoys the process of getting it made, the relationship may continue.

In the middle of this scale are the design professionals who offer direction and some degree of specialization. They bring not only expertise to the table, but also a degree of professionalism.

At the far end of the scale stands the design consultant. She is able to serve in an advisory role, guiding the client through the design problem-solving process. As design problems become more complex and require broader collaborative thinking, advisors provide not just solutions, but insight and depth, and they help synthesize information amassed or created by collaborators. A design consultant positions herself as a collaborative partner, whose job it is to facilitate the problem-solving process. As Jagdish Sheth notes in his book *Clients for Life*, "In the twenty-first century, the knowledge workers who excel will be those who transcend simple expertise and are able to provide insights to clients in the context of a collaborative, learning relationship."

Designers who make the leap from craftsperson to collaborator, who don't necessarily have all the answers but at least boast a methodology for facilitating design thinking, will be able to position themselves as trusted consultants. As such, a designer does not push ideas, but rather listens. Nor do they try to dominate, but instead work collaboratively. They bring a high level of design expertise and also the ability to manage the increasing complexity of design problems, design "in context" to their target audiences, and remain accountable through measurement.

WHAT MAKES A GOOD DESIGNER?

Good designers are multifaceted. They are able to manage the complexity of design problems through finely honed design thinking. They also work collaboratively, understand cultural and business contexts, and assume accountability for the outcomes of their work.

From a client relationship perspective, they are client focused and work with a transparent process that supports collaboration. They are active listeners who ask thoughtful questions. They are professionals and manage their emotions in difficult situations. To a great degree, these "soft skills" are as important as traditional design skills. Good designers, at a glance, are:

- talented
- client focused
- collaborative

They utilize:

- interpersonal skills
- managed emotions
- transparency

Talent

Visual design literacy is the price of entry into the design field. If your design craft skills are substandard, and you have no sense of the context for design, no amount of interpersonal or organization skills will help you. Designers must be masters of the elements of design (that is, line, color, shape, form, value, size, texture, motion and space), as well as have an understanding of design as it relates to—and impacts—culture.

Client Focused

We've all heard clients use the term *artist* when describing designers. The distinction between these two disciplines is clear to any professional designer. Artists are about personal expression. They are interpretive and define the success of their project based on their own criteria. Designers, on the other hand, are client focused, rely on data as well as intuition, and base their work on measured outcomes. They design for people, not themselves. They take the time to understand the goals of the client and develop solutions that get them there, on time, on budget and on target. As hired professionals, clients are their *raison d'être*.

A Collaborative Partner

Designers cannot expect to work in a vacuum. The client–designer relationship is one of interdependence. As Tim Larsen, founder and CEO of Larsen Interactive, says, "It seems in the past, where designers were asked to do more tactical solutions, it was pretty well outlined, like 'we need a brochure or an identity.' Now, clients are coming to us saying, 'We have a problem, and we don't know what the right solution is. Is it a branding problem? Is it a direct-marketing problem? Is it a website?'" Larsen goes on to say, "We are much more consultative than we were in the past. It's much more difficult to work on your own, as teams are more collaborative... There will probably be an account executive, a writer, someone from interactive, and some research involved. In the old days, a typical meeting would involve the designers and someone from the printing company. Now we have developers and others who help develop the sites, or we may be working with a direct-mail company to do fulfillment." As project dynamics change, the designer's role changes too. No longer can designers expect to fly solo.

Thomas Walton, editor of the *Design Management Journal*, says, "Consultant–client teamwork, grounded in trust, research, and sensitive communications, can [deliver] design objectives and uncover options that are more creative and more effective than anyone's perceptions." This "designer as collaborative partner" perspective has gained much credence in the last decade. We've witnessed the rise of new areas of design consultancy and design research techniques that bring designer, client, and audience together.

Tim Bruce, principal of the Chicago-based design firm LOWERCASE, INC., takes collaboration seriously. Bruce believes that involving clients at key points in the process is critical. As he puts it, "We involve the client for certain projects, like annuals. We do this for several reasons. One, they have good ideas. Two, it brings them along because they help create it so they end up supporting it."

Interpersonal Skills

The ability to be an active listener and ask insightful questions is a key skill for designers. Without these qualitative skills, designers cannot gather the data they need to develop smart designs, nor will they be able to achieve a level of chemistry with clients. Interpersonal skills include the following:

Managing emotions: Client interactions can at times be frustrating. They can make you angry or defensive, particularly if clients fail to grasp an idea or direction that you've labored over. But getting too invested in any direction can be dangerous. Bruised egos can quickly turn a potentially productive relationship into drudgery. As a professional, you must be able to manage your feelings by separating who you are from your work.

Taking it personally: *Passion* is a word often used to describe how designers approach their work. Designers feel more connected to their work than some other professionals do. When their work is criticized, it's easy to take it personally. However, doing so can lead to souring the relationship, and impede good work from happening.

Maintaining perspective: Another aspect of the client–designer relationship involves retaining a mind-set that allows for detachment. By not becoming emotionally involved in every wave and trough brought on by the client, the designer is able to maintain a healthy degree of independence. This can be difficult, as many creative people have a personal investment in their work. Criticism and other forms of feedback are hard to absorb without feeling defensive. The fiscal nature of the relationship can produce additional anxiety for the designer. However, holding on to a sense of independence frees the designer to take corrective action when necessary.

Managing the design ego: The designer assumes she is being hired for her creative expertise. She provides insights that are of value to the client and are also expected to nudge the client in a strategic direction. Knowing when to push and when to concede requires experience, judgment, and an understanding of the client and its needs. Push too hard, or for too long, and trust may evaporate.

The design ego is a double-edged sword. On the one hand, it supplies the confidence to explore uncharted territory and lends strength to the designer's convictions. On the other hand, it can become an emotional barrier to meeting client needs. In the end, it is the client's money and reputation on the line, and they will absorb most of the burden of the success or failure of a project. The designer is a consultant; in this role he provides design concepts, offers advice and recommendations on various options, and then allows the client to choose the creative direction that best suits them. If the process for developing options proves collaborative, the chance of arriving at a mutually beneficial solution is higher. However, in the event that the client ultimately insists on an option the designer cannot live with, the designer reserves the right to withdraw from the project.

Designers are experts in their field. They may have more experience and training than their clients at solving communication problems and should take a leadership role, guiding the client through the process to take them to the best possible solution. This position requires a level of tact and judgment, as there is a delicate balance between being assertive and being aggressive. The latter is often evident in the "trust me, I'm a professional" response designers sometimes give clients who challenge their direction or advice. Seemingly a reaction to the marginalization of designers in the past, this type of bluster comes across as a weak attempt to position oneself as an authority figure, one who knows "what's good for the client." Unfortunately, the end result is often a breakdown in the previously established trust between client and designer.

Transparency

As a collaborative partner and guide, designers offer a transparent process so that their clients can be active participants in the process. Design process provides the framework for creating a productive working environment.

WHAT MAKES A GOOD CLIENT?

Noted author, educator, and designer Ellen Shapiro describes great clients as having "a vision, a great story, and a great budget." Shapiro believes that even difficult clients can be "the best kind to have," as they push you to do your finest work. Generally, good clients provide meaningful work and profits for the designer, they are aligned around a common goal, and have staff and monetary resources to fund a successful outcome.

How do you know who will be a good client? David C. Baker, the principal of the management consulting firm ReCourses, Inc., has had a lot of experience helping design and advertising firms position themselves, structure their organizations, and develop systems for moving away from a deadline-driven environment to a profit-driven environment. Baker recommends several approaches to help vet the appropriateness of clients. "You can talk about money up front and see what their reaction is. If it slows the conversation down, this might be an indication that the client might not be profitable. You can also make some true, astute, and bold observations about their situation before they even become a client to see how they react. Will they be open to your point of view or perspective on their situation?"

Profitable

When asked what designers should look for in a client, Baker believes that the most important thing a client can provide the designer is a profit. Designers cannot be expected to produce high quality work without sufficient funding. Along with the ability to generate profits, Baker advises that designers work with clients that give them the opportunity to have a significant impact on their situation. This can only come from a relationship that is appropriate for both parties.

Experienced

Clients that have previous experience working with designers ease the learning curve. One of the challenges designers often face is having to educate their clients about processes; the value of design; roles and responsibilities. Baker provides some caveats about the types of clients designers should be wary of. These include clients that have not worked with a professional design firm before; clients who are spending their own money; clients who do not have full budget authority over the money; and clients who are not forthright about the project budget.

Decisive

A decisive client ultimately saves time and money. Decisive clients know what they want and are able to articulate it clearly. They have an understanding of their business goals and audience's needs and know enough about what constitutes good design to make smart choices.

Open

A big issue for designers is how to deal with clients who are not open to the designer's advice. Should they "fire" the client? Or continue to fight for a creative direction they strongly prefer? Or just do whatever the client asks, collect a paycheck, and move on? This issue is at the crux of the client–designer relationship. How do the designer's creative vision and the client's organizational needs fall into sync?

Like any professional, a designer needs to maintain a clear set of values and standards. She needs to know what she will and won't do, and be clear about this with the client at the outset of a project. Without personal standards, designers are simply service providers carrying out the demands of a client. A client hires a designer for more than a technical skill set; clients value designers' unique insights and sense of perspective. Thus, it makes sense for a designer to stand by her ideas and ideals. This may call for diplomacy and judgment when meeting with a client. Knowing when to say when is critical, if a designer wishes for the relationship to continue. An overly persistent designer runs the risk of exhausting a client—to the point that the client may choose to no longer work with him.

Aligned

Too often designers view clients as opponents who care little for the nuances of design, and are quick to make changes without regard for the impact on a designer's work. Certainly, a client's oft-repeated plea, "Just finish the project, already," can be thought of as a barrier to creativity and a hindrance to excellence. As a result, designers often distrust clients, purposely keeping them at a distance from the design process to prevent the client from hijacking or squelching the creative direction. Without alignment, the critical interplay of ideas cannot exist.

CLIENTS TO AVOID

Gather any group of designers together and inevitably the conversation will turn to clients. Stories about the "perfect client" who is appreciative and gives ample creative freedom to the designer are rare. More common are tales of woe involving the "bad client." The bad client oftentimes serves as a scapegoat when something goes wrong. However, most breakdowns are not solely the result of client interference or mismanagement. Typically, both client and designer—and inadequate communication—are at fault.

As business owners, designers reserve the right to accept or reject offers of business. While most designers welcome new opportunities for work, there are times when saying "No, thanks" makes more sense. Clients who are overly demanding and offer little in the way of profit should be avoided. Identifying such clients is part of the learning curve and is best chalked up to experience. What follows are a few red flags for designers to be aware of when doing business with clients.

Mo' Money

Designers are passionate about their work, but passion will not put food on the table, pay the mortgage, or put shoes on their children's feet. Successful designers place as much value on the profit associated with a project as the project itself. Clients that have no budget set aside for design are generally not worth engaging. Equally dangerous are clients who won't disclose their budgets. This scenario often makes it impossible to plan properly.

R-E-S-P-E-C-T

Certain clients assume a designer is at their beck and call 24/7. Or they consistently make requests that fall outside the scope of the original contract. Either such clients are unclear about the parameters of the work agreement or they assume that because of their size or reputation they will always get what they want, whenever they want it. If the designer feels the relationship is worthwhile, or necessary to long-term success, an exception might make sense. But it's a bad habit. After all, the designer is basically training such clients to forever expect more for less.

She's So Vain

Too often, a designer's smallest accounts prove to be the most demanding. When a designer finds himself spending too much time handling the minor issues of one client at the expense of neglecting more profitable work, it's time to reconsider the big picture. You may need to terminate such "low value/high maintenance" accounts.

A Matter of Trust

Trust is the foundation of any good relationship. Once trust has been breeched, only time will prove if the oversight was unique or part of a troublesome pattern. Clients that habitually break the bond of trust with a designer, or consistently act in a deceptive manner, should be dropped.

(I Can't Get No) Satisfaction

Then there's the client who apparently will not be satisfied, no matter how many concepts a designer presents, no matter how many revisions the designer executes. This is often a sign that a client doesn't know what they want (even if they insist they do). Alternatively, other stakeholders involved in the project cannot reach a consensus as to what creative direction will meet their needs.

Take This Job and Shove It

We all work to make a profit, but for many designers, deeper motivation stems from something greater than the need to earn a living. Designers take pride in a job well done. For some, the line between the professional and the personal blurs entirely. A designer's body of work becomes part of who he is, a reflection of his unique passions and talents. When clients are disrespectful or unappreciative, it can be deflating. It can even deprive a designer of the sense of satisfaction she normally gets from her work. As in any relationship, a lack of positive feedback can lead to confusion and sap motivation.

WALKING IN THE CLIENTS' SHOES

As in all relationships, empathy is important. Designers would benefit by experiencing at least one design project from a client's perspective, and they should do so early in their careers. Until this is done, designers may not understand the unease, frustration, and anticipation that the client too often experiences. If you can't be a client yourself, then imagine yourself as a client. You ask a designer to reflect the ethos and character of a business or organization, an endeavor into which you have poured considerable time, money, and talent. How would you want the designer to proceed? What do you want the designer to know about you and your goals? What if the designer doesn't ask? And what if the process remains undefined? How would you feel? What would the designer need to do to earn your trust?

On the other hand, clients sometimes assume designers have fragile egos and inflexible approaches. The designer is thus perceived as lacking strategic focus, someone working reclusively with little regard for the input of others. This further alienates the client, increasing friction and dissolving trust. In this context, design decisions can seem overly subjective to clients, without explanation or justification, based on little more than whimsy and self-satisfaction.

At the end of the day, clients and designers need each other. Without a client, the designer is an artist, pursuing exclusively individual work. A client makes a designer a designer by establishing requirements and constraints that a designer must address. Conversely, a client benefits from the creativity and fresh thinking that a designer can lend to problem solving. Therefore, a designer skilled at cultivating relationships built on mutual respect, who can focus on a client's needs while maintaining her own individuality, will create the most opportunities for trust and profit.

RELATIONSHIP FUNDAMENTALS

Stefan Bucher, principal of Los Angeles design studio 344, describes the client–designer relationship in terms of dating. "You go into it thinking this is going to be a good match, we look good together, we have an easy rapport… but at the same time it may crash and burn. It is somewhat ineffable." The similarities between dating and the client–designer relationship don't end there. Consider that two people tentatively come together in the hopes of making a connection. Personal chemistry, communication skills, and background all play a part in the success or failure of the relationship. Like a marriage, it generally takes several years to reach the level of trust and understanding that enables a happy union. The design consultant's relationship with a client is no different. It must evolve incrementally, from an initial meeting to increased levels of connectedness, before a long-term relationship is possible.

Designers hope to create long-term relationships with clients by fostering mutual goodwill. To maintain a strong relationship, both parties must have a clear understanding of the values each party brings to the relationship, as well as the needs of each party. Through effective communication and managed experience, designers can forge more profitable and meaningful relationships with their clients.

Businesses realize that the most profitable relationships are not with one-time buyers; rather they are with the repeat buyer, who consistently uses their products or services over an extended period of time. The ability to retain clients is the goal of most businesses because long-term customers are less expensive to maintain. They require less education about processes, are less likely to switch to other design firms, are less price sensitive, create word-of-mouth referrals, and because of their familiarity with the designers process, projects generally run smoother.

Developing long-term clients is a process. Most clients begin as prospects who are then turned into customers. A customer who returns with additional projects may then be termed a client. Clients whose value to the designer continues to increase eventually become supporters, advocates, and ideally, partners. Like all relationships, developing faithful clients in this way takes considerable time and effort. Once a customer becomes a client, retention becomes a key focus.

INTERPERSONAL COMMUNICATION

"I've seen people who are poorly organized accomplish great things because they work well together," says Emily Carr, project manager and brand strategist for Gensler, the global architectural, design, and planning firm. "I think overall that is the thing that you really need. To be able to work well together—if a team works well together, they'll get it done no matter how difficult it is. It all comes down to people."

When asked what role interpersonal skills play in the client–designer relationship, designer, teacher and author Ellen Shapiro answers succinctly, "Everything." From a client perspective, great design skills are expected, but being a good listener is seen as a real added value. "I don't think there's a major client I've ever interviewed who didn't say that the ability to listen was a top characteristic of a designer who did great work," she says. "Conversely, clients who complain about designers always say, 'They didn't listen and just went ahead and did what they thought was cool without understanding what we're trying to accomplish and communicate.'"

A designer's ability to communicate on a personal level is the foundation for making connections with clients. Designers communicate volumes to the people around them not only with words, but with listening skills, and tone of voice, and body language. Communication and empathy are the keys to building a foundation for rewarding and profitable relationships.

One of the first steps in the design process is to gather information. Ways of doing this include interviewing the client, administering a survey, and conducting visual research. These activities are the equivalent of listening and asking questions, usually the first step when interacting with a client. Once information is collected, a context is established, and the business model is understood, a client's specific need or problem—what they are asking for a designer's help with—must be defined. This, too, is similar to one of the steps in building a personal relationship.

Listening

Petrula Vrontikis, award-winning principal of Vrontikis Design Office, author and design educator, has coined a phrase that should be quickly added to the design lexicon. Vrontikis believes that designers should be "working with their ears" before they begin working with their hands. "If I'm in an interview with a potential client, I'll ask them, 'What do you value in a relationship with a graphic designer?' Eighty percent of the time, they will respond with, 'I want somebody who is able to listen.'"

Vrontikis believes that strong listening skills place the designer in the position of trusted partner in the mind of the client and that only when a client perceives the designer as an expert do they feel comfortable giving that designer the information needed to perform quality design work. "So you've got to ask them really good questions," she says. "And really listen to the answers. Then ask a lot more really good questions, to help them delve deeper. You will impress the client with your questions and the way you use their answers to inquire further."

Designer and in-house design management guru Andy Epstein understands that designers and clients tend to have different communication styles, and that these differences can have a significant impact on how designers communicate with clients and peers. "As designers, we tend to take our work very personally because we are passionate about it," he says. "As a result we're also very sensitive about the feedback that we get from clients and might feel that they are criticizing us or our work. I think that this gets in the way of hearing what the client is really saying."

For example, a client can say, "I think the logo is too large." If the designer has his ego in the way, what he hears is, "The logo stinks." When designers get caught up in the emotional response that they perceive as criticism, then they don't hear the facts. This causes two problems—they don't absorb what has been said to them, so they don't hear "The logo is too large" or some marketing directions, and they don't remember the facts and can't execute on them. Secondly, they won't know how to ask good follow-up questions, because they didn't hear what the client said.

Listening is the first step toward establishing a client's trust. Before design work can start, a client's needs must be understood. This deceptively simple act of empathy not only allows a client to be heard, but lets them know that the designer cares about what they have to say. Listening is an active skill, one that can be developed only through practice. To become an effective listener, a designer needs to know what to take note of while listening. Communication research contends that listening consists of several distinct levels.

We have all conducted a conversation while performing other tasks, such as checking e-mail or filing paperwork. When we are not fully engaged with the person who is speaking to us, however, we generally only hear them. We understand the basics of what they are saying, but only on a superficial level. We may hear the words coming out of their mouth, but miss (or misunderstand) their true meaning or more subtle intent.

When we eliminate distractions and focus on one conversation at a time, we are able to not only hear a conversation, but understand it. This allows us to make meaningful comments that in turn raise the level and enrich the quality of a conversation.

At the highest level of listening, we are able to make judgments about what is being said. Are there points in the conversation that don't make sense? Were the ideas expressed believable? How should I best respond?

Active listening requires a listener to remain engaged with a conversation and not let other activities distract her. To be an effective listener, a designer needs to focus on what is actually being said, so she can evaluate and contribute to the ideas being presented. Listening is not passive; it requires practice, desire, and commitment. Here are some tips for active listening:

Restate the idea. One cue that indicates you understand what is being said is to repeat the main points back to the speaker. This allows you to demonstrate your understanding of what she said—thereby establishing a connection with her. Do this and you become more engaged and more engaging.

Focus on content. Focus on the main ideas. Sometimes we are distracted by one another's body language, tone, or delivery. Instead, try to judge the value of ideas on their own merit, not by how they are presented.

Be aware of body language. During a conversation, faces can say a lot about how engaged people are. Facial expressions, eye contact, tone of voice, body language all play a part in communication. Eye contact helps you focus and lets the other person know you are paying attention. Physical feedback, like a nod of the head, along with simple verbal cues, also help. A receptive listener encourages people she communicates with by sending signals that say, "I'm interested," or "Oh, now I get it," or "What a great idea!"

Manage your emotions. Designers are connected to their work in a unique way. It's often hard for them to talk about it without revealing a strong emotional tie. Emotions can also influence the way you hear a conversation. If the subject is a sensitive one, it can be hard to divorce yourself from your feelings and stay objective. Designers must maintain a reasonable amount of emotional distance between themselves, their work, and their clients.

Prompt for further details. The more a client explains what he is thinking and feeling, the better chance a designer has of understanding the client's point of view. A wise designer endeavors to keep a client talking by probing for details, using "why" questions as a way to get deeper into the client's thinking.

Suspend judgment. By giving in to an urge to respond too quickly to a client's problem with a nifty solution, a designer runs the danger of appearing random, lazy, or even worse, arrogant. Again, a designer must focus on the client first, not himself. Jumping to conclusions or interrupting a speaker is impolite. It can also make a client feel like she is not being allowed to express her thoughts.

Questioning

The most powerful tool designers have to work with is not a design skill; rather, it's the ability to ask meaningful questions and expand his understanding of a client's businesses and goals. From a client perspective, asking the right questions can transform a designer from an artist into a strategic business partner. Questioning challenges clients to think beyond assumptions and approach projects with fresh thinking. In many ways, it is the most effective way of educating clients about the power and value of design, and guiding them toward efficient design solutions.

For Todd Wilkens, senior practitioner and manager at Adaptive Path and coauthor of *Subject to Change*, questioning is his stock and trade. As an expert design researcher/strategist, Wilkens understands that in order to truly connect with an audience, you have to dig deep.

"I always push toward the *why*—the internal human motivational why," says Wilkens. Wilkens will often ask clients a seemingly simple question such as, "Tell me how everyone in the organization knows you're successful at your job?" The response will oftentimes be very practical and centered around basic metrics: the number of conversions per customer or the number of new accounts opened. However, when asked, "How does the company know you are doing a good job?" clients will say something along the lines of, "Well, I said I would complete the project by March and we finished in February, and so they gave me a raise." By asking questions, Wilkens is able to get beyond superficial answers to the real motivators, in this case understanding that success is based around organizational metrics (getting the project done early) and not customer-based metrics, as we initially indicated. "As much as they talk about customers, it's often organizational things that are driving clients," Wilkens says.

Questioning strategies have their origin in the education process. The Socratic method employs questions to help students arrive at their own logical conclusions, rather than having answers spoon-fed to them. It enables them to engage the problem on a deeper level, thereby enhancing the learning experience. It also teaches students to think for themselves, not just regurgitate facts. The basic Socratic format begins with a question, and then suggests a hypothesis. The hypothesis is then cross-examined; students search for examples that do not agree with the hypothesis. The hypothesis is then either accepted or rejected.

When explaining design concepts to clients, designers can use much the same method. Like many philosophical questions, design concepts can be somewhat hard to pin down. For example, how will an audience interpret certain images or graphics? Convincing clients that one direction is more appropriate than another can be a challenge if the client is not visually literate. By walking a client through a thought process via questioning, a designer can move them toward better design solutions and transcend assumptions. Plus, this method is collaborative, allowing the client to feel they arrived at a decision in tandem with the designer, or by themselves, as opposed to having the designer push a direction at them.

Open-ended questions are a big help for opening up a client–designer discussion. Kick-starting the conversation is the first step toward making room for options. Letting a client see the opportunities that exist, through questioning, helps the client break free from misguided or preconceived directions. Journalists often begin an interview with an open-ended question, then wait quietly while the other person comes up with an answer. Next, the reporter follows up with a "why" or "explain what you mean" question, allowing the interviewee to refine or elaborate on their answer. Most people don't possess ready-made answers to many questions. It may even take them several attempts to come up with something accurate. By digging deep to uncover the real reason something "must be done this way," designers open doors to innovation and foster creativity.

Giving Feedback

The ability to give clients positive and negative feedback is an important part of the collaborative process. By letting a client know what is and isn't working, the designer establishes a productive dialogue, allowing the client to clarify directions or options.

"If it's a good client relationship that has started out on the right foot, what I find is that the more I've met people personally, getting feedback tends to be okay," says Stefan Bucher of 344 Design. "When its feedback that is well founded and the client affords me the respect of saying, 'Here is the feedback and here are the things we are not happy with, and here is why,' I tend to do really well with it. What I don't do well with is if I get it back without comments, and they say, "Change this and move that." Then I say, "Why?" and they say, "It's because of sales." That does not give me a whole lot to go on. If it is coming out of nowhere, then I have a hard time with it."

Positive feedback is easy enough to deliver. But it is not enough just to say, "Atta boy!" or "You go, girl!" Meaningful feedback requires specifics about what went right—so everyone involved can ask questions and expand on how success was achieved.

Giving negative feedback can be difficult. Not many people relish the thought of having to tell someone they disagree. In Ron Carucci and Toby Tetenbaum's book *The Value-Creating Consultant*, they note that in the course of researching client–consultant relationships, delivering bad news emerged as the most difficult task to perform. A consultant will often go to great lengths to avoid confronting a client, even rationalizing the problem's existence to minimize its potential negative effect. For handling such confrontations, Carucci and Tetenbaum recommend a direct approach, one that is "straightforward, unfiltered, un-couched, and nonjudgmental."

Below, several steps have been identified to help keep the exchange focused, free of judgment, factual, direct, and running smoothly. The following eight principles are generally applicable, regardless of whether feedback is positive or negative.

1. **State your intent.** By clarifying the intent of a conversation, the designer allows the client to prepare himself, while offering an opportunity to participate more fully in the project.

2. **Review the goals.** Restating the goals of a project helps remind people why they are doing what they are doing. Positive or negative feedback has little meaning unless it's based on pre-established goals. Otherwise, there is nothing to work toward, and nothing to measure against.

3. **Be specific.** Feedback needs to be specific to be meaningful. Vague comments don't have much impact; they are too easily perceived as

random or insincere. When delivering positive feedback, the designer should tell the client specifically what she did right, and how it helped move the project toward an intended goal. In the case of negative feedback, the designer should give specific reasons why the client's actions didn't help.

4. **Get to the point.** It's often difficult to be direct when delivering negative feedback. It may create stress and anxiety for both the designer and the client. And yet, as much as people dislike receiving such bad news, they usually come to appreciate it if it is delivered in a respectful and direct way. Dancing around the issue prolongs the client's anxiety and makes the designer less confident in what he has to say.

5. **Don't qualify.** Many people tend to sugarcoat negative feedback. However, consistently burying negative comments within positive ones can backfire. The client may end up feeling that the designer is being manipulative or disrespectful. Besides, sugarcoating is a transparent ploy, solely intended to alleviate the pain of negativity. In actuality, it does little to soften the sting. Again, a direct and sincere path is more effective. Sugarcoating makes for insincere delivery. In turn, this makes feedback easier to challenge or deflate.

6. **Do it face-to-face.** Feedback may constitute a highly charged experience, especially for someone on the receiving end. It makes more sense to deliver it face-to-face, to avoid misinterpretation. It's easy enough for a designer to send an e-mail to a client outlining comments and concerns. True, this can be a quick and effective means of delivering feedback—but only after a positive client–designer relationship is firmly established. In a relatively new relationship, face-to-face feedback helps establish the tone of the relationship as sincere, making the designer appear both confident in their ideas and respectful of the client.

7. **Do it right away.** Feedback needs to be given quickly after the event in question. Delayed feedback becomes diluted and is ineffectual, especially if there are negatives that require immediate attention. The

only exception is if an issue has become notably emotional, such that a "cooling off" period may be prudent.

8. **Finish on a positive note.** Once feedback is given, restate the desired outcome. Explain how it will feed into the overall goals associated with the project.

MANAGING CREATIVE TENSION

In the classic film noir, *The Third Man*, Orson Welles's character, Harry Lime, gives a memorable speech on the creative aspects of conflict. "...In Italy, for thirty years under the Borgias, they had warfare, terror, murder and bloodshed, but they produced Michelangelo, Leonardo da Vinci and the Renaissance. In Switzerland, they had brotherly love, they had five hundred years of democracy and peace—and what did that produce? The cuckoo clock."

In Peter Senge's book *The Fifth Discipline*, Senge states, "The gap between vision and current reality is also a source of energy. If there were no gap, there would be no need for any action to move towards the vision. We call this gap creative tension." Designers are very familiar with the gap. In fact, to a great degree, designers live and work in the gap. Design is about problem solving, so more often than not projects start without a defined end. This "gray area" of design creates a great deal of anxiety in clients who are accustomed to working in a black-and-white world.

As collaborative partners, designers need to be able to challenge clients to think differently about their projects. This often leads to some resistance on the client side. Yet strong designers don't back away from this resistance. They embrace it as part of the creative process. Designers need to be assertive during discussions, as well as diplomatic. By expressing points of tension honestly, designers become less adversarial and more likely to move a client in a productive direction. Assertive does not mean aggressive or even passive/ aggressive. Assertive is being straightforward while maintaining diplomacy. Remember, the client owns the project, while the designer is a paid consultant who creates options to help solve problems. The choice of the "final" outcome belongs solely to the client.

SEVEN PRINCIPLES FOR
MANAGING CREATIVE TENSION

- Eliminate qualifying statements that demean a response
- Demonstrate that you understand the client's point of view
- State a problem clearly; explain why a change is necessary
- State a position clearly; explain why you believe it is correct
- Use "I" statements as opposed to "you" statements
- Concentrate on behaviors, not personalities
- Repeat a single key fact that reinforces your point

Tension between clients and designers is par for the course. As designers try to lead clients in a useful direction, inevitably there will be instances where the two parties don't see eye to eye. When the designer and client come into conflict over a project's direction, the designer's interpersonal skills become crucial to achieving a satisfying resolution.

SELLING IDEAS VS. GUIDING DECISIONS

Being able to influence clients is an important part of getting them to make good design and communications decisions. Some people use influence through personal power, while others use their position in an organization or relationship to gain control. Only on rare occasions can designers expect to use their "position" to influence clients, as the power typically resides with the client.

Every client is unique and carries with him his own experiences and perspectives. According to Robert Miller and Gary Williams, cofounders of Miller-Williams Inc., a leading consumer research firm, clients fall into one of five categories of decision-making style. *Charismatics* are intrigued by new ideas, but experience has taught them to make decisions based on balanced information, not emotions. *Thinkers* are risk averse and require as much data as possible before they will make a decision. *Skeptics* are suspicious of data that don't fit their worldview; thus they make decisions based mostly on gut feel-ings. *Followers* make decisions based on how other trusted executives, or they themselves, have made similar decisions in the past. And *controllers* focus on the facts and analytics of decisions to overcome their own fears and uncertainties.

Miller and Williams note that most design presentations aren't designed to acknowledge these different styles—much to their detriment. With so many different decision-making possibilities, it can be difficult for a designer to find the proper way of getting an idea across to a client. However, there does exist one time-tested method for getting people to accept your ideas: Invite them into the process. When clients are active in the creation of the idea (or believe the idea was theirs in the first place), they are more likely to support a pro-posed direction. As an old adage puts it: People support what they help create.

NEGOTIATION STRATEGIES

People use negotiation techniques every day when they decide what to make for dinner, what television program to watch, or what brand of cereal to buy. To move clients in a smart and sophisticated direction, a designer may have to employ considerable and specialized negotiation skills.

Design negotiation is not a winner-take-all proposition; rather, the aim is to reach an agreement that benefits everyone. Like any business activity, negotiation requires planning and should not be done spontaneously. First, a meeting is scheduled so that everyone has time to prepare his or her thoughts and objectives. The designer should define what is being negotiated and decide what she is willing to give in return for what she hopes to get. Negotiators must be keenly aware of their limits and must not promise things they are reluctant or unwilling to give up. Additionally, the designer as negotiator must know what it is that the client wants and what the client might be willing to give up to get it.

Sensitive Issues

Consider this scenario. The client is pleased with the new website a designer crafted for them. Now they want the designer to add their new logo to the site, which their amateur designer brother-in-law designed. Unfortunately the logo is poorly executed and does not meet basic standards for quality, and will ultimately degrade the overall aesthetic of the site. Does the designer risk insulting the client by addressing the concern? It's human nature to dance around sensitive situations like this. Typically, however, such evasive behavior confuses people and leads to frustration and disappointment.

A better strategy is for the designer to be direct about the issue and invite the client to participate in the conversation. By declaring their concerns outright, the designer can make a difficult conversation easier, and clarify expectations. Difficult conversations require effort; letting participants know the intent up front allows them to prepare mentally and feel comfortable giving consent. Declaring intent also helps project stakeholders understand each other's goals and roles. Thus, they are able to comprehend what is being said and respond with meaningful feedback. The client and designer are also prepared to address a difficult issue head-on, one they might otherwise strain to avoid.

The Center for Nonviolent Communication identifies five messages you can include in a conversation to help get your listeners to empathize. If you communicate what you saw or heard, what you felt, why you felt that way, what action you will seek, and what result you intend, you will inspire deeper understanding in others. Articulate communication, free of diagnosis and judgment, results in less defensive responses and inspires communicators to describe their needs in a constructive manner. When people feel they are being blamed or ordered to act, they instinctively block communication.

Express what you saw or heard: Begin by stating what you observed. Do this without emotion or unnecessary qualifiers. Use specific information about time and place.
Example: When I saw the logo your brother-in-law created...

Express what you felt: Use words that clearly articulate how you felt. Avoid words that cast blame on the other person.
Example: I felt uneasy...

Express why you felt that way: Make a statement that ties what you experienced and felt to your interpretation of the event.
Example: I think that we can do better...

Express what action you will seek: What do you want them to do?
Example: I want you to think about not using it...

Express what final result you intend: What will you do?

Example: Our goal is to represent your firm in a sophisticated way.

Managing Emotion

When negotiating, it's important to focus on the problem at hand and not the personalities involved. Clients and designers need to find common ground and maintain alignment. By reviewing shared goals, there is less of a chance for one side to make a power play. If strong-arm tactics are employed or a client proves uncooperative, the designer should be direct and describe what he is experiencing. Next, take a break. Everyone can reconvene once the strong emotions have died down.

Negotiation requires a thick skin. If you are highly emotional or cannot accept criticism, much less an outright attack, you won't be able to negotiate effectively. Good negotiators don't let personal issues get in the way of what they really want. If a negotiation has been a success, both parties should end up with something desirable. Also, the final agreement should be documented so that both parties have a physical record of what was said and what was agreed to. This can be included in the design brief, along with other relevant project information.

Roger Fisher, director of the Harvard Negotiation Project, and author of the classic negotiation text *Beyond Reason*, believes that managing emotion is the key to successful negotiating. Fisher and his colleague, Daniel Shapiro, identify five core human concerns that influence emotional states:

- Appreciation of one's thoughts and feelings
- Affiliation with, or treatment of, people as colleagues
- Autonomy, and respect for people's freedom of choice
- Status, and recognition of one's standing
- Having a fulfilling role to play

These are the keys to building collaborative environments in which a designer and a client can work together and understand not only their needs and problems, but also the emotions behind them. As Fisher says, "Negotiation involves both your head and your gut—both reason and emotion." Fisher says that emotion can become an obstacle to negotiating when it diverts attention away from the real matter at hand. Strong emotions left unchecked can severely damage or destroy a relationship, and be used to exploit a vulnerability or a weakness.

Win/Win

Roger Fisher developed the win/win approach to conflict resolution, though Stephen Covey made it famous in his landmark bestseller, *7 Habits of Highly Effective People.* In his book, Covey describes taking an integrative or collaborative approach to conflict. Win/win changes a conflict from an attack/defense model to one of cooperation and consensus. People are instinctively drawn into conflict when they feel they are being challenged or attacked, necessitating a defensive reaction. This happens when we don't have enough time to evaluate a situation, and consider an appropriate and measured response. The result is often a battle of attrition, such that even the winner may feel more like a loser in the end.

Covey describes three paradigms of conflict: win/win, win/lose and no deal. Win/lose uses power to dominate a conflict. Win/win or no deal lets both parties walk away from the conflict if a satisfactory solution cannot be reached.

Win/win seeks a third solution, and offers a give-and-take where both parties are able to satisfy their most important needs. By evaluating both client and designer needs, an equitable solution can often be reached. Many people assume that conflict resolution is an all or nothing, win/lose proposition. But such thinking only addresses the problem from one perspective. By asking clients why they want something done a certain way, and determining their true needs, opportunities may arise for compromise.

To achieve a win/win resolution, both parties must agree that a mutually beneficial solution exists, that a new approach is indeed necessary. "Win/win is a belief in the third alternative," explains Covey. "It's not your way or my way; it's a better way, a higher way." This stems from the conviction that there will be an opportunity for each party to end up with something of value, that success for one party does not exclude the other. Both parties must enter the negotiation process with the goal of arriving at a fresh solution together. Both parties must also have a keen understanding of each other's needs. Armed with determination, a willingness to adapt and a passion for working creatively together, the client and designer can form an increasingly fruitful, collaborative relationship.

COMMUNICATING THE VALUE OF DESIGN TO CLIENTS

Even with the prominence of design in the media, clients still misunderstand its value. At times, even experienced design professionals have difficulty articulating its value in a clear way. Because of this, designers need to be prepared to explain the strategic importance of design.

Communication design is about influencing audiences, whether it's changing their thinking about an important social issue or motivating them to go out and buy a new car. All clients—from small businesses to corporations—share the common need to motivate people to act. Communication design provides a means to inspire this action.

We make sense of the world through our visual processes. Images define our social, political, and cultural understanding. We view, filter, interpret, and create meaning in an instant of looking. We use visual codes to create meaning. The designer's skill at connecting with an audience by employing visual codes can determine the success or failure of a communications project.

Culture is steeped in visual imagery. These images motivate us, change our thinking, and move us to act. The motivational power of images has been used throughout the ages in religious, governmental, and other entities to move people in common directions and create a shared understanding of complex social systems. One need only think of how soldiers rally around a flag or how religious icons give strength and unite people.

The cognitive processes that people use when interacting with images happen automatically. That's why, even as visually immersed as we are, there remains a gap in understanding concerning the power of design to motivate. Graphic design exists because people make meaning from, and are motivated by, words and images. Yet people mostly react to visuals on a subconscious level; thus they are unable to articulate what they are experiencing.

DESIGN VALUE

Three important points can be made with clients about design's value.

Design as consumer motivator. Design has the power to create perceptual value. It is often a consumer's first impression of a product or service, and in that way it initiates and establishes a relationship.

Design as differentiator. As a competitive strategy, design offers a means for a firm to differentiate its products or services from those of its competitors.

Design as risk-management tool. Design process offers a structure that takes into account the strategic purposes of the communication being developed. Process aligns client and designer, offers opportunities for collaboration and innovation, and manages risk—by creating a common understanding of goals and roles, and a structure for diagnosing problems.

The bottom line for organizations is to influence thinking and motivate people to act in a certain way. Visual communication and design do this by helping create and influence perception.

DESIGN AND CONSUMER BEHAVIOR

An audience's decision-making process is complicated at best; and multiple models have been created to better understand it. It is generally understood that people undergo a four-step process regarding purchasing.

Step One: Perception of Need

The audience becomes aware of a need through advertising, social interaction, or other interaction. In this first step, design is the stimulus that pushes consumers to react.

Step Two: Prepurchase Planning

Once need is determined, the audience looks for ways of satisfying the need, by reviewing options offered in the marketplace. At this point, many people do at least some research via the web. The look and feel of a website, its message, its ease of use—each of these factors can make or break the customer experience.

Step Three: Making a Purchase

Consumer decisions about brand, price, availability, and payment all factor into a final purchase decision. Along with practical issues—Is it affordable?

Is it available? What are the payment options?—how the brand is perceived plays an important role in the decision-making process.

Step Four: Postpurchase Behavior

The goal of a business is not just to sell but to sell consistently. Brand loyalty is therefore the prime objective. Customers satisfied with their purchases, who have had a positive purchasing experience, are more likely to become repeat buyers. Did the product or service live up to its brand promise? Buyers are concerned with the functionality of a product as well as what the product represents, in the context of their social environment and core values.

To a significant extent, motivation depends on a consumer's interpretation of particular messages, both visual and textual. The four steps are thus influenced by multiple factors including attitudes, beliefs, values, and cognitive style. A buyer's method of processing information is key to how they make decisions. A person's cognitive style, as identified by the Myers-Briggs Type Indicator Test, plays a large role in how that person makes decisions. Each person filters a message through personal experience, such that no single message is interpreted in a single way.

DESIGN AS COMPETITIVE STRATEGY

A great deal of audience's perceptions are created through visual communication. Brand and style are some of the primary vehicles through which an organization's ethos is mostly conveyed. The offering must be unique and valued by a target audience. The intent is to express a meaningful, unique quality that captures attention and resonates. This is the essence of branding, and a key to differentiation strategy. To a great degree, they are the responsibility of the designer.

Differentiation is one of three proven, generic competitive strategies. It is expressed primarily through brand. A strongly differentiated organization or product tends to create brand loyalty. This loyalty is created when customers connect to a product or service on a level beyond what competitors offer. Think of the subtle differences between rival brands like BMW and Mercedes, or Nike and Adidas, or HP and Dell. Each product line is similar in character, price, and status level, yet each speaks to a unique group of buyers. Vehicles by BMW and Mercedes are both targeted at well-to-do, success-oriented consumers who are concerned with status. Where they differ has to do with age and peer groups. BMW is perceived as the car of choice for newly minted MBAs, along with other up-and-comers in the business arena. Mercedes cars are aimed at the older, more seasoned professional, those who others think of as having "made it" in business. This differentiation is the basis for stiff competition between the two companies. Each struggles to define and maintain an area of control, and if possible, gain ground on their rival.

DESIGN AS PROCESS

Design process is considered an important component in the development of new ideas and a tool to manage problem solving. It works by generating increased communication and stronger alignment between designers and clients. It's a tool for increasing creativity and innovation, for promoting risk management and enhancing success rates, and for ensuring smooth project management and measurable outcomes.

DESIGN AS RISK MANAGEMENT TOOL

Design projects are fraught with opportunities to fail. Designers and clients often play a game of Marco Polo, calling back and forth until at last the designer figures out what the client is really thinking. One person's idea about what *contemporary* means can contrast sharply with another person's. In addition, production issues, client miscommunications, scope creep, schedule breakdowns, and budget busters all contribute to potential design train wrecks. Design process offers a risk-management tool to help avoid these and other design obstacles.

IN CONCLUSION

The client–designer relationship is based on trust, respect, and mutual benefit. Designers that have strong interpersonal skills and methodologies for design problem solving can position themselves as trusted consultants offering both specialized and a broad range of knowledge.

Designers invest a great deal in their work and often see finished pieces as reflections of themselves. This commitment is essential to creating quality work. It can also, however, distract from the prime objective: to meet the needs of a client. For many in the creative field, this constitutes a difficult balancing act.

- Put clients first
- Develop an understanding of the client's needs
- Help the client solve problems; do not push ideas at them
- Provide multiple options to the client, not only a "best" one
- Act in a spirit of partnership with the client

chapter 4
DESIGNING IN CONTEXT

EMPATHIC DESIGN
THROUGH RESEARCH

In the late 1950s, Charles Eames said, "The recognition and understanding of the need was the primary condition of the creative act. When people feel they have to express themselves for originality for its own sake, that tends not to be creativity. Only when you get into the problem and the problem becomes clear, can creativity take over." As Eames suggests, design is not an artistic indulgence but a discipline, one that solves problems. Design research is a tool to help clarify a problem, taking into account a wide range of business and audience needs.

Eames points out that effective design cannot depend solely on designer preferences; it must be informed by business goals and customer perceptions. As professors Craig Vogel, Jonathan Cagan, and Peter Boatwright point out in their article, "A Strategy for Directing Innovation and Brand," "Creative insights must be connected to customer value and not simply the result of talent operating in isolation and throwing concepts over the wall to marketing and engineering." Design research not only creates a framework for design problemsolving, it ensures that any solutions a designer produces will meet the needs of both a client and an audience.

DESIGN RESEARCH DIY

When design agencies are called on to develop visual solutions, they traditionally outsource the research part of the project to specialized market research firms. This is understandable, as most design consultancies do not have the skill or bandwidth to conduct such research. But the question remains: How much information is lost in translation, when original audience responses are pushed through a marketing department's various filters, then incorporated into a final design brief, which in turn is handed over to a design team? Several steps removed from the original source of information, designers are typically left with little more than a diluted understanding of the real needs of an audience and insufficient knowledge about what motivates that audience to act.

"I've been doing research for so many years," says Luis Fitch, principal of UNO Hispanic Branding, "I couldn't believe that other designers were not already doing this. How can you start any project without it? I've worked in places where they've done lines of package design and the designers have never tasted the product, or never talked to the person who's going to open the product. Nothing. They just do 'beautiful stuff.'"

Another all-too-common scenario finds the designer lacking the resources to do meaningful research that would allow them to make informed decisions about how to connect with audiences. Because most designers do not have access to marketing research, understanding how they can gather it on their own is critical to any designer who wishes to affect business goals. When designers participate in the research, they can get the information they need.

Design research also offers a means for keeping design projects focused. Chris Rockwell, founder and principal of the design research firm Lextant, has said that designers need an accurate frame of reference, a clear definition of the problem and an "understanding of the 'solution space' where the best solution might reside" before they can apply creativity to solve a problem. Design research provides a tool for achieving that frame of reference, helping to define the problem and align project stakeholders through a common focus.

Joe Duffy, CEO of Minneapolis design firm Duffy & Partners, considers design research an essential part of his firm's design process. "I think, many times, particularly with advertising agencies, all of the front-end work, which I think is the most critical, is done by people outside of the creative department, which is ridiculous." Duffy goes on to say, "All of our people are involved in the beginning. They are not handed something and told this is the direction, now run with it. They are actually part of creating it. And it makes the design more specific to what the audience is asking for."

WHY DESIGN RESEARCH?

Designers that conduct research provide themselves with several important advantages. Most significantly they are apt to develop more insightful design solutions by aligning business goals and audience needs, and in doing so provide their clients a competitive advantage. Lastly, research provides an imperative for moving design forward.

Many designers use intuitive processes for developing ideas. Intuition often gives birth to great ideas that may never have surfaced otherwise. But before ideas can be born, a designer needs to prepare her mind with information. Thus, the information stage is critical to the design process. Ultimately, it shapes and informs the direction of the project. As HCI pioneer, educator and design entre-preneur Brenda Laurel puts it, "Good design research functions as a springboard for the designer's creativity and values." Bad information tends to result in proj-ects that are "off the mark," while good information fosters a better outcome.

RESEARCH PROVIDES ACTIONABLE INFORMATION

Brenda Laurel suggests, "One must frame the research question and carefully identify the audiences, contexts, and research methods that are most likely to yield actionable results. Those last two words are the most important: "actionable results." As Laurel points out, research must be targeted at a spe-cific problem and must yield meaningful information. As a practical matter, focused research maximizes the designer's time, so that he is not wasting his efforts acquiring irrelevant information.

Consider how Sean Adams, principal of the design firm AdamsMorioka, made design research a key phase in one of his most important projects. Adams recalls that his first big breakthrough developing a strategy happened soon after he and Noreen Morioka started their firm in 1994. Working on posters and collateral for clients like SCI-Arc, the Getty Museum and the Museum of Contemporary Art in Los Angeles, Adams and Morioka enjoyed the work they were doing; however, they soon realized that they could do more if they looked at design from their clients' business perspective. When VH1 decided they needed a new identity, AdamsMorioka were one among several firms asked to bid on the project. Their competitors were big well-known New York firms.

Through business analysis, AdamsMorioka immediately understood that the problem VH1 was facing was not directly related to design or identity, but to programming. Instead of pitching new logos, Adams took a different tack. "We came back and said that it was really about content, and we could come back and make things pretty by applying Band-Aids on top of something. So we came back to them and said here is a strategy, a position you can own. Here is the criteria you should be using when developing or acquiring programming. From there, the corporate identity is easy, it just falls into place."

After six months of working with AdamsMorioka, VH1's rating increased 154 percent. The new identity was a part of that success, but Adams credits the programming staff for coming up with hit shows like *Behind the Music* and *Concert of the Century*. "Once you have that success under your belt," says Adams, "it is a lot easier to go and help someone else. You have a reputation of raising the ratings. That's billions of dollars of revenue for the client."

From that experience, AdamsMorioka went onto work with Nickelodeon, ultimately helping that network gain its highest profit in history. "Design is just one part of many moving components," says Adams. He echoes Paul Rand's idea that a good logo can never make a bad product better when he says, "I like to think the actual design part of it, the visuals and identity program and the package around it, is critical. That's how you're communicating the message. But in the end, it's just a really nice necktie or a brand-new suit, and if you don't have the inner workings of the content in place, it won't work. You're just dressing up the hog."

Adams reflects on their design research approach. "We were really just listening to people," he says. "Whether it was Nickelodeon, VH1, or any of the Disney projects we were working on, they already had research. They gave us these big books of research, which they had probably never read. Five hundred pages that no one wanted to read through. We read through it, and we listened to them, and then we got to the point of asking some very pertinent and difficult questions. And I think [we were able to do that] because we are designers and we are trained to take lots of complex dissimilar information and coalesce it into a very simple and understandable point of view. It was not easy, but we were primed for it. It just had a lot to do with good design thinking."

RESEARCH LINKS BUSINESS GOALS AND AUDIENCE NEED

One of the goals of design is to connect an organization's goals and values with an audience's needs and desires. It's a relatively simple equation, but it requires a great deal of understanding of both groups. Organizations strive to create an image that will connect and engage their audiences, while audiences have a need to project who they are through the products and services of organizations they interact with. Designers can excel at the role of "matchmaker" when they understand enough about these two groups, enabling them to identify an effective way to communicate with each other. Design research must be conducted in order to establish this connection between organizations and audiences.

When VH1 initially approached AdamsMorioka, they had predetermined that an identity was what they needed. However, through research, AdamsMorioka was able to move beyond these assumptions by challenging their client, ultimately taking it in another direction. Organizations strive to meet audience needs in a way that is profitable and allows for growth. A primary goal of design research is to clarify where the organization is going and achieve alignment with audience needs. This is done by asking questions about an organization's strengths and weaknesses, and the environment in which the organization operates. The simple act of questioning places the designer in a guiding role. Once pressed to articulate a strategy or direction, organizations often find they are unclear about their goals. By initiating the conversation and acting as moderator, the designer challenges the organization to clarify what it is doing, subsequently moving the designer beyond the role of stylist to strategist.

UNDERSTANDING THE BRAND

"I don't just design a package," says Paul LaPlaca, creative director for Graco, "I try to find ways that leverage the brand and what the brand stands for. And if I don't know what the brand stands for, I find out." Through a rigorous research process that includes understanding the long-term business strategy, as well as the brand position, brand character, positive and negative brand attributes, consumer perceptions, competitive dynamics, benchmarks, segmentation, category trends, consumer insights and unmet needs, LaPlaca looks at design from a business and audience perspective. "I use a fact-based approach. I don't just throw graphics at a package and expect it to work."

LaPlaca starts his projects with a brand-emersion session. This session brings all the brand stakeholders together, including the internal team, retailers, and customers, and provides an opportunity to discuss the project goals, share information, and develop an overall understanding of the brand, the consumer, and the category. The ultimate goal is to ensure that the communications that are developed are cohesive across all touch points. "Coming out of those meeting and discussions, you may be able to tap into something that you have not been able to tap into before," says LaPlaca. The brand-emersion meeting expands the boundaries of the brand by identifying new opportunities or ideas that can be leveraged later. Says LaPlaca, "Basically what we are doing is hypothesizing the perceptions and drivers of the brand, and identifying equity challenges of the brand."

RESEARCH PROVIDES AUDIENCE INSIGHT

Digital design pioneer April Greiman believes that "design must seduce, shape, and perhaps more importantly, evoke an emotional response." To create design that resonates with audiences on an emotional level, designers must understand what motives them. Darrel Rhea, CEO of Cheskin Added Value, describes design as an empathic act and believes that designers should design for people. If this is the case, then designers need to be more aware of who they are designing for, what those people think, and how they perceive value. Cheskin Added Value was founded by Louis Cheskin, a pioneer in investigating how design impacts consumers perceptions and acts as a motivator in purchasing decisions. "Making meaning is the new core competency of design," says Rhea.

But how can a designer connect to an audience on this deep level when clients and audiences often find it difficult to articulate what is meaningful to them? Consequently, research needs to be conducted to coax this information out of them—prior to producing a design solution. By looking beyond functionality and benefits, and zeroing in on audience need and context, designers take a step closer toward making a connection with audiences.

Connecting at the "heart and soul" level requires new approaches to information gathering. Markets used to be fairly homogenous, with marketing departments dictating much of an organization's tone and message, and the look and feel of its products and collateral. Today, however, the expectation is that the individual customer, with all of its unique needs and specific experiences, must be addressed directly. Customization and customer relationships are key concepts among organizations that now look to create personalized experiences for audiences. The goal for many organizations is to relate to audiences on a deeper and more personal level. For organizations that embrace this philosophy, involving an audience in the conversation gives them an opportunity to work closer with customers as active participants in the development of products and services.

In the last decade, research has provided better insight into how consumers engage organizations through visual communication, bringing design research to the forefront of design discussions. However, such activity is hardly a new idea. Half a century ago, for instance, legendary industrial designer Henry Dreyfuss wrote the following:

"The products we design are going to be ridden in, sat upon, looked at, talked into, activated, operated, or in some way used by people individually or en masse. If the point of contact between the product and the people becomes a point of friction, then the industrial designer has failed. If, on the other hand, people are made safer, more comfortable, more eager to purchase, more efficient—or just plain happier—the industrial designer has succeeded."

Dreyfuss helped usher in a new era, one that witnessed people driving design in new directions. Several topics that presently dominate design discussions—including usability, human factors, human–computer interaction and ergonomics—evolved out of his thinking. Today, a customer-centered approach is common.

EMPATHY OVER EGO

But even with the widely held understanding that connecting with audiences is key to design success, it is surprising how often a designer, having just begun work on a project, will within minutes decide what type of paper will be used, what style of photography will be employed, and what kind of layout will be developed. When this occurs, it is often the designer's personal vision that is being expressed, rather than a user's or even a client's. Frequently this is when the design process turns problematic, as a designer's vision is brought into direct conflict with an audience's need. In fact, initial ideas and concepts generated by designers rarely consider all aspects of audience and organizational needs. A more empathic approach is simply smarter as it takes more variables into account and can even lead the designer into fresh and uncharted territory.

RESEARCH PROVIDES A COMPETITIVE EDGE

Along with considerations about audience needs and organizational goals, design research gives designers an opportunity to understand the competitive environment. Design as a business tool is competitive, after all; it defines an organization's position relative to its competitors and distinguishes it with audiences.

Michael Porter, professor of business administration at Harvard Business School and a leading authority on competitive strategy, describes three generic strategies that organizations use to compete: overall cost leadership, segment focus, and differentiation. Each strategy can be used alone or in combination, with the express goal of outperforming competitors.

All three of these strategies can be leveraged by designers. However, differentiation is the most accessible strategy designers can employ. Consider how a company that manufactures a commodity like candles can transcend marketplace malaise by using differentiation as a strategy.

Blyth Industries

Candles are a commodity. They are easy to manufacture and any benefits, like color, size or scent, are quickly copied by competitors. In spite of this, candle making is a booming business for Blyth Industries, with sales of $500 million and a market value of $1.2 billion. Much of their success is the result of differentiating their products and services from their competitors'. They do this by conducting audience research, and considering their customers every step of the way. Their competitive methodology is clear and straightforward. First, map the customer experience with their products and services. Next, consider the context of their experience. This creates opportunities for finding niche areas they can target with unique products. Finally, balance such opportunities against the company's strengths and capabilities. Adhering to this simple formula, the company has been able to dominate the market by constantly developing new candle products and accessories, and create new uses for their product by moving candles from their traditional place in the dining room to all areas of the consumers home.

Harley-Davidson

Much of differentiation is expressed visually through branding. A strongly differentiated organization or product can do wonders for brand loyalty. Such loyalty is created and enhanced when customers connect with a company on a level beyond what competitors can offer. Harley-Davidson is a classic case study.

Harley sells more than just a physical product. They foster a sense of community and experience that its competitors cannot easily duplicate. Competing at a "belief and values" level, Harley has managed to create a virtually impenetrable market position. The trigger for these beliefs rests not only in the design of motorcycles, but in the logo, in collateral materials, on the website, in the showroom, in a vast array of specialized clothing and merchandise. Any item associated with the Harley-Davidson brand has a look that conveys a certain spirit, evokes feelings of personal freedom, and speaks of the open road. The brand resonates with customers on an almost spiritual level. Harley is the only American company among the top five motorcycle manufacturers, and according to a 2004 survey, it controls about a quarter of the market. Because of its peerless ability to connect on a personal level with customers, Harley is able to charge about $5,000 more than its nearest competitor. To achieve this kind of loyalty, an organization must understand its customer's "heart and soul." This cannot be achieved through quantitative research alone. A deeper level of personal engagement is needed.

Target

Retail giants Target and Walmart are also putting differentiation strategy to the test. Gerald Storch, vice chairman of Target, says that when Target reviewed the three competitive strategies available to them (cost leadership, segment focus, and differentiation), only differentiation offered a way for the company to move past its main competitor. Walmart already had a lock on low cost, and limiting the focus of the Target audience would mean limiting growth. Differentiation, however, could create a unique position for the store in the minds of consumers. Through clever advertising and joint-venture projects with such globally renowned designers as Michael Graves and Philippe Starck, Target was able to position itself as a stylish alternative to other discount stores.

For Blyth, Harley, and Target, design is the primary vehicle through which their brand is conveyed. Through design they are able to express a meaningful, unique quality that captures attention and resonates with audiences. This is the essence of design and a key to differentiation strategy.

RESEARCH PROVIDES A RATIONALE FOR DESIGN DECISIONS

For a designer to fulfill her role as a trusted business partner, design decisions must be defensible and verifiable. Design research is crucial to this effort. It creates a context that informs the design process and influences others to view design as a competitive tool, one closely aligned with a client's goals and objectives. Designers that engage in design research can thus elevate their work to a strategic level that positions them as valued business partners.

When presenting designs to clients, designers must be prepared for "group think." The typical scenario is that of a design presentation, where the designer provides a direction to project stakeholders, who then begin to redesign the piece according to their own ideas of what it should look like. The design integrity is often eroded at this point, and the designer is left with only a shadow of his original idea.

Research provides a rationale for designers to defend their design decisions. By having evidence to back a decision, the designer mitigates the need for the client to make arbitrary design decisions. Presenting information about audiences' needs and trends, as well as business objectives, creates a more convincing argument when defending design decisions and controls the need for the client organization to direct the project.

RESEARCH PROVIDES A BASIS FOR MEASUREMENT

Collecting information from audiences about perception and emotion, as well as more quantifiable measures like behavior and performance, creates the foundation for building measurable outcomes when done at the beginning of the design process. Did the audiences do what we wanted them to do? Did we create the right experience for the audience? By establishing criteria for measurement and collecting data for comparison, design can better define its strategic role.

Without a clear understanding of what is valuable and meaningful to an audience, a designer is unable to establish a connection. A designer needs the tools to dig deeper. While demographics are somewhat useful, a greater degree of interaction is necessary to compete today. To attract and retain audiences, features, and benefits no longer suffice on their own.

Communication designers, by and large, don't receive formal training in design research. However, by employing a few time-tested and relatively simple research methods, such as focus groups and interviews, co-creation, and participatory methods, designers can extract meaningful information from clients. This will enable them to better understand what messages are likely to make sense to an audience.

THE 360° VIEW: THE BUSINESS AND AUDIENCE PERSPECTIVE

In order to represent organizations, designers must first know who they are, what they do, and why they do it. Without a basic knowledge of an organization's activities, designers cannot make informed design decisions. Organizational research focuses on four areas of business: goals, the customer, the competition, and the environment.

British Airways

In 1994, British Airways was on the brink of a crisis. The world's most profitable airline was facing competition from rivals, soaring oil prices, and management battles with unions, all of which were draining profits. On top of this, British Airways' reputation had taken several hits over the preceding decade with allegations of unfair practices leveled by competitors. As part of a plan to turn around the embattled airline, British Airways decided that an identity overhaul was needed. Research indicated that the airline's identity did not resonate with customers, nor did it reflect the company's long-term vision.

Before the designers put pen to paper, British Airways began an intense research phase to better understand how they would compete in the changing aviation environment, knowing that their organizational strategy would need to be reflected in their identity.

The London design firm Newell and Sorrell worked with British Airways to develop a plan for moving the airline forward. They considered not only how the company would represent itself, but how it would compete. The process was inclusive and collaborative, involving more than 3,000 British Airways managers and suppliers. Through their research, Newell and Sorrell identified several key factors for moving the troubled airline forward.

Like all businesses, British Airways' priority is to be profitable and competitive. British Airways is one of the largest airlines in Europe, just behind Air France, KLM and Lufthansa, and is the leading airline in the United Kingdom. Once a struggling company, British Airways rose to become the most profitable airline in the world after it was privatized under the leadership of Sir John King. British Airways had positioned itself as a premium long-haul air carrier with a distinctly aloof British personality. But British Airways customers were now asking for something different. Customer research revealed that British Airways needed to present itself as less provincial and more global, as well as more focused on the individual needs of passengers.

Drawing from interviews with British Airways passengers, researchers identified several opportunities to improve service. Many thought the carrier too formal and even a bit dated, as reflected in comments concerning BA uniforms. Sixty percent of British Airways passengers turned out to be from outside the UK. Among their requests was more respect for individuality. They also expressed a desire for a more cosmopolitan style. Passengers were not only interested in getting from point A to point B, they wanted some of the "romance of travel" restored as they did so.

These insights provided the foundation for how Newell and Sorrell would revitalize the British Airways brand. Simon Jones sums up the brand in the following statement: "For British Airways, the defining idea is of a company that is a true citizen of the world—efficient and effective, inspiring and involving—a world brand whose essence would be the genuine and passionate commitment of its people to serve and bring together people from all over the globe." With these ideas in mind, Newell and Sorrell began charting a direction that would reposition British Airways as a responsible and caring "citizen of the world."

Articulating design

Newell and Sorrell designer Rodney Mylius designed a new typeface for the airline's wordmark, with the intention of exuding a warmer, more human tone. Complementary text fonts were developed for use in brochures and various collateral materials. Attempts were made to soften the angular, red, speed mark logo. Eventually it was reborn as a dimensional, flowing, red and blue ribbon, one that projected a less rigid, more natural image. The company's corporate blue color was tweaked so that it reproduced more consistently. Additionally, Newell and Sorrell added a photographic element—a broad swath of people and scenes from around the world—for use in both business and collateral communications. These images reinforced British Airways' commitment as a global provider that celebrates diversity.

Once the new identity was vetted and approved by company managers and suppliers, staff was offered the opportunity to review the new approach before the official launch, reinforcing British Airways' new commitment to transparent management and equal opportunity.

British Airways is proud to claim that it "takes a total design approach to every aspect of the customer experience, engaging all the key interested parties from start to finish. On every project, customers are involved to make sure that the design being developed reflects what they want. This mixture has resulted in some award-winning and novel solutions, such as the Club World flat bed, launched in 2000."

By understanding how it needed to grow, how to counter competition and listen to customers, British Airways was able to alter passengers' perceptions through design. As a direct result, it was also able to maintain its leadership role in the airline industry. "It goes much deeper than the paint on the aircraft or the ink on our publications," says Bob Ayling, company CEO. "It is the physical manifestation of a fundamental review of our mission, our values, and our corporate goals."

As illustrated in the British Airways identity redesign, an understanding of audience need, as well as a solid knowledge of the business, is critical for the designer to make informed design decisions. Business analysis looks at all of the internal and external forces that impact an organization (where the business needs to grow and who is it competing against), and forms a basis of competitive strategy that the organization might choose to employ.

IN CONCLUSION

Designers who conduct research provide themselves several important advantages over those who don't. Not only are they apt to develop more insightful design solutions by aligning business goals and audience needs, they also provide their clients a competitive advantage. Lastly, research provides an imperative for moving forward. Research provides:

- Actionable information
- Business goals
- Audience need
- Competitive advantage
- A rationale for design decisions
- A basis for measurement

chapter 5

UNDERSTANDING
THE BUSINESS

LINKING DESIGN AND BUSINESS

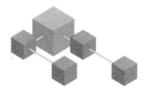

For years, the design community has longed to be recognized by the business world. This yearning has been captured in the phrase "a seat at the table," which is understood by designers as having the full acknowledgment of design's importance in business decision-making. Design's significance in business, once understood primarily on an intuitive level, can now be measured through multiple metrics, including customer experience, financial performance, and brand relevance. The ability to measure design's effect plays no small part in business's acceptance of design as a strategic tool. Seen as a way to gain a competitive advantage through differentiation and customer satisfaction, design holds a new place in the minds of business leaders—and these leaders are now looking for ways to bring design thinking into their organizations. The integration of business and design is best exemplified by Roger Martin, dean of the Rotman School of Management, who has been one of the most vocal proponents of design thinking as a means for invigorating organizations. With the belief that the only way for organizations to compete in a global economy is through innovation, Martin has stated that the world is moving from the information economy to the design economy, where business leaders not only need to understand the value of design, but also need to think like designers.

Now that business is ready to talk to design, the question is, do designers know enough about business to keep the conversation going?

Alonzo Canada, directing associate of the San Mateo, California–based design strategy firm Jump Associates, believes that design must be linked to business strategy. With clients ranging from Clorox to Nike, Canada helps identify new business opportunities through the discipline of design thinking. While working at Deloitte Consulting as creative director, Canada learned the value of design and its ability to help business achieve its goals. With an understanding that design and business have a symbiotic relationship, Canada thinks of design as a powerful strategic lever that helps a business deepen customer loyalty, increase margins, and find new ways to differentiate products. "While business strategy may show you where the hunting grounds are, it does not necessarily show you how to get in and begin hunting," says Canada. Design helps business craft strategies that are viable, and that consider audience needs and business capabilities. On the flip side, business helps designers stay focused on measurable outcomes. Canada says, "You can go off and design a new product or service, a web experience that you think is the coolest thing in the world, but if it doesn't make money or is too expensive to make or it's not going to be able to be sold through certain channels or it does not resonate with your core audience, it's not going to go anywhere; it's not going to have any impact."

Though both design and business are willing partners, several issues may hamper their ability to work together. These include challenges in communication, lack of business understanding on the part of the designer, and difficulty in communicating design return on investment.

PROBLEM: COMMUNICATION

Nathan Shedroff, chair of the MBA in Design Strategy program at the California College of the Arts, believes that when designers share a common language and understanding of business protocols, they position themselves to push for design innovation. The majority of designers justifiably believe that they should have more influence in their organizations than they do. Shedroff points out that this can only happen when designers are able to communicate the strategic role of design in business terms. The trouble is that design and business are distinct cultures and disciplines. Designers speak one language, and finance and marketing speak another, which makes finding common ground difficult. Business has adopted design thinking into its culture, but most designers have not embraced business. For designers, understanding basic business concepts like competitive analysis, business environmental considerations, cost reduction, increase in margins, and customer acquisition helps them position their design directions so that they resonate with their clients. By learning the language of business, identifying where design can have impact and creating metrics that measure the impact of design activities, a designer can earn the coveted "seat at the table."

PROBLEM: INVOLVEMENT IN ALL FACETS OF THE BUSINESS

Compounding the communication issue is designers' reluctance to get involved in other aspects of the organization, including operations, finance, manufacturing, marketing, and human resources. "Historically, designers have barricaded themselves into a little world of their own because they don't want to deal with these other issues," says Shedroff. "However, to be involved strategically with an organization, we (designers) can't ignore all the other constraints on the organization. And, we need to speak to these issues in the language of those whose primary responsibility they are."

It is clear that if designers are to take a strategic role, they need to know the basics of operations, finance, sustainability and marketing, and more importantly, how success is measured within the organization. Says Shedroff, "You get what you measure, so if the metrics are all based on financial or organizational trivia, and not customer satisfaction, then designers need to develop new metrics and models for the organization. Otherwise, nothing will ever change."

PROBLEM: SHOWING ROI

Return on investment (ROI), in all its forms, is critical to organizations and businesses. For designers, being able to communicate the return on their work is key. Alonzo Canada identifies two important things designers must do if they expect business to recognize them. The first is to link design to business frameworks and mental models so that design becomes less subjective. Most clients don't understand what is good or bad design, nor do they have any way to judge whether it is successful, which makes them reluctant to invest in it.

Because of this, designers need to frame their work in terms that are meaningful to the their clients. Ultimately a good design solution that is presented from a quantitative or a qualitative standpoint increases the odds of the design solution going through the organization. On the quantitative side, Canada suggests that designers need to know the financial drivers for the organization and what is the expected design ROI. Understanding ROI is also important when it comes to resources allocation, as most organizations have limited funds to spend on design. By having a better idea of the outcomes, they can make better decision about how they spend money on design activities because they understand what the expected ROI is going to be.

SOLUTION: BUSINESS ANALYTIC TOOLS

What analytic tools can designers use to help understand the client's business and help them articulate their business strategy? Fortunately, there are a number of useful analytic tools available for designers to call. These tools help designers and clients identify new opportunities by looking at the goals of the organization, its strengths and weaknesses, the environment, and the competitive landscape. When married with an understanding of audience behavior, motivations, needs, experience, and demographics, designers are able to create a more vivid picture of how design can help organizations succeed.

To be clear, we are not suggesting that designers become business mavens. Design and business are distinct skill sets and cultures, and they attract different types of people. But designers that take the time to understand who their clients are, how they work, and what their goals are position themselves for better design opportunities. As an example of why designers must understand the businesses they hope to work for, Victor Lombardi, product development consultant and visiting professor at the Pratt Institute, recalls this incident: When responding to a request for proposal (RFP) for a large nonprofit foundation, several firms claimed that they could, through their good design work, increase donations to the foundation. Such a claim was a big red flag for the foundation, as foundations generally have large endowments and are the ones who award grants to others. This was a fundamental aspect of the client's business that the design firms got wrong, and ultimately eliminated them from further consideration.

Like any process, the quality of the input determines the quality of the output, and the following "Tools for Understanding Business" are not substitutes for deeper exploration. Shedroff warns that the problem with most business analytic tools is that they're used as templates. "I've seen so many organizations use a positioning statement like a Mad Libs template by simply plugging in the blanks with whatever they think the answer should be," says Shedroff. The tools do, however, provide designers an advantage on two fronts: first, they provide a way for designers to ask their customers strategic questions through a shared language and framework; and second, they provide the designer a way to make design decisions based on business criteria.

TOOLS FOR UNDERSTANDING BUSINESS

Many designers enter projects at the brand-strategy level, working with marketing to understand how to take the business imperative, and through design, bring the brand to life. It is at this point in the process that context building begins. The big questions are asked: What is the business is about? What does the business do? How will it do it? Once business strategy is worked out, designers have an imperative for design.

The purpose of business analysis is to understand and help define the goals of the client. For the designer, an analysis leads to intelligent design decisions. It also makes it possible for the designer to have informed conversations about the direction in which the client wants his business to go. Ultimately, such in-depth work is the only way for a designer to develop a design solution that goes beyond style to something that is strategic. Beyond its use as a strategic tool, a designer's business research proves that she is serious about helping the client and is concerned about the outcome of her work. This goes a long way in forging long-term relationships.

DEVELOPING BUSINESS STRATEGY

How do you go about collecting business information? It can seem a daunting task, especially if you don't have a background in business. The good news is that there are a few basic pieces of information that designers can collect without first having to earn an MBA. Essentially, designers need to know the right questions to ask. By asking the right questions, they can initiate important conversations within the client organization. During the questions-and-answer phase, designers have more in common with therapists than creatives. Instead of asking, "How does that make you feel?" a designer might ask, "What are your strengths?" and "Who is your primary audience?" and "What can you tell me about your competition?"

Generally, there are four key facets to strategy development. An overall approach includes the setting of objectives that the organization wishes to achieve, an evaluation of the organization, the environment in which the organization exists, and the competitive landscape. By understanding each of these key areas, designers can develop a deeper understanding of the constraints and possibilities that exist for the client. It would be inappropriate to assume that designers will formulate strategy for their clients—that is not their responsibility. It is, however, crucial for designers to have an understanding of how their client's strategy was developed and the forces that dictate how they will maneuver in the future. The expectation for the designer is not to know the answers but to be able to ask the proper questions that will initiate conversations on the client side.

THE FOUR BASIC ELEMENTS OF STRATEGY DEVELOPMENT

1. Setting objectives—Vision and mission statements, SMART goals and focus
2. Client business evaluation—SWOT
3. Competitive evaluation—Competitive analysis
4. Environmental evaluation—PEST, Five Forces

SETTING OBJECTIVES

The foundation of business strategy lies in the setting of specific objectives. The vision and mission of the organization must be understood. The vision is a description of how the organization sees itself growing, specifically the objectives it will it pursue and how the company will differentiate itself in the marketplace. Mission statements focus on why the organization exists, what they do, and how they do it.

Next, the issue of how the organization will achieve its goals must be determined. Without a clear focus, an organization cannot properly allocate resources critical to achieving its goals or create alignment among leadership and staff. For designers, it is critical to help mitigate the all-too-common scenario of designing everything for everybody.

DEFINING A VISION AND MISSION

Von Glitschka, a Salem, Oregon–based graphic designer and illustrator, tries not to assume anything in terms of what the client does. "Let's say they are a dry cleaner," he says. "Even if I think I know about what they do, I still ask them questions as if I don't know. I usually stumble upon little insights that I normally would not have discovered if I had not taken the time to inform myself on what they do." Most clients don't think about the nuances of their professions because that's what they do for a living and it's routine, so they unintentionally assume that their design partners already know everything about them. It is important that designers saturate themselves in the business's culture and subculture, their industry-speak, so that they can fully understand who their clients are, what they do, and who they cater to. One method Glitschka uses to get clients to think deeply about their business is to ask his clients to describe how *their* clients describe them. "That really brings out a lot of interesting insights," he says.

Not only is it critical to understand how the business functions, it is equally important to understand the underlying ethos that inspires and drives the business. A way to understand this dimension of the client business is to look at the mission statement. The mission statement is made up of two elements, the core ideology and the vision. James Collins and Jerry Porras, educators, business consultants and authors of *Built to Last: Successful Habits of Visionary Companies*. Collins and Porra provide defintions of *ideology* and *the vision* in the text that follows.

CORE IDEOLOGY

Businesses must remain nimble to survive. In a turbulent business environment, strategies must be altered to meet the constantly changing needs of clients, trends and social demands. However, at the heart of every business must reside a set of core principles that remain constant through all of the activities and in all environments. Understanding the core ideology is not about logistics, strategy, or even customers. It is about the heart of the business, its reason for existing, and why the business leadership and staff dedicate their time to the enterprise.

> **Core values:** Individuals who build companies are usually driven by a set of tightly held beliefs that go beyond the demands of the marketplace. Core values are timeless and unchanging and reflect the ethos of the business.

> **Core purpose:** Another timeless dimension of a business is its reason for being. Core purpose describes not the functional aspect of what the business does, but its higher calling. Collins and Porras provide an interesting test of determining the purpose of the business. The "Random Corporate Serial Killer" test asks the question: If someone would buy the company at a generous price, guarantee that the employees would maintain their salaries, albeit in a different industry, and that the buying company would destroy the firm and eliminate all its offerings, causing the company to no longer exist, would the business owners accept the offer? The question gets to the heart of why the business owners want and need the company to exist.

VISIONARY GOALS

In 1961, John F. Kennedy presented what is considered to be one of the most audacious goals in human experience: land a man on the moon and return him safely back to earth within the decade. Facing increased competition from the Soviet space program, and with limited experience in space flight, many questioned the United States's ability to meet Kennedy's goal. However, on July 20, 1969, Neil Armstrong set foot on the Sea of Tranquility, the first man to walk on the moon. Four days later Apollo 11 safely splashed down in the North Pacific. Goals of this magnitude are made up of two basic components: an audacious goal and a vivid picture of what the future will look like.

> **BHAGs:** Having a goal is one thing, but to be successful, organizations need to have big, audacious goals. Often termed BHAGs (big, hairy, audacious goals), organizations that strive for excellence aim high. BHAGs provide a rallying point that engages and energizes staff, and provides a clear vision of what victory looks like. Visionary goals are long-term and often seem unattainable at the present moment, but their very audaciousness is what compels people to take them up.

> **Vivid description:** The second part of a visionary goal is the vivid description of what achieving the BHAG looks like. These statements provide an image of success in the minds of individuals. Filled with passion and emotion, these statements vividly describe the dream. The visionary goal goes beyond reason and judgment, and instead provides motivation for moving forward.

The vision statement is a picture of how an organization sees itself in the future. It formulates the goals, or milestones, that an organization hopes to achieve by way of a strategic plan. After all, without a vision statement firmly in place, how will an organization ever know if they are succeeding? Organizations seek to create a realistic, credible vision that stakeholders can believe in and put to use. The vision statement tells an organization where to go and how to prioritize its activities. It is also a tool for inspiring people toward a common mission.

The vision statement is built around questions: What are we about? Who is our audience? How do we benefit others? The vision statement is also an indicator of where the organization wants to go, including accommodations for change if necessary.

As mentioned earlier, another place the designer can seek valuable information is the mission statement. The mission statement explains why the organization exists, what it does, and how it does it. Traditionally, it also outlines the beliefs and values of the organization. Consider Apple's mission statement:

"Apple ignited the personal computer revolution in the 1970s with the Apple II and reinvented the personal computer in the 1980s with the Macintosh. Apple is committed to bringing the best personal computing experience to students, educators, creative professionals and consumers around the world through its innovative hardware, software and Internet offerings."

This statement tells us why Apple is in business, who its customers are, and what it produces. It even throws in a bit of history, so that we understand Apple's historically significant position in the marketplace as the first to introduce personal computing.

A caveat about mission and vision statements: Sometimes they are vague or poorly written. Such cloudy statements oftentimes became the butt of jokes—especially when they are so padded with arcane jargon, recondite lingo, and business-speak as to render them meaningless. An effective vision or mission statement is clear, concise, and written in basic language—such that anyone can understand it.

MISSION QUESTIONS

What do we do?
Who do we support?
How do we do it?

VISION QUESTIONS

Where do we want to grow?
Will our current strategy take us there?
What objectives will we pursue?
What differentiates us from our competitors?

Understanding the client organization's mission and vision, and linking them to the needs of audiences is important. The mission and vision statements act as tools for aligning stakeholders, making clear to them where the organization is headed. It also sets important design parameters. A company that can clearly articulate where it's going and how it plans to get there gives the designer key information about what messages need to be developed and how strategy can be visually communicated.

GOALS

Business objectives and goals are developed from the mission and vision statements. Although mission and vision play an important part of defining where the organization wants to go, they are not the only factors in determining strategy. Organizations must look not only internally at their various competencies, but they also must look outside, evaluating trends in technology, society, and the environment in which they compete, if they are to determine what goals are achievable.

Goals outline the most important priorities the organization needs to achieve. They are deeply rooted in the organization's mission and vision, and should provide a clear framework for meeting these ends. Goals determine how resources will be allocated and which projects will have priority. They also influence all levels of decision-making. A common framework for thinking about setting goals is the mnemonic SMART. SMART goals are *specific* in their description of what is to be achieved. You must be able to *measure* their success in some meaningful way. They must be *achievable*. They consider circumstances that might cause roadblocks, and are therefore *realistic*. And finally, SMART goals are *time based*.

QUESTIONS FOR DEFINING GOALS
What are the specific outcomes?
How will we know if we reach the goal?
Can we achieve the goal?
Are the goals realistic?
When will we achieve the goal?

DEFINING BUSINESS FOCUS

Often organizations will develop multiple goals that ultimately end up competing with each other for resources. When analyzing the client's business, one of the challenges designers often face is that of focus. Clients tend to have numerous initiatives, multiple stakeholders, and interdepartmental rivalries. Clarifying the goals and objectives of the client and the communication are a critical first step. Without this clarification, communications often end up being too broad to be effective, targeting no one in particular.

Consider the case of Changemakers, the nonprofit social innovation firm that uses a crowd-sourcing model for solving the pressing problems that face the world. With a community of over 50,000 participants, Changemakers hosts several competitions per year, challenging its participants to come up with innovative solutions to such problems as ending global slavery or developing financial security for the poor.

Changemakers uses its website as the primary means of communicating and engaging its participants. Developed several years ago, the site had usability issues and needed a redesign so that participants could more easily access information. With an understanding that the site needed an update, Changemakers contacted Henning Fischer, design strategist for Adaptive Path.

The first step for Fischer was to help Changemakers decide what they wanted to achieve. Like most organizations, Changemakers felt that several of its objectives were important. "Changemakers wanted to move into a more social networking direction," says Fischer. "They wanted to enable connection within the community. They believe that groups of people are more effective at creating their brand of change than individuals." Changemakers also had several other business needs it wanted to address, including a means to provide a turnkey template for its competitions so that they could shorten the amount of time it took to launch a competition.

DEFINING FOCUS

Fischer had to remind his clients that strategy is about saying "no," and it's about identifying achievable goals. "Firms need to understand that they cannot be all thing to all people," says Fischer, "and that a focused business strategy is a key to success." Using a viability/feasibility matrix, Henning quickly mapped out all of the requested needs for the site and rated them based on their importance. Business needs were listed, then rated on a 1–5 scale of importance and feasibility. Changemakers leadership needed to ask themselves how crucial to the business is the need and how much impact they will gain by addressing the need. Points were then assigned to each need. These prioritized needs were then graphed onto a matrix with axis of importance/ feasibility. Those needs that are ranked highly in the importance/feasibility quadrant were selected as those to be focused on for the design. Fischer advises that client then do a "gut" check to see if the focus points are accurate.

Fischer recalls, "We did have to leave several painful things on the table for them, in particular the turnkey solution,"

As Fischer points out, clients need to understand that if they are going to have a strategy, they are going to need to make trade-offs in what activities they choose to participate.

QUESTIONS FOR DEFINING FOCUS

What are the most important things we should be doing?

Given our resources, which of these things can we do?

SELF-EVALUATION: THE SWOT CHART

Once an agreement is reached regarding both the mission and vision of the organization, and opportunities have been prioritized, the conversation can turn to the context, or environment in which the organization operates. The most common tool for viewing the big picture is a SWOT chart. This chart is a simple matrix that compares *strengths, weaknesses, opportunities,* and *threats.* The four quadrants making up the SWOT in turn can be divided into two areas. Strengths and weakness are considered internal characteristics, while opportunities and threats are considered external; that is, they reflect circumstances and realities in the business environment.

INTERNAL REVIEW

Strengths describe what the client organization is doing successfully. These may include, for example, assets, competencies, and processes that are key to moving the organization forward.

STRENGTH QUESTIONS

What do we do best?

How do customers perceive us?

What resources do we have at our disposal?

How loyal is our customer base?

How healthy is our financial picture?

Weaknesses indicate areas where the organization is lacking. These may include processes that need improving, resources that need to be developed, or functional areas that need strengthening.

WEAKNESS QUESTIONS

What do we do poorly?

What negative perceptions do people have about us?

What resources do we need to move forward?

How can we restructure to improve performance?

Where can we cut costs?

EXTERNAL REVIEW

Opportunities project where the client organization can grow, based on environmental factors. These may include new business and economic, technological, political, or social trends.

OPPORTUNITY QUESTIONS

Which trends currently offer the best opportunities?

What can we do that will provide a competitive advantage?

In what areas is the competition weak?

Threats are similar to opportunities, except they emphasize negative factors based on business, economic, technological, political, or social conditions.

THREAT QUESTIONS

What negative trends can be identified at present?

What do we need to avoid in the future?

What is our competition doing that could hurt us?

CONDUCTING A SWOT ANALYSIS

The SWOT chart provides a quick overview of important factors that warrant attention. To take it a step further, you can conduct a SWOT analysis. A

SWOT analysis can be done in several ways, including via surveys or face-to-face meetings. It's a good idea to gather the stakeholders for a SWOT analysis—if you have a particularly large group, you can break them into smaller groups.

Begin by briefing the groups on the purpose of the SWOT and its four component parts, so they have a clear understanding of what each component represents. Groups should then brainstorm on each area of the SWOT, record their comments, then share their findings. Each group gives a report, one SWOT section at a time. All insights are collected in a common place (whiteboard, flip chart) so the entire group can read what each group came up with.

The next step requires making connections among the four SWOT components. What strengths work with the opportunities presented? Can any weaknesses be resolved by opportunities? Drawing connections between SWOT areas empowers strategy, and suggests ways to build on strengths, mitigate weaknesses, exploit opportunities, and avoid threats.

SWOT QUESTIONS

What is the organization's vision?

Is the vision attainable given current strategy?

What are the organization's strengths?

What are the organization's weaknesses?

What areas represent opportunities for the organization?

What areas constitute threats to the organization?

What patterns or trends characterize the environment?

What should the business be doing?

You can also use SWOTs to analyze the competition. The same process of determining strengths, weaknesses, opportunities, and threats can show where competitors are and where they might be going.

UNDERSTANDING THE COMPETITION

Organizations do not operate in a vacuum, but in fact position themselves relative to their competition. To a large degree, it is your competition that defines you. Although being defined by another organization may seem like a negative, the competition provides an important parameter for how you will communicate value to an audience. Take for example the subtle differences between Coke and Pepsi, or Miller Lite and Bud Lite.

Competitive strategy guru Michael Porter developed the definitive model for understanding how organizations compete. In his landmark book *Competitive Strategy*, Porter says, "The objective of a competitor analysis is to develop a profile of the nature and success of the likely strategy changes each competitor might make, each competitor's probable response to the range of feasible strategic moves other firms could initiate, and each competitors probable reaction to the array of industry changes and broader environmental shifts that might occur." Porter's competitive analysis framework answers the key questions of what drives the competition and what the competition is currently doing. Porter's analysis considers the competition's future goals, their current strategy, assumptions about the industry and the firm, and its capabilities.

Porter's Five Forces framework looks at the competitive environment through several lenses including economic, social, and industry specific. By understanding the impact of these forces on the client's business, designers can help their clients develop strategies for competing. The idea that competition is not solely driven by competitive firms, but by the environment in which the company functions, is critical to understanding competitive strategy and industry profitability.

INTENSITY OF RIVALRY AMONG COMPETITORS

Numerous and equality balanced competition

Slow industry growth

High fixed or storage costs

Lack of differentiation

Capacity augmented in large increments

Diverse competitors

High strategic stakes

High exit barriers

BARGAINING POWER OF BUYERS

Purchases made in large volumes

The products purchased are undifferentiated

Switching costs are few

Product is unimportant to the quality of the buyer's product or service

Buyer has full information about demand, costs, and market price

THREAT OF NEW ENTRANTS

Economies of scale

Product differentiation

Capital requirements

Switching costs

Access to distribution channels

Cost disadvantages independent of scale

Government policy

BARGAINING POWER OF SUPPLIERS

There are few suppliers

The supplier does not have substitutes

The industry is not an important customer of the supplier

The supplier's offering is differentiated

THE THREAT OF SUBSTITUTES

Cost of switching

Price of substitute

Level of perceived differentiation

Ease of switching

GENERIC COMPETITIVE STRATEGIES

Porter also identified three generic ways that firms compete. These include cost, focus, and differentiation. Based on the firm's strengths, they can determine what position they want to hold within an industry. Porter points out that the strategies are, for the most part, exclusive, and warns that firms that do not claim a high market share (cost) or a low market share (niche) run the risk of getting "stuck in the middle." Firms that pursue a cost strategy will have difficulty combining it with a differentiation strategy. The exception is the combination of focus strategy, which targets a niche audience and differentiation strategy, which provides a unique offering.

COST

Cost leadership helps organizations compete by achieving a low-cost position. Businesses are able to increase returns, create a defensive position against competitors, and defend against buyers and suppliers. Companies like Walmart and Costco are strong proponents of this strategy.

FOCUS

Segment focus emphasizes a specific audience in order to "out-specialize" competitors. Consider how a clothing store like Anthropologie targets a specific group of thirty-something women who have outgrown what parent company Urban Outfitters has to offer. Or the way that Abercrombie & Fitch appeals to teens and twenty-somethings who are highly trend conscious and buy into the preppy lifestyle. Conversely, think of how Gap has surrendered its once prominent market share by trying to appeal to everyone from the newborn to the elderly—all under one brand.

DIFFERENTIATION

Differentiation strategy focuses on creating and communicating unique customer value. Differentiation can take the form of unique products, services, or a brand. By offering a unique value to a segment of the market, organizations create a defensible position. As Rodney Fitch, CEO of the design firm Fitch, reminds us, "Only one company can be the cheapest—the others have to use design."

DEVELOPING A UNIQUE SELLING PROPOSITION

Another approach to understanding the competition and finding opportunities for a unique and meaningful position is USP, or unique selling proposition. Organizations can get a competitive leg up on their rivals by offering unique and valuable products or services that competitors cannot easily copy.

Determining unique value begins by understanding what audiences value. Through interviews and focus groups, relevant criteria can be established that the client organization and its competitors can be rated against. Once ranked, the data can be mapped onto a chart that plots the various criteria based on high or low relevance to the audience. This method provides a quick picture of how the client organization competes on various values, and provides an opportunity to address unmet audience needs. By understanding where the client organization ranks, a USP statement can be created that outlines an analysis of what strengths are defendable over a long period of time.

This method is instrumental in developing what W. Chan Kim and Renee Mauborgne call "Blue Ocean Strategy." Using the examples of Cirque du Soleil and Yellow Tail Wines, Kim and Mauborgne illustrate that to move beyond the competitive fray, organizations must reinvent the category they compete in by creating a new market space. For Cirque du Soleil, they took the dying circus industry and bolstered it with theater, artistic sophistication, and high production values, thereby creating a new type of entertainment for adults. Similarly, the Australian vineyard Yellow Tail developed a line of easy drinking accessible wines for the every day, bypassing both low cost and premium wine competitors.

DIFFERENTIATION QUESTIONS

What do customers want from us?

What unique value does the competition offer customers?

What unique value can we provide them?

What new offering can we provide?

BENCHMARKING THE COMPETITION

Before investing time and effort in design explorations, taking a quick review of the competition's material is an easy way to compare how organizations stack up. Placing competitive designs side by side produces immediate feedback. For designers, benchmarking represents an opportunity to compare design approaches, messages, and branding strategies. By monitoring the competition and identifying key factors for success, designers can develop designs that best position their clients in the marketplace. The benchmarking process helps answer the crucial question, How will we visually differentiate ourselves from our competitors?

When conducting an audit, designers should first determine what areas they will be benchmarking. Will it be solely the visual design, or the messaging? Criteria for deciding what makes one piece more effective than another should also be agreed upon at the outset of discussions. Once a comparison is made, designers should determine how the new piece to be developed could exceed the competition.

Much design benchmarking focuses on two things: message and visuals. The goal of benchmarking is differentiation. By looking at how others are representing themselves, you are able to avoid clichés and find distinct and unexpected ways of communicating the client's unique value.

Publix Super Markets

How does competition influence visual design? Consider how the Publix Super Markets chain created their store brand identity. Publix, the employee-owned, privately held corporation, was ranked 99 on Forbes Fortune 500 list of companies at the time of this printing. With locations across the southern United States, Publix employs over 140,000 people, owns its own distribution centers, and manufactures its own brand of dairy, deli, baked goods, and other food products. Publix offers both mainstream brands and "up-tier" offerings that include their Publix Premium and GreenWise brands.

For most store brands, the design strategy has been to mimic the leading brand packaging as closely as possible. Colors, type treatments, and design elements are aped in order to position the store brand closer to the national brand. The execution of these designs is often poor and does little to influence consumers who are savvy enough to know the difference. This "me-too" approach fails on another level, in that the packaging fails to distinguish itself from its competitors.

To commemorate their seventy-fifth anniversary, Publix decided on a redesign of its store brand packaging. Prior to the redesign, Publix also used the "me-too" strategy described above. Tim Cox, director of Publix's in-house design team, took a decidedly different tack when approaching the redesign of the Publix store brand. To compete on the shelves, he decided that Publix's products needed to stand out by communicating their unique character. Cox and his team aimed to position Publix as a reliable brand that consumers would trust and respect.

After creating a brief, the in-house designers developed concepts that were then reviewed by a cross-functional team. With a stated goal of creating a package that is decidedly different than its competitors, Cox and his team reviewed competitors' designs and noticed a trend toward the use of busy graphics on most packaging. To counter this, Publix adopted a clean, contemporary, simplified packaging solution that was flexible enough to carry over multiple categories of food products. Using the Publix logo in a black circle, set across a band of bright color, product names are written in all lowercase sans serif fonts. With a single hero image of the product set against an open field of white space, the design successfully distinguishes itself on store shelves, standing apart from the clutter and noise of national brands.

Implementing a system to keep packaging "simple and engaging," Publix managed to extend new design standards across its entire product line. By taking this approach, Publix positions its store brands not as suspicious knockoffs of national brands, but as brands that can stand on their own. As a result, they are widely respected by consumers for both their high quality and low cost.

Publix illustrates an interesting trend in packaging. In the last ten years, store brands have evolved from the anonymous starkness of packages that simply said "Corn" or "Paper Towels," to more developed designs that rival national competitors. Consumers who not long ago were reluctant to admit they bought store brands now buy them without feeling the least bit self-conscious. According to a recent industry survey, people believe there is little difference in quality between store brands and national brands. With the quality gap successfully bridged, store brands are now designed and presented with the same care as national and name brands, allowing them to compete head to head. And, as store brands gain in popularity, they drive down the cost of national brands, which must now consider them direct competition.

REVIEWING THE BUSINESS ENVIRONMENT (PEST)

The final aspect of understanding the client organization is to review the environment, or business arena, in which the organization competes. Organizations must consider a wide array of factors when determining how to move forward. These include *political, economic, social,* and *technological* (PEST) trends.

THE POLITICAL ENVIRONMENT

The government plays an important role in determining how businesses operate by developing policies, making capital accessible, creating regulations, and regulating market forces. One of the more important functions the government plays in business is as an advocate of everything from health to the environment. Some examples of how the government and overall political feeling can influence organizations are illustrated in the following paragraphs.

With obesity on the rise, the U.S. Government has put increasing pressure on food manufacturers to clarify the nutritional content of their products so that consumers have the information they need to make healthy choices. With these growing concerns, packaging design has been affected. Companies like Kraft Foods are reacting quickly to avoid increased government interference, and have voluntarily changed their packaging to accommodate nutritional information. The same is true in the UK, where companies are considering the adoption of the "traffic light" system, where green, red, or amber color-coded bars would indicate the health rating of a product. This trend will certainly continue to influence the design of packaging.

The packaging of fast foods is affected as well. As Eric Schlosser's landmark 2001 book *Fast Food Nation* points out, America loves fast food so much that a staggering 96 percent of schoolchildren can identify hamburger icon Ronald McDonald, and the average American eats fast food three times a week. Our obsession with fast food and concerns about childhood obesity have prompted consumer groups as well as the FDA to pressure McDonald's to provide nutritional information including calories, carbohydrate content, and fat percentages, not only on its website and in printed materials such as pamphlets, but directly on its food packaging.

The political environment can affect how people interpret certain messages. In January 2007, Turner Broadcasting engaged in a guerilla-marketing campaign for its cartoon, *Aqua Teen Hunger Force*. The tactic did indeed garner attention, although not in the way the company probably intended. On the face of it, the stunt seemed like a typical guerilla-marketing tactic and was essentially harmless. An outlined figure from the cartoon, created with LED lights, was placed via magnetic backing on various public structures in the Boston area. The figure is a block-like character, with a scowl, who appears to be making an obscene gesture with its left hand. Ordinarily, such a campaign would be seen as a clever stunt and little more. However, in a post-9/11 world, the stunt managed to incite chaos, ultimately closing down parts of Boston and the Charles River. Two men were even arrested and charged with creating a hoax. It turned out that America—particularly Boston, from which two of the doomed 9/11 flights departed—was not ready for this type of guerrilla marketing.

THE ECONOMIC/INDUSTRY ENVIRONMENT

In his book *Competitive Strategy*, Michael Porter writes, "Although the relevant environment is very broad, encompassing social as well as economic forces, the key aspect of a firm's environment is the industry or industries in which it competes." Porter goes on to outline the forces that drive competition—the threat of new entrants, the bargaining power of buyers, the threat of substitute products, and the bargaining power of suppliers. These forces impact the economic environment of the industry.

The threat of new entrants: The California firm Obopay provides customers the ability to transfer money from their cell phones. Less expensive than the venerable Western Union, Obopay is challenging Western Union to break from its long-held systems, forcing them to consider new technologies in order to stay competitive.

The bargaining power of buyers: Walmart is the biggest supplier-retailer of consumer goods in the United States. It has been estimated that a third of the U.S. public visit a Walmart in any given week. Because of Walmart's size and influence, it is able to get the lowest prices on the products it buys and can dictate price to suppliers.

The threat of substitute products: Substitutes can occur when audiences are given choices of similar products for the same or lower price. Examples include soft drink companies switching from glass to plastic or aluminum cans, or switching from sugar as a sweetener to high-fructose corn syrup. Another example: consumers can select generic drugs over pharmaceutical brands.

The bargaining power of suppliers: When there are few suppliers, or limited substitutes to a given industry, suppliers have an upper hand in establishing price. Suppliers that are able to differentiate their offering are also positioned to negotiate with their clients.

Along with these forces, organizations need to be aware of changes in the overall economic environment as well, including economic growth and inflation indicators, labor costs, unemployment, and labor supply.

THE SOCIAL ENVIRONMENT

In the late 1700s, with its control of colonies and plantations in Jamaica, Barbados and Trinidad, the British Empire was the largest producer and consumer of sugar in the world. However, through a series of events which included slave revolts and calls for the abolition of slavery from the Quakers, British citizens stopped buying the sugar produced by slave labor, based on the understanding that slavery was morally and ethically wrong. This is one of the first recorded attempts by consumers to dictate to corporations their wants and values. Today, firms are scrambling to be the next "socially responsible brand" and show that they are as conscientious as the audiences they serve. Ethical consumerism has flowered in the last decades, creating greater awareness of health and safety, and the treatment of workers, animals, and the environment. These trends show that consumers are not only interested in the sustainability of the products or services they use, but also the process of how the products were made.

Many won't remember the days of the polystyrene clamshell hamburger carton, but not too long ago, this was the norm for the fast-food industry. McDonald's, a long-time target of consumer groups, faced growing criticism from environmental and health groups on the grounds that the polystyrene packaging was not biodegradable and was also considered a possible carcinogen. In 1993, McDonald's made the switch to the more familiar cardboard microflute clamshell based on research conducted by Perseco, the manufacturer of McDonald's packaging. Though more expensive to produce, the microflute clamshell was lighter, and was made of recycled fiber, thereby creating less of an impact on the environment. In addition, the packaging was printed using soy-based inks. With this move, McDonald's took steps to position itself as a responsible corporate citizen.

Conversely, the British cosmetics store The Body Shop was created on the basis of environmentally-friendly and socially-responsible design. "Design becomes responsible when it gives shape to a responsible corporate culture," says Alan McDougall, head of design for The Body Shop. The Body Shop doesn't advertise; however, through their well-defined philosophy and distinct design, they are able to communicate and educate the public about who they are and what they believe. As a result, the company that started out in 1976 as a small storefront run by a homemaker with children rode the wave of an environmentally-conscious society to achieve a market value of more than $550 million in 2004.

Or, consider the Ecofont developed by the Dutch marketing firm SPRANQ. The Ecofont is essentially a sans serif font, with holes throughout the body of the letter, the idea being that this font uses up to 25 percent less ink. Primarily developed for at-home use, the font appeals to the public's desire to use fewer resources.

Along with consumer values, firms are striving to meet the exact needs of their audiences, providing methods for customization of everything from sneakers to jeans to automobiles. These "Long Tail" strategies aim to sell a large number of unique items to a small group of customers. Amazon, eBay, and Netflix exemplify this trend, with their ability to store and distribute a wide range of popular and equally unpopular items cheaply. Customers are also able to search for and find rare items through the use of search engines and peer recommendations.

Along the same lines is the trend of customization. Organizations have been striving to connect one-on-one with consumers. Consider Nike's design-it-yourself online shoe store. Customization gives individuals the ability to create their own products and connect to companies as participants in the design and purchasing experience. Mass customization is not a new trend, but got started back in the early 1990s, with computer companies like Dell offering customers the opportunity to build machines to their own specifications. Now customers can create everything from footwear to house décor online and have it delivered to their doorstep, sometimes overnight.

Customization affects not just physical products but content as well, as we see in the case of RSS feeds online or variable data printing. For designers, this means considering a specific audience for every mode of print communication. Organizations often need a way to target brochures to specific audiences with the goal of providing information "at the right time, in the right scenario, to the right person." Through customer message management (CMM), organizations are able to use variable data printing to create brochures, presentations, and other collateral materials, each reflecting the unique needs of individual customers. This on-demand solution cuts costs, reduces time to market, and allows for increased responsiveness.

THE TECHNOLOGICAL ENVIRONMENT

Technology moves fast. Those that fall behind the curve often lose business opportunities. If we look at the latest technology trends, many are related to communication. From blogs to video on demand, technology continues to make it quicker and easier for people to connect to each other. Businesses that embrace such trends stay ahead of the curve. Consider the freedom and accessibility of mobile computing, the cost per click advantage that online advertising has over traditional advertising, and the ability to connect to customers via customer relationship management tools.

The most significant impact tech has had in the last five years is democratizing communication by empowering citizens with the tools and resources that allow them to communicate with as much authority and impact as corporations. In Thomas L. Friedman's book *The World Is Flat 3.0,* he identifies the rise of the personal computer, fiber-optic micro cable and workflow software as the driving force behind several seismic shifts, including globalization, democratization of communication, and information abundance. Simply put, the Internet has democratized communication. Access to information is now available to a huge section of the population in the United States, Europe, and Japan. Today, the Internet is growing in areas as remote as North and sub-Saharan Africa, and the Middle East. Communication opportunities like video, wikis, social networking sites, blogs, and text messaging are now available to just about anyone. Consider that in 1996 there were 18,000 websites, whereas today it is estimated that there are 156 million.

Along these lines, C.K. Prahalad, former professor of corporate strategy at the University of Michigan Stephen M. Ross School of Business, identifies four key drivers that are changing the competitive landscape. These include global connectivity, digital technology, convergence of features on digital products, and the rise of social networks. Technology is allowing for a one-consumer-at-a-time personalized experience. Beyond just providing products, more companies are providing "platforms," or means for customers to create their own experiences. The iPod allows users to create their own playlists. Apple does not own the content or the device. The experience of using the iPod is co-created. You provide your own value through the content you choose. Apple supplies the platform. This experience cannot be done without the collaboration of many independent players.

QUESTIONS ABOUT THE BUSINESS ENVIRONMENT

What political considerations do we need to be aware of?

What is happening in the environment?

What social trends and consumer values do we need to consider?

What technological tools can we take advantage of?

STRATEGY IMPLEMENTATION

It's understood that the development of strategy is critical for organizational success. However, without implementation, strategy is meaningless. The two activities are very different. Strategy development requires analytical and visioning skills; implementation requires project management and planning skills. Some tools that aid in implementing strategy include the following.

ORGANIZATIONAL ALIGNMENT

Like project management, implementation considers a range of key organizational elements that contribute to the success of strategic initiatives. A model for analyzing these elements was developed by Tom Peters and Robert Waterman while working at McKinsey & Company consulting firm. What they call the 7-S Model looks at the organizational *strategy*, the *systems*, the organizational *structure*, the *skills* and *staff* of the organization, and overall leadership *style*. Overlapping these six elements is the *shared values* of the organization. For successful strategy implementation, all of these activities need to be aligned throughout the organization.

ACTION PLANS

Once the organization has determined its mission and vision, determined its goals, and done analysis of both internal and external factors, they can start to break down the goals into actions. Like the Work Breakdown Structure (WBS) in project management, goals are broken down into specific activities that are then broken down further into tasks and subtasks, until the work can no longer be subdivided. The Action Steps are then looked at in terms of roles and responsibilities, resources and time needed to complete the activity.

BALANCED SCORECARD

As an ongoing part of strategy, measurement provides the organization a means of determining if the strategy is working or if it needs adjusting. The primary measures organizations use for evaluating their strategy are financial. However, financial measures are outcomes of the organization's activities and do not point to where the company needs to improve. A method that considers a broader range of activities is the Balanced Scorecard performance measurement tool. This tool allows managers to focus on areas that are critical for implementation of the organization's strategy and provides them with a "dashboard" of strategic objectives.

The balanced scorecard looks specifically at four areas of measurement, including financial, customer experience, internal factors, and innovation and learning. Goals are established for each area. These goals are then compared across the four areas to see if they interrelate and support the overall strategy.

Financial: How is the implementation of the strategy affecting the finances of the organization?

Customer experience: How is the implementation of the strategy effecting customers?

Internal factors: Are the activities of the organization supporting the strategy?

Innovation and learning: Does the organization have the skills to support the strategy?

Tools for Strategy Implementation

7-S Model: Alignment of people, resources, and culture.

Action steps: Defining the specific activities for achieving the goals, including activities, tasks, subtasks, roles and responsibilities, and time frames.

Balanced scorecard: Measuring the activities that influence the success of the overall strategy.

IN CONCLUSION

"Strategy is incredibly important to design, if you want to have any impact on the world," says Alonzo Canada. "Impact meaning that you are actually putting offers out into the world that people care about, that are improving their lives, or better yet are having a societal impact, an economic impact for the companies."

The purpose of business analysis is to understand and define the goals of the client. For the designer, this leads to intelligent design decisions, informed conversations about the direction of the client, and ultimately the ability to develop a design solution that goes beyond style to strategy. Beyond being a strategic tool, business research lets the client know that the designer is serious about helping them, is concerned about the outcome of his work, and takes great interest in his work. This goes a long way in forging long-term relationships.

chapter 6

UNDERSTANDING
THE AUDIENCE

DESIGNING FOR PEOPLE

With an increased appreciation for audience needs, designers are taking steps to better understand audience motivations and behaviors. Before sketching or designing, designers are seeking out audience insights by going on shop-alongs to view purchasing behaviors, as well as conducting visual audit analysis and equity asset research. They are asking audiences what the client brand and competitive brands mean to them. They are asking about the graphics, trying to understand what resonates with consumers. All along, they are looking for ways to ground the creative work by incorporating the consumer's perspective into the process.

For Luis Fitch, understanding the Hispanic market is at the heart of his business. Fitch is the founder of Minneapolis-based UNO Hispanic Branding, a leading branding and design agency dedicated to building brands that connect with Hispanic consumers. Their first step is always to understand the demographic. From there, they are able to determine not only the needs of the audiences they are serving, but also the context and meaning behind the product or services. "We want to know what is the latest trend and what's in their heads," says Fitch. "That's what our clients want. It's more than making it look authentic or making it look Mexican… It's 'What is the next big thing?'"

UNO takes an ethnographic approach for much of its research. "If you don't go out to the streets and ask, you won't find it," says Fitch. Fitch and his team conduct interviews and focus groups, and they even go to consumers' houses to see how they live with and use the product. Sometimes the people they talk with even help UNO develop the product.

To better understand what will resonate with its target audience, UNO uses a visual and verbal collage method they call "Filtros." Pulling from their vast collection of books, magazines, and images related to Hispanic culture, they create mood boards that inspire and help the design team focus on the audience's particular cultural language, based on their level of acculturation. Filtros acts as a reminder for the design team by helping them discover not only new things about audiences, but things they might have forgotten or things they were not aware of, and more importantly, things that they can combine with the U.S. culture.

Filtros sometimes involves user participation by using visual references like pictures, books, and magazines, and letting the consumer put collages together using writing, drawing, and photography. Consumers may be given small cameras and told to take pictures of how they use the product, or what's inside their refrigerator, or to document their week in a diary, and then those pictures are categorized and Fitch and his team start to look for patterns. Often the results reveal insights into how consumers use the products or services.

Consider how the Tech Museum in San Jose, California, called on its patrons to help design exhibitions. With entries coming in from around the globe, the museum was able to develop these exhibitions in months, as opposed to years, while building ownership and interest at the same time. Or, consider how the U.S. Army calls on everyone from generals to officers to privates to help update several army field manuals. Through a wiki, the Army is able to collect and integrate the experience of all of its personnel, thereby developing a deeper, more meaningful document.

"Design really needs to be based on the consumer," says Paul LaPlaca, creative director at Graco. LaPlaca observes that when consumers buy a product like coffee, they generally have a brand in mind. If they find a lower price offering, they may switch. Designers need to understand how consumers shop the category and what it is they are looking for. Is it brand then price? Is it brand, feature, benefit, then price? Is it price first? Understanding the hierarchy of how consumers shop is critical for making strategic design decisions. Says LaPlaca, "Understanding how they shop that category is very important to designing a good package. You need to know, is it brand, is it price, is it feature?" LaPlaca points out that some products are very feature focused, listing the features and benefits on their packaging. Some products don't need that information because consumers have already made their decision. By understanding the consumer—and what the consumer hopes to find on a package—designers can create a hierarchy and determine what should be on that package.

AOL Living Network

"We do everything around our audience," says Allison Bucchere, former vice president and creative director at AOL Living Network. Bucchere starts each of her web projects with research. Whether it is formal or informal, research is the anchor for all of her design decisions. Working with usage data from the websites she directs, she and her team are able to understand what is and what is not important to her audiences. "For instance, if we are going for more of a coastal audience, our design decisions will change, or if it is mid-America, our design decisions will be different. We also look at pathing data to see how people are navigating the sites and what areas are most popular, where they are coming from, where they are exiting the site, URLs that are referring them to our sites. All of this information is helpful in knowing how to design [the website] differently when we are approaching a redesign, so that we can keep people on the site and give them what they need. We can see what the most clicked-on items are. This helps us decide what to keep and what to delete. We also do competitive analysis to see what is successful and what is not successful in the marketplace."

One of the most important types of research Bucchere does is quite simple. She reads the audience site feedback on a weekly basis. "We are reaching about 16 million people monthly. They are very vocal and leave a lot of feedback. That really helps guide our work, because we can respond to their needs right away."

How do designers translate research into design solutions? Bucchere starts with a brief that focuses on user goals and outlines the scope of the project, tone and voice, client insights, strategy, marketing and syndicating strategies, and how they will measure success.

To help brainstorm solutions, Bucchere also creates basic personas. These personas are weighted. For AOL's food site they are speaking to "family life managers," maybe 70 percent of the audience who mainly want to know what to put on the dinner table. But they also speak to people who cook only once or twice a week. A third audience might be people who like to entertain. Bucchere will weight these audiences, then take the features of the site and assign a value. This helps prioritize what features to build first.

Bucchere then moves into low-res sketches to convey the direction of the brief. This is done fast and cheap, and helps all involved illuminate the features and understand the scope of the project. These sketches are shared with all of the stakeholders, including audiences, to further refine the direction.

AOL engages audiences early in the design stage. Bucchere shows them sketches to see what they like, and then once in the design phase, Bucchere's team creates three mock-ups and asks audiences what they think. For instance, when AOL Living created a new brand for Stylelist.com, the number one style and beauty site on the web, they created multiple designs and brought them to their audience to ask what they thought. Bucchere uses this audience feedback when presenting to AOL executives.

Hallmark

For over ninety years, the familiar handwritten script and crown logo belonging to Hallmark has been associated with sincerity, emotion and warmth. The success of the Hallmark brand has allowed it to expand from greeting cards to merchandise to a television channel. In the 1990s, Hallmark determined that it needed to evolve its identity system, so it contacted the design firm Libby Perszyk Kathman (LPK) to guide it through the process. LPK's first task was to determine which identity elements resonated with audiences and which required further development. They also set out to develop a deeper understanding of Hallmark's business goals and objectives. Through this process, LPK was able to evolve the Hallmark identity so that its target audience more clearly understood it.

With the primary business goal identified as increasing Hallmark's presence in retail environments, LPK used exercises with audiences to test for recall and awareness of Hallmark identity elements. Using a simple recall test sample, audience members were asked to draw the Hallmark logo from memory. The results would determine which identity elements, both visual and verbal, the audience was retaining, and therefore which element of the brand held the most value. The familiar crown logo was easily identified; some audience members even managed to pick it out of a lineup of other crown logos.

From their research, LPK concluded that the identity element of color proved very important. As John Recker and Jerry Kathman of LPK recall, audiences consistently identified yellow as the color that best expressed Hallmark's "sense of optimism and warmth while increasing its presence." The selection of yellow, along with a position adjustment to the logo and the word mark, helped increase Hallmark's recognition across all brand assets. Through audience research LPK was also able to "incorporate the customer's voice," making the Hallmark brand identity a more effective marketing tool.

The Hallmark identity update illustrates the importance corporations place on their audience's perceptions of their brands. By looking outward to the perceptions of customers, identifying and closing the gaps in understanding, Hallmark not only created a tighter bond with audiences but also was able to clarify its positioning in the retail environment.

CO-CREATION AND PARTICIPATORY RESEARCH

The first case of HIV/AIDS in Kenya appeared in 1984. By 2003, the number of Kenyans afflicted with the disease had reached over 6 percent of the population, killing nearly 150,000 people. The effects of HIV/AIDS not only affects individuals, but also impacts the ability of countries to grow economically, strains resources of international agencies, and most devastating, leaves millions of children orphaned. Awareness programs launched in cooperation with the World Health Organization have helped stem the tide of the epidemic. Most significantly, in Uganda the percentage of the population that are HIV positive, which peaked at 13 percent in the 1990s, has dropped to 4 percent since.

Understanding the impact that communication has had on managing the disease, Audrey Bennett, associate professor of graphics at Rensselaer Polytechnical Institute, reached out to the small town of Kusla in Kenya, and engaged the people of the town to explore more effective approaches to communicating HIV/AIDS awareness. Bennett's approach was unique. Whereas most prevention campaigns were developed by government agencies and clearly had western influence, Bennett engaged the audience as co-creators in the design of the communication. More than just collaborative, Bennett says that her participatory process "involves the audience directly in the decision-making activities that affect the final output, as well as empower the audience by giving them control over the design propaganda that affect their community."

Bennett started with field research. Through a virtual studio, she was able to better understand the cultural aesthetics of the people she was working with. Bennett's process consisted of problem identification, audience analysis, ideation, prototype development and final design development. Each phase went through rigorous steps of hypothesis, selection of an appropriate research method, documentation and analysis. Collecting information in lab books, the Kenyans documented their process from beginning to end, with Bennett's team of U.S. educators acting as consultants.

After defining the problem, the Kenyans conducted audience analysis to better understand the environment in which they were communicating. They then carried out brainstorming sessions using words and metaphors. Once concepts had been developed, prototypes were created. Copy, visuals and sketches were run through Bennett's "empirical" process to make sure they were appropriate in tone and message. These prototypes were then reviewed until the strongest prototype was selected.

The Kenyans had no prior graphic design experience, but more importantly had life experience. Several of the participants had dealt directly with the death of parents and siblings, poverty and cultural challenges. With Bennett's team as guides, the Kenyans developed their own concepts using visuals and language that were culturally meaningful to them.

"Had we not used a participatory design approach," says Bennett, "we would have used an intuitive approach which may have yielded aesthetically pleasing graphics that did not communicate effectively to the Kenyans. With a participatory approach, we yielded effective cross-cultural graphics, though the final aesthetic outcome might not measure up to the western graphic design standards."

A PEOPLE-DRIVEN ERA

Todd Wilkens, senior design researcher at Adaptive Path, believes that too often companies oversimplify their view of people. When thinking of the conventional approach organizations take with clients and audiences, Wilkens invokes a quote from the *Cluetrain Manifesto*, citing that organizations often see their audiences as "a gullet whose only purpose in life is to gulp products and crap cash." Wilkens says, "We need to see people as people. Not as Homo Economicus, or people who want the most for the least amount of effort, unemotional, rational actors, or as docile and gullible pawns like sheep."

What is missing from these outdated marketing perspectives is the complexity of people and their lives. Wilkens reminds designers to consider the complicated nature of their own relationships, their emotions, the groups that they interact with, the technology they use, and the social and cultural world they live in. Furthermore, when they consider audiences, he suggests they embrace the complexity of a human life and to "try to understand people as you think of yourself."

Elizabeth Sanders, president of the design research firm MakeTools, believes that, "The market-driven world has given way to the people-driven era." She notes that a great deal of people without design backgrounds are actively participating in design, and that the distinction between the various aspects of design disciplines are blurring. These factors have put a great deal of emphasis on the collaborative nature of design, particularly on the front-end phases of the design process.

Consider Coca-Cola. This ubiquitous brand connects with people all around the globe on many levels. For many years Coke sold itself on the basis of connectedness, that is, that people could connect to others through the shared enjoyment and good feelings associated with the product. Some might remember the classic Coke television spot from the early Seventies in which people from all walks of life stood atop a grassy hill and joined in a chorus of "I'd Like to Buy the World a Coke." This ad clearly showed the product as a means for connecting. However, Coke later discovered that there was another side of the brand that they had not understood. Coke was not only a way to reach out to others, it also represented a way of connecting inward to the individual. Coke offered a moment of "me time" for people as they went about their busy day.

This revelation came about through the work of Harvard Business School professor Gerald Zaltman, developer of ZMET, a process for uncovering the hidden associations that people hold about products. Zaltman asks client to find pictures that express their feelings about the brand. These images are then analyzed by Zaltman's team with the client through a rigorous self-examination process. By using techniques more readily associated with psychology, Zaltman's teams probe clients for the hidden meanings behind their image selections, while helping the client build a collage from the images.

Similarly, Patricia Seybold has been using her "Customer Scenario Mapping Sessions" for twenty-five years. Seybold, a strong proponent of the power of user-generated innovation, believes that companies that find the "smartest customer" ultimately win in the marketplace. Seybold says that working directly with customers to find ways in which products and services work best for them makes designers money and streamlines their operations. In her book *Outside Innovation*, Seybold outlines the process for Customer Scenario Mapping (CSM). Seybold has team members work in groups to identify four ideal scenarios that answer their needs. CSM uses lead customers, experts and stakeholders to actively help co-design products or services. The team members focus on the "vision" of the ideal state. Customer satisfaction metrics are also established.

MIT economist and innovation expert Eric von Hippel believes that by tapping "lead users," or audiences that use a product or service and have identified a need that is yet unknown to other users, organizations can make innovations that meet the hidden needs of their audiences. Through his research, von Hippel has helped establish a change from manufacturing-centric innovation to user-centric innovation. He says lead users have two characteristics: "First, they have a high incentive to solve a problem. Second, they are ahead of the target market. What they want in the present is what the market as a whole will want in the future."

Lead user studies help identify the unmet needs of users. The first step is to create an internal team from various disciplines within the organization. This team prepares the user study. Markets and interests are identified, secondary research is conducted (periodicals, professional journals, books, etc.), and interviews are conducted with lead audience members to better understand trends and unmet needs in the marketplace. These trends are then analyzed to identify more specific needs that can be met. Once identified, these needs are used to develop ideas for new products or services. Onsite visits are conducted to see how end users will actual employ new ideas. Teams come away from these visits with concepts that they can then test. Next, "lead user workshops" are held where users, experts and the project team meet to engage in concept development. Participants are given specific deliverables at this stage. The group is broken into teams to develop product concepts, taking time throughout the process to meet as a group to refine and evaluate ideas. Recommendations are then made to management. From there, winning concepts go into prototype development.

Hilary Cottam of the Design Council is harnessing audience participation in design to address England's public services and systems. As the team leader for the Design Council's RED initiative, Cottam has taken a co-creative approach, more formally known as "transformation design," which engages users to help improve government services. RED uses design thinking to tackle complicated problems such as how user participation can strengthen the health care system; how prison systems can help reform and not just incarcerate; how homeowners can reduce the amount of energy they use; and even how members of Parliament can establish more productive relationships with their constituents.

The key behind many of these approaches is that they actively engage users in the design process. Unlike "user-centered design," which traditionally engages the user at the end of the process or treats them as an object of study, co-creation views audiences and users as vital to their goal of creating communications that connect on a meaningful level. By understanding how an audience perceives and interacts with the client's products and services, designers gain valuable insight into which visual styles work best to reach that audience.

TOOLS FOR UNDERSTANDING AUDIENCES

Designers can look at both demographic and psychographic information to gain an understanding of audiences. Traditional demographics include information such as age, sex, financial, geographic and marital status. Psychographic information looks at how the audience makes decisions, what they value and what is meaningful to them. This section outlines several well-established tools and methods for gaining insights into audiences.

SEGMENTATION

Marketers use segmentation to divide large groups of people into small distinct groups. These smaller groups, called segments, usually share similar demographic characteristics and are more closely related to each other than the overall target market. Segmentation allows designers to understand audiences on a basic level, and communicate with them in a way that that is more likely to resonate. Segmentation is an aspect of one of the primary generic competitive strategies (cost, differentiation and audience focus) and allows firms to focus their resources on one target market. This strategy, sometimes called a focus strategy or niche strategy, concentrates on a few select target markets.

For designers, segmentation provides tools to better understand audiences on several dimensions.

DEMOGRAPHIC

Age
Gender
Location

PSYCHOGRAPHIC

Lifestyle
Beliefs

Values

Attitudes

Behavioral

For instance, Choice Hotels International offers a variety of hotels tailored to fit specific needs of audiences ranging from luxury to economy. From its Quality Inn brand, CHI introduced Comfort Inn and Clarion Hotels as midlevel brands that offered comfortable accommodations. At the extremes, CHI provides economy hotel lines Econo Lodge, Rodeway Inn, and Sleep Inn, all of which offer basic, no-frills lodging. At the high end, Cambria Suites, a distinctive all-suite hotel, offers guests an upscale experience.

The design of each brand identity, from logos to interior design, reflects its personality. Cambria positions itself as "thoughtful, contemporary and stylish." This is reflected in the architecture of the buildings and the interior decorating. Cambria Suites proudly offers a luxury experience, including the latest technology and state-of-the-art fitness centers, spas, and bars. Econo Lodge, on the other hand, positions itself as "Bright. Easy. Affordable." Econo Lodge offers basic rooms with minimal decorating, and an economical experience for families with kids or the business traveler on a tight per diem. Econo Lodge is an offer of value. Each hotel is designed and marketed to appeal to the needs of specific types of travelers.

DEMOGRAPHIC SEGMENTATION

Demographics help define audiences based on such categories as gender, age, location, and social class. These characteristics help designers create a mental picture of the target audience.

GENDER

It is generally believed that men and women have different communication styles. Research has shown that although men and women have some distinctions in how they *communicate*, what is more important is how they *perceive* messages. According to Georgetown University linguistics professor Deborah Tannen, women look at dialogue as an opportunity for connection and closeness, whereas men use conversation to assert status. These distinctions contribute to the feelings of frustration that men and women have communicating, and provides an added level of complexity for organizations that wish to communicate with both genders.

On a product level, consider Daisy Rock. Founded in 2000 by Tish Ciravolo, Daisy Rock guitars offer ultralight, handcrafted guitars made specifically for women and girls. With their slimmer necks and lighter bodies, Daisy Rock guitars are more ergonomic and provide their customers the freedom to play without the constraints of more male-centered guitar designs.

From a packaging perspective, house-painting tools and supplies have traditionally been marketed to men. However, Dutch Boy, with an understanding that women make most of the home purchasing decisions, took a decidedly different tack with the development of its Twist & Pour line of paint cans. With twist-off lids that eliminate the need for additional tools like screwdrivers and mallets, the lightweight packages provide an easy-to-use handle, making lifting and pouring easier for women.

From a design research perspective, Heidi Dangelmaier, founder and director of the girl-centric market research firm 3iying, provides deep insights into how companies can connect with girl culture. Using a deep therapy approach, Dangelmaier probes girl's emotional vulnerability and looks for what unites them as females. "We get deep and dirty and emotional," says Dangelmaier. Through in-depth and emotionally revealing conversations over a course of weeks, Dangelmaier looks for emotional patterns first, then searches for bigger trends—which are then tested in focus groups.

AGE

Over the last decade much has been written about generations and their distinctive traits. Boomers, Gen-Xers and Millennials all have unique qualities and respond differently to messages and visual cues. Strauss and Howe's book, *Generations*, theorizes about the idea of history being defined through the experience of the generations. For designers, understanding the drivers of these distinct groups is an important communications consideration.

Strauss and Howe have labeled the generations of the twentieth century as follows: Missionary, Lost, G.I., Silent, Boomer, Gen-X and Millennial. Each of these generations reflect the circumstances of the era in which they grew up and helped create. Generations have a strong influence on marketers and businesses as they strive to connect with audiences. By segmenting generations and analyzing their defining traits, designers can develop a manageable persona for each generation. As a group, these personas act as a broad foundation for achieving a better understanding of the markets.

Boomers (1946–1964)

Born into the economic prosperity of post-war America, Boomers are known as the "Me" generation. The first generation that experienced television and rock and roll, these are the rebels, the ones who defied the status quo of work, play and family. They protested the Vietnam War and worked their way into the boardrooms of Fortune 500 companies. Now boomers are heading into late middle age, with the last boomers entering their forties. Boomers make up the largest retail market; more than 80 million people who spend in excess of $900 billion annually. They see achievement and status as important to identity.

Gen-Xers (1965–1981)

In Douglas Coupland's novel *Generation X*, twenty-somethings Dag, Andy, and Claire struggle to find a life without being trapped in the over commercialized world they live in. Working their "McJobs," they find little meaning in the culture that surrounds them. These characters came to epitomize the slacker culture of the generation born between 1965 and 1981. They grew up with AIDS, crack, faltering families, downsizing and a sense of crisis. They have redefined the job market, marriage and consumerism. Gen-Xers make up about 18 percent of the population—over forty-five million people—and spend $125 billion annually.

Millennials (1982–2000)

Born between 1982 and 2000, Millennials have never known a world without the Internet, DVDs and cell phones. They are defined by major events, like the First Gulf War, the September 11th attacks and the War on Terror. Millennials (or echo Boomers) are the children of Boomers. Access to technology defines this group, along with global awareness.

Generation C

Generation C is not defined by a birth date. Instead, they are defined by their desire and ability to develop original content. Through the widespread availability of video, photo, text, and the public platform of the web, today almost anyone can become a content provider. This generation has embraced the democratization of communication, providing reviews of movies, products, and books, becoming journalists through blogs and forums, authors through self-publishing sites like blurb.com, performers through YouTube and MySpace, and designers through the online customization websites for sneakers, jeans, and automobiles.

PSYCHOGRAPHIC SEGMENTATION

Demographics by themselves are helpful, but they provide only one dimension of an audience. Psychographic profiles allow designers to get an even deeper understanding of the audience with whom they are communicating. With this kind of understanding, designers can create targeted communications that are meaningful to audiences, communications that reflect their attitudes and values, as well as the social environment in which they live.

LIFESTYLE

Lifestyle is about activities, interests and ideas that are shared among groups of people. Information about spending habits, use of time, and opinions are reflected in lifestyle categories. Lifestyles help complete information about audiences, and help designers imagine personas around audiences by creating a handle for understanding the harried mother, the busy manager, the slacker student.

ATTITUDES

Attitudes are predispositions that people have about events, ideas, behavior or other people. They play an important role in linking audience's emotions and thoughts about organizations, products and services. Attitudes are learned over time and are not inherent. Attitudes are broken into three categories: beliefs, liking/disliking and behavior.

BELIEFS

Beliefs are subjective understandings that are based on perceptions. Beliefs are the foundation of our attitudes. They act as a way for people to filter information and messages, and make decisions.

VALUES

Audiences accept or reject messages based on how well the messages match with their existing values. Values help people make decisions about behavior and are based on our earliest experiences.

MOTIVATIONS

According to noted psychologist Abraham Maslow, an audience's needs are established in ascending order from physical, safety, love, esteem and self-actualization. Each need must be satisfied before moving to the next (higher) level. Once a need-level is fulfilled, the desire for the next level is established. Maslow's theory is a cornerstone of contemporary marketing philosophy (for example, advertisers focus not on features, but on socio-psychological desires that feed an audience's needs for social self-actualization). Motivations can be seen as a way for people to address these needs.

BEHAVIORS

By understanding what people do, as opposed to how old they are or where they live, designers can target audiences based on when they buy, how they buy, and how much they buy. Behavioral data tells us what audiences have done in the past, and helps us predict what they might do in the future.

AUDIENCE INFORMATION

Generally the problem with identifying audiences is not lack of information. Most organizations make a point of collecting as much information as possible about their audiences. The real issue is determining what information is the most relevant to creating a meaningful design solution.

When requesting audience behavioral information from clients, designers should use a few simple rules to ensure that the information they are requesting is actionable. Audience information must give the designer insight into how the organization will be relevant to audiences. The information should specifically address what the audience wants from the organization, and it should give the designer insight into how to communicate with the audience in a meaningful way. Once all of this information is collected, a picture of who the audience is can be developed.

DETERMINE AUDIENCE VALUE

Once the audience is identified, the next step is to determine which audiences provide the most long-term value to the organization. Value can be defined as anything from overall lifetime spending to their role as evangelists for the organization. This audience is known as the "Most Valued Customer" and serves as the target audience for the design strategy. By taking this approach, designers are able to filter out audiences that are too expensive for the client to acquire, or do not give an acceptable return, or take a long time to become profitable. By eliminating these audiences and focusing on just the most valuable, designers can help clients target their efforts, and maximize their design and marketing costs. Why spend money on low-return audiences?

Ellen Reid Smith, CEO of Reid Smith & Associates, an Austin, Texas-based e-loyalty marketing consultancy, and author of the book *e-loyalty,* wants designers to understand that all customers are not equal. In her book, Reid gives the example of standing in a long twenty-person line at the airport, while a gold member for the same flight gets into a line of two people. You feel like it's not fair, but you know that gold members spend more because of their frequent flights and therefore are going to get the perks. Most folks in the twenty-person line start planning how to become gold members. The airlines know that loyal customers are ultimately more profitable, easier to service, and have less chance of defecting to another brand, since they have a vested interest in staying with their current brand.

AUDIENCE DECISION-MAKING

A way that audiences distinguish products they like or dislike is through the visual cues they receive via packaging, design and promotion. If the messages resonate with them, they are more likely to remember products even though they might not have a lot of information about them. Thus, the first stage in the audience's decision-making process is awareness. The next stage in the process starts when audiences become interested in the product because of publicity or advertising. At this point, they begin to look for more information about the product—to learn if it can satisfy their needs. Once interested, the audience decides whether or not to try the product, but they still need to be convinced that the product is what they need. To a great degree, it is the designer who prompts this behavior. If convinced, the audience makes the purchase. The true test, however, is whether the audience will make a repeat purchase—the sign of product loyalty that is the treasured goal of most marketers.

One important consideration to make is that most decision-making is emotional, not rational. Consider the wine industry. In Robin Goldstein's book *The Wine Trials,* he conducts a classic taste test using scientific evidence to show that "wine tastes better when you know it's expensive." He enlists the help of five hundred wine drinkers and has them sample six thousand unlabeled glasses of wine. The results are impressive. Two thirds of the people preferred lower-cost sparkling wine (under $15) to the venerable $150 Dom Perignon. For wine drinkers, price plays an important role in their enjoyment of the product, even if in reality they cannot tell the difference between a $10 bottle and $50 bottle.

PERSONAS

With so much audience data available, it can prove unwieldy for a designer to manage and utilize. Thus, a means for boiling down so much information into a readily accessible stew becomes quite important. Creating personas is one way to do this. It helps a designer envision the type of person for whom she is designing. Personas are fictitious people who represent the needs and characteristics of a broad range of audience members. They help designers understand an audience's goals and expectations, based on relevant research and interviews. The persona represents the composite of a typical audience member. Not only are personas helpful for creating audience profiles, they help define design objectives and targets, making it easier to prioritize needs, correct assumptions, and dispel misunderstandings.

Universal Studios

Universal Studios Orlando has consistently managed its online presence to maximize traffic. After years of incremental advances, Universal was eager to speed ahead by addressing several new goals, including improved visibility, clearer differentiation, and a stronger appeal to mothers. Key to making such a leap was to gain a better understanding of its audience. Universal worked with New York web marketing firm FutureNow to help them understand who their audiences really were, and the psychology that drove their audience's decision making. Personas were developed for six customer archetypes that included motivators and unique needs. Demographic and psychographic data was collected for each persona, allowing Universal to better understand the drivers for its primary audiences. Refining its website based on persona research, Universal increased its likeability—and ultimately increased ticket purchases by a whopping 80 percent.

Personas are generally based on interviews with audience members. Through the interviewing process, information about the audiences' attitudes, values, beliefs and lifestyles are captured. This helps give dimension to the persona, so that it's more than just a flat description of a person, their job and other demographic information. Every characteristic of the persona can be tracked back to something that was reflected in research.

This method has some pros and cons. On the pro side, it helps designers create for someone specific, which makes the task a lot easier. On the other hand, interviews can take a long time to conduct and there is no guarantee that the persona you create will be accurate. In other words, there is a considerable amount of subjectivity involved.

CONDUCTING AUDIENCE RESEARCH

Matt Cooke, creative director at Iron Creative Communication, a full-service marketing firm that specializes in brand strategy, advertising, and design in downtown San Francisco, had his "aha" audience research moment in 2001, when he was a production editor and designer for the World Cancer Research Fund in London.

At the time, Cooke had run across a government report titled, "Exercise at Our Age," which explored ways to promote physical activity to seniors. It was in this report that he came across a bit of information that would change his approach to communications. "There was some qualitative research that the British government had done," says Cooke. "In a nutshell it said people who are sixty years and beyond categorically don't want to hear from younger people about exercise. They want to hear from their peers, or people older than themselves. They don't want some young upstart telling them what to do. And I thought that type of insight is absolutely critical in terms of a communications campaign."

As a result Cooke went on to develop a physical activity education outreach program. He found a former gymnastic and ballet dancer and teacher who was in her sixties to act as a spokesperson. With this step, Cooke had taken a leap forward in how he addressed the users' preferences, thereby producing work that would work as opposed to things that were aesthetically pleasing. Cooke recalls that as a design student he'd been trained primarily in aesthetics, but not in user-centered design.

After reading the report it became obvious that there were certain things Cooke needed to find out qualitatively before he entered into a large-scale public outreach program. He believed that it was not only good design practice, but also the socially responsible thing to do. Cooke believes that in circumstances where you are spending other people's money, and you are trying to change public behavior for the good, designers need to do everything they can to achieve client result. As a driver for his design approach, Cooke was attuned to where the funding for design projects were coming from, always asking himself if he was doing everything in his power to help change public behavior. Cooke understood that changing behavior was a very difficult thing to measure, and that it was a very difficult thing to attribute solely to design. "It's really about doing due diligence," he says, "not about saying what I'm going to do is about changing behavior, but what I can do is the best I can do. What is the responsible thing for me to do?"

By using observation and questioning, qualitative research delivers insights into the audience's attitudes, beliefs and values—all of which play an important part in crafting meaningful messages. As designers seek to better understand their audiences, qualitative research offers insight into how audiences think and behave. The tools provided by qualitative research allow for increased customer satisfaction through better product development and more targeted messaging.

QUANTITATIVE RESEARCH TECHNIQUES

Although designers tend to rely mainly on qualitative research, quantitative research can also be a rich source of information. Quantitative research focuses on measurable data and uses statistical modeling and analysis of data as a means of understanding a problem. Quantitative research usually starts with a theory or hypothesis, and then statistical methods are applied, comparing various relationships of data.

There are several straightforward quantitative methods available to designers. Through the use of questionnaires and surveys, designers can collect valuable information about attitudes and opinions of audiences. Additionally, with the low learning curve and availability of online survey tools, designers can easily create cost-effective real-time surveys that reach a broad range of respondents.

QUESTIONNAIRES

Questionnaires are self-administered surveys that offer a cost-effective means of collecting information from a large audience. Because the researcher is not present to administer the questions, he has less of a chance to influence the respondent's answers, thereby offering a bias-free method for collecting information. Additionally, questionnaires are less obtrusive and allow respondents to answer at their leisure.

Conversely, one of the drawbacks of questionnaires is that they do not allow the researcher to have direct contact with participants. Since questionnaires are self-administered, there are few opportunities for follow-up questions. There is also no way to gauge the "mood" of the audience, since there is no opportunity to read the participants' body language or inflections.

Overall, questionnaires offer designers the ability to gather broad data to initiate projects. Quantitative data should not be used on its own; it is most useful when bolstered with additional qualitative research, in the form of focus groups and projective techniques. These methods complement quantitative research, allowing designers to get a deeper understanding of the motivations of audiences.

DEVELOPING A QUESTIONNAIRE

Questionnaire development follows the path of problem identification, information gathering, analysis and implementation. The design of questionnaires is critical to their success. Response rates and questions that provide actionable information are two primary considerations when developing questionnaires.

WHAT IS THE PROBLEM?

As with any kind of research, a well-defined goal is critical. Without a clear understanding of the problem to be solved, there is little chance of developing questions that will reveal actionable information. The more specific the problem definition, the easier the survey will be to construct.

WHAT QUESTIONS SHOULD WE ASK?

The key to having a strong response rate is developing questions that are clear, simple and meaningful. Questionnaires open with an introductory overview of the reason for collecting the data, and the importance of the audience's participation, along with clear and concise instructions for completing the survey. Questions should be posed in an unbiased way, so as not to influence participants. Complex sentences and language should be avoided as it can confuse participants and reduce their desire to complete the questionnaire. Question styles should be varied, so that audiences do not become less engaged by falling into a repetitive pattern of answering questions. The more convenient the survey is for the participant, the better the response rate. Questions should be grouped in a meaningful way, so that they have a natural flow to them. Important questions should appear at the beginning of the survey, as respondents tend to drop off as they go along. To be useful to the designer, every question should have an actionable answer.

WHO AND HOW MANY PEOPLE WILL WE NEED TO SURVEY?

Based on your goal definition, you should be able to identify key audiences that will help you provide feedback relative to reaching your project goals.

As a rule, the larger the number of participants, the more accurate the survey results will be. For most, however, it is impractical to create large surveys. Smaller surveys generally provide sufficient data for most projects. Finding a balance between too few and too many is the key.

PRETEST

Before launching the survey to the entire target audience, it is wise to pretest it with a small section of the group. Once completed, you can determine if the questions asked are providing actionable feedback and if the questions are clear.

PRESENTING DATA

Final survey data is usually presented in a brief document that contains information about the goals of the survey, who participated, and general findings. Each question is presented along with the statistical data associated with it and general findings. Alternatively, survey results are also presented through presentation software such as PowerPoint.

QUALITATIVE RESEARCH TECHNIQUES

Although quantitative research allows marketers to understand audiences on a broad level, it does not tell them *why* people make decisions. To answer those questions, qualitative research is used. There are several qualitative research techniques that are appropriate for designers. Among the most popular are focus groups, interviews, projective techniques and ethnography.

FOCUS GROUPS

When dairy product producer Penn Maid needed to revitalize packaging and labeling for its entire line of dairy products, they enlisted the help of Hanson Associates, a Philadelphia brand strategy and design consultancy. As an integral part of their research, Hanson organized a series of focus groups to better understand customer perceptions about the Penn Maid brand.

Penn Maid is a large regional brand, encompassing the six million people of the Pennsylvania, Southern New Jersey, and Delaware tristate area.

It was important that Hanson understood the equity of the design elements, because they not only wanted to maintain the market share but increase it as well. Competing against Kraft, a big national player that could invest more money into their own brands than a regional company could, it was important that Penn Maid was as good as or better in appearance than Kraft's national brand Breakstone's.

When forming the focus groups, Hanson narrowed its selection to a specific segment—tristate area moms. Hanson looked at two groups: those who were loyal to the brand and those who were transitional into the tristate region (and therefore new to the Penn Maid brand). Focus groups were shown the old Penn Maid packaging, 3-D mock-ups and concept boards, and taste testing was done, alongside competitor packaging. A second focus group was shown new packaging against the competitors' packaging.

Through the focus groups, Hanson was able to identify the brand equity of the black Penn Maid package, the company name, and "Queenie" the Penn Maid "spokescow." The research was pivotal in creating new packaging that was contemporary, friendly, and had better "appetite appeal." Gathered information divulged that customers liked the old lettering of the Penn Maid word mark. The "Queenie" logo was given a subtle update and took a more prominent place on the packaging. The overall packaging retained the positive features focus groups connected with but was refined to create a more premium feel. These focus groups also revealed that the current package design had strong connotations of "down on the farm, homey, and dependable," and a strong history with consumers as being "part of their family." Hanson would build upon these strong feelings for the brand, as opposed to trying to reinvent them, which would only erode the goodwill created over the past eighty years.

Without direct input from consumers, the redesign could have gone in any number of other directions. By understanding how consumers connect visual cues on packages, the design team was able to make updates that enhanced existing feelings. In the end, the packaging update helped increase sales.

Qualitative and quantitative market research helped Hanson to know that they were on target with their design ideas. The market research also provided Hanson the credibility necessary to promote design directions inside Penn

Maid, which in turn gave them the opportunity to get the Penn Maid sales team and management excited about the idea. Put in simple terms, the focus groups gave Hanson a rationale to take to their clients.

Focus groups have long been a staple component of marketing research. They help organizations better understand how audiences perceive offerings, while enabling them to validate and test new products. In focus groups, a moderator uses a scripted series of questions or topics to lead a discussion group. These sessions take place at neutral locations, sometimes at facilities with videotaping equipment and an observation room with one-way mirrors. A focus group usually lasts for one to two hours. It takes at least three groups to get balanced results. The goal of focus groups is to gain insight into an audience's attitudes about a particular product, service or organization.

Much has been written about the weakness of focus groups. While focus groups offer an excellent opportunity to discuss topics or brainstorm with audiences, they can also lead to inaccurate information if not facilitated properly. People are inherently reactive. When put into groups, they tend to mask their true feelings. This can lead to a "group think" phenomena. In turn, this can lead to "false positives," the appearance that the group responded favorably, as illustrated by Pepsi's use of online focus groups to vet a new cola, Pepsi Edge. Based on positive feedback from focus groups, the product was launched, only to flounder badly in the marketplace. Rarely are focus groups used as a sole source of feedback. They seem to work best when complemented with interviews and other design research methods.

CONDUCTING FOCUS GROUPS

Focus groups are comprised of a moderator, a prescreened group of six to ten participants and a scribe. The moderator leads the group through a series of open-ended scripted questions that will reveal insights about the attitudes, beliefs and values held by members of the group. The format is loose, which allows for conversation to flow among the group's members while the moderator maintains focus. Groups are often recorded or videotaped, so others can view the discussion and capture nonverbal communication (such as, facial expressions and body language).

TRAITS OF AN EFFECTIVE GROUP MODERATOR

- Superior listening ability
- Excellent short-term auditory memory
- Well organized
- Quick learner
- High energy level
- Friendly, personable
- Ability to think clearly under stress

SIX STEPS TO A SUCCESSFUL FOCUS SESSION

Step 1: Define the objective. Determine a clear objective at the beginning of the session. By knowing what you don't know, and what pieces of information you need to collect, you can develop questions to address the problem to be solved.

Step 2: Develop the questions. A minimum of six questions should be crafted. The questions will answer the objective defined in step one. Take care to ensure that questions encourage active participation and discussion. Information from previous focus groups can also be used to create future focus group questions.

Questions should be open-ended and allow participants to answer them on a personal level. Questions like "What can you tell me about...?" or "What do you think about...?" encourage participants to speak from their own experiences, giving designers insight into how they think and feel. Open-ended questions can be analytical, comparative or evaluative.

Your questions should elicit reflection from the participants and prompt conversation. Questions should be presented in a conversational way so they don't sound stiff or preplanned. They should flow with the conversation. Questions should be clearly stated so participants don't get hung up on jargon or intent. Even though focus groups only last one to two hours, questions should not be rushed. Moderators should use affirmative statements to lead participants in directions that meet the focus group's primary objectives.

Focus groups employ a set of phased questions, each with a different purpose. Opening questions give the group a chance to answer and get comfortable with speaking. These questions are generally based on facts, rather than opinion. Next, introductory questions introduce the topic for discussion. Transition questions illustrate differing opinions within the group. Major questions focus on the most important items of discussion. Closing questions allow participants to express final thoughts.

Step 3: Plan the meeting. Focus groups generally last from one to two hours. Give participants an agenda that outlines the goals of the session and discusses how the session will proceed. Sessions are usually best held at neutral locations so that participants feel free to speak without constraints. Food is always a great way to put participants at ease, again allowing for candid conversation about the topic.

Step 4: Screen the participants. For focus groups to achieve success, there must be an adequate number of participants who have an understanding of the topic and fit the target audience. When contacting potential participants, designers should identify who they are and explain the topic of the focus meeting, including the goals of the research and what the participant can expect during the session. A series of screening question can help determine appropriate participants. Inform them that participation is confidential, so they feel comfortable giving honest answers. Any payment should be mentioned at this time as well.

Step 5: Hold the meeting. Once the prescreened group has been assembled, the moderator should make a brief introduction that outlines the goals of the session, the roles of participants, and ground rules for the session. The mention of any recording equipment or process should also occur at the beginning. Remind participants about the confidentiality of their responses.

Establish ground rules, then ask participants to introduce themselves (name, title, company or division) and state their relationship to the topic.

The moderator can then begin the questioning, allowing for free conversation. The moderator should be aware of any lulls in the conversation and be ready to either dig deeper into a response with a "why?" or move onto the next line of questioning.

Step 6: Conclude the Meeting. At this point, the moderator should ask participants for any last-minute insights about the topic; then thank the participants and distribute any payment or premium. At the end of the session, collect data and compile it into a readable format. This enables the designer to share the information in a concise way with project stakeholders.

ONE-ON-ONE INTERVIEWS

One-on-one interviews are similar to focus groups. They use open-ended questioning and have a conversational tone. A typical interview lasts about an hour, and it is based around scripted questions aimed at illuminating a specific problem or issue. The primary advantage of a one-on-one interview is that the participant cannot be influenced by the answers of others, and is therefore more likely to give an honest reflection.

Like focus groups, the information gleaned is not statistical, but subjective. Interviews reveal insights about audiences' attitudes, beliefs, and behaviors, giving designers data from which to base their design decisions. As the name suggests, a one-on-one interview takes place between a single interviewee and interviewer, and can be held almost anywhere, but they are most effective when done in a contextual space. Interviews can extend in the actual purchasing environment, at a person's home, or in an office building.

Beside the ability to get isolated responses, one-on-one interviews also allow participants to interact with prototypes and designs—a critical part of design research. Participants can explore sensory factors that are a part of many designs, for example, the feel of a particular paper stock, how a particular piece feels in one's hand, or how a person navigates a website. Additionally, participants may feel more comfortable talking at length with an interviewer who they are sitting face-to-face with, as opposed to a more impersonal approach such as talking over the phone or through an Internet survey.

DYADS AND TRIADS

By interviewing two or three individuals at once, designers can often gain understanding of topics that might be hard to ferret out of a larger group. Dyads and triads offer cost-effective approaches for gaining insight into audience needs.

Dyads are conducted with two participants who have an existing long-term relationship with each other. This technique is good for getting honest responses out of participants, since they are more likely to keep each other truthful. Dyads can last an hour and require a moderator using a scripted series of questions.

Triads are interviews that use three people who are similar to one another in some way, or different in a specific way. An example of a triad group might include three levels of philanthropic donors. This technique is good for gathering comparative information about a particular topic.

PROJECTIVE TECHNIQUES

Why do people really smoke? This was one of the questions Ernest Dichter set out to answer in the mid-1940s. Dichter, a psychologist and marketing research guru, was one of the first consumer motivational researchers to rely on psychoanalytic techniques to uncover the hidden motivations of consumers.

In *Psychology of Everyday Living*, Dichter identifies eighteen reasons why people smoke. After interviewing over two hundred people and asking the question, "Why do you smoke cigarettes?" Dichter discovered that though advertisers focused on the benefits of taste and mildness, most cigarette smokers had deeper reasons for their habit. Through his projective analysis, Dichter discovered that smoking was a reward to some and a way to combat loneliness—"with a cigarette I am not alone"—for others. Smoking helped some people relax and gave them time to think by creating a "smoke screen that helps shut out distractions." By employing projective techniques, Dichter was able to get beyond the superficial outward benefits of the product and to discover the real motivations behind the act of smoking.

Projective tests allow designers to dig deeper into the thinking of audiences, revealing feelings that might not surface because of self-defense mechanisms. Through the use of intentionally ambiguous images or scenarios, audiences are free to respond without the constraints of their subconscious. Common techniques include word association, collage-making, and drawing—each allowing the audience to fill in missing information without making them feel self-conscious. Most are familiar with the classic projective technique, the Rorschach test. As designers look to delve deeper into the motivations of an audience, projective techniques allow for honest opinions and help them express the inexpressible.

PHOTO SORTS

Photo sorts are a technique that use images for eliciting audience feelings about brands. A typical photo sort might use decks of images showing a diverse cross section of people (audiences are asked to match the people with the brands they might use) or as a random stimulus technique for helping participants break from conventional thinking. The origins of photo sorts can be found in the Thematic Apperception Test (TAT) developed at Harvard in the 1930s by psychologist Dr. Henry Murray and his partner, the artist Christina Morgan, to study personalities. Through the use of random images, subjects project meaning onto the images by developing a story around them. The stories are then analyzed to find patterns of meaning, with the goal of revealing underling feelings and ideas.

DRAWING

Asking audiences to draw their feeling about a brand offers a nonthreatening way to uncover their true feeling and dispel assumptions. Pioneered by psychologist Emmanuel Hammer, the author and teacher of numerous books and articles on the practice of therapeutic drawing and its clinical impact with children, prisoners, and the mentally challenged, projective drawing techniques offer designers a way to better understand their perceptions of a brand or experience. Designers can simply ask participants to draw an experience they had with a product or service and then have them describe the drawing.

"Storyboards have been very successful in the past when we have a client that wants to go in a certain direction but isn't sure how," says Henning Fischer of Adaptive Path. He recalls one project in particular in which storyboarding played a role in helping the client identify business opportunities from a customer's perspective. There was no way to do research because he was without access to customer data. In this case, scenario building and sketching possible outcomes and possible journeys ended up being very valuable because they allow you to walk in someone else's shoes and through their process. After identifying a number of business opportunities, participants developed posters for each opportunity. The poster illustrated the constraints and opportunities and the customer experience. Participants mocked up three scenarios for each opportunity. Both Fischer and the clients worked together to think through the various scenarios. The clients drew stick figures to help get all the ideas out there. The ideas were critiqued and refined further. The rough sketches were redrawn professionally with a greater level of detail.

At the start of this exercise, Fischer takes his client through a five-minute class on how to draw a stick figure. "People are comfortable drawing boxes and things that appear on screen," he says. "They are less comfortable drawing people. But if you can draw a triangle, a circle or a square, then chances are that you can draw a stick figure in action. Sometimes we'll do a warm-up exercise, because everyone knows how to draw when they are five. If people are more comfortable working with text, we let them start there, then gently start to sketch stuff in. It does not have to be a work of art."

At XPLANE, the visual-thinking company, Scott Matthews, head of design, helps companies across the globe better communicate their process, plans, and ideas through visual language. Matthews often works with senior executives from enterprise companies, helping them convey what is going on to their staff, their employees, and stockholders. "We communicate stories and results," says Matthews. Moving from high-level communications down to specifics on the ground, Matthews keeps on eye on how the organization is communicating, identifies what problems workers are encountering, and takes note of how they are managing these problems.

In some corporate situations the delivery of messages can be very dry. While today's organizations make attempts to liven up their meetings, there is still a great deal of uninspired communication that quickly becomes monotonous. "We want to bring the joy back to meetings," says Matthews. Matthews works with groups of up to fifteen people over the course of one to two day sessions to facilitate their conversations. Using drawing techniques, he is able to get information out of their heads and onto paper, enabling them to synthesize ideas. "Once everyone can see the idea, it drives understanding." Matthews has his clients draw as early as possible in the process. Acknowledging that the CEO's top-level executives may not be comfortable drawing, Matthews gets the group going immediately to "loosen them up." Participants are asked to draw self-portraits, their favorite animal, or pictures of themselves in their favorite Halloween costume. "The goal is to pull out that 'fearless child' and the imagination that we all have," he says.

One example of an exercise Matthews uses to help develop personas is the "big head" exercise. On a large whiteboard participants are asked to draw a large square with rounded corners, similar to the profile of a person, with eyes, nose, mouth, etc. Participants draw lines from the eyes and ears, then draw what the CEO is seeing and hearing, allowing participants to climb inside the head of the CEO. Participants fill out sticky notes identifying things that the CEO is seeing, then post them up on the big head profile drawing. This exercise helps employees get over their insecurities of speaking up in a meeting, and creates a sense of freedom, getting them up and moving, talking and drawing, and most importantly working collaboratively with each other. When participants get their work on the whiteboard, they see it in a way that is different from just boxes, lines, and circles; they see pictures and contexts, and they quickly see their efforts more clearly, which helps them identify areas of improvement.

Can this all be done more conventionally with words? Possibly, but Matthews says that drawing sessions are more fun for people, who instinctively react to the drawings as opposed to the written word alone. People tend to tune out when reading business reports. Drawings make the key points clearer and faster.

On the power of images, Matthews muses, "Communication is flying around the globe at an unbelievable rate, and really the only barrier that exists between people is language. The word *dog* might be referred to in hundreds of ways around the world, but a picture of a dog, everybody knows what that is." For global companies that want to tell stories, visual language is the effective pairing of words and pictures to convey meaning.

STORYTELLING

Few people think in terms of pure fact. Instead, people tend to think in terms of stories. As Daniel Pink, author of the best-selling book *A Whole New Mind,* points out, "Stories are easier to remember—because in many ways, stories are how we remember." For designers, this is a critical point, particularly when it comes to designing collateral for brands. Many clients will use a "data dump" approach to their communications, providing endless information about their product or services. Most of this is lost on the audience, who would better connect and recall the brand through storytelling.

Storytelling is also a very powerful tool for eliciting the hidden meaning behind an audience's thinking. Allowing audiences the opportunity to share their experiences, storytelling can be done verbally or by using images. A typical storytelling exercise might have a participant draw an experience related to a brand or service. Stories help identify the phases or steps associated with an experience, as well as their corresponding emotions.

Methods similar to storytelling include sentence completion and bubble drawing. Sentence completion works by asking audiences to finish a sentence and from that, discerning their feelings about a brand. "What is the first thing you think about when hear the brand name _____?" For bubble drawing, audiences are shown a simple drawing of a person (or people) talking. The characters have blank speech bubbles above their heads, which participants fill in with conversations based on the topic at hand.

ETHNOGRAPHY

Ethnographic research is a technique used in the fields of cultural and social anthropology. It provides in-depth information about attitudes, beliefs and behaviors. The research uses firsthand observation of people as they go about their daily lives. This allows researchers to gain an even better understanding of how they live. Over the last ten years, ethnography has played an increasing role in market and design research as organizations take greater interest in developing a deeper understanding about customers and audiences.

Dori Tunstall has helped companies as diverse as the U.S. Army, Nokia, Allstate, General Motors, and Sears understand and engage customers. She has also lent her unique skills to the world of technology, consulting with the marketing services agencies Arc worldwide and Sapient. In her teaching role as design anthropologist at the University of Illinois at Chicago, she teaches design research to graphic design students in a class she calls "creative conceptualization boot camp." The class asks students to make design decisions that ignore assumptions and to base decision-making on the reality of the user. Tunstall walks her students through a rigorous process in which they gather primary and secondary research, including interviewing, observation, self-documentation and analysis.

Says Tunstall, "From an anthropology perspective, we try to understand how the processes and artifacts of design help define what it means to be human. If design is the artificial world, the man-made world, then it's the perfect match for anthropology, which is about studying all aspects of the human world." Through her work, she challenges her students to understand the role of artifacts in mediating meaning.

Students start out with a design-related question and are asked to think about what it means in a broader context. They try to identify assumptions about the subject and compare that to reality.

One student looked at the use of typography in terms of font choice and spacing, along with its effect on readability, as experienced by third graders. After reviewing current research and conducting research of his own, he came to understand that much research focuses on the speed of reading, or on legibility, while neglecting the most important part—comprehension. As a graphic designer, he now has to think about how design principles aid comprehension, and about the relationship between comprehension and layout and imagery, as well as about how typographic choices are made.

Tunstall explains that ethnography is not about a series of techniques or methodologies. Rather, it is a philosophical orientation that asks you to understand an experience from the perspective of the people you are observing. It's only by getting close to an experience and trying to understand it that you open up new pathways for graphic design practice.

Innovative firms like IDEO, Doblin and Jump Associates all have ethnographic capacity. But for a small boutique design firm it might prove highly impractical to employ an ethnographer whose minimum qualification is a master's degree in anthropology. The cost alone is typically prohibitive. There is also the difficult job of convincing clients about the value of ethnographic research.

Another issue for designers is the ephemeral nature of graphic design. Much of what designers create does not last more than a year. And if something is going to last six months or less, you are obliged to consider if it's worth the money. Thus, longer-term projects like websites, evergreen marketing material, and information design can benefit from an ethnographic study.

In lieu of engaging an ethnographer, designers can consider conducting some research on their own. Depending on a designer's knowledge and expertise, and the level of complexity involved, designers can often perform basic research without professional help. However, if a designer has no knowledge whatsoever of the culture or language of a community, and is not skilled at analytics, then they would be wise to partner with an appropriate professional.

At high levels of design, it is ethically irresponsible to go into an ethnographic project without ethnographic understanding. If you are planning to make definitive statements about certain peoples and the way they exist in the world, ethical consideration is important. The communicative power of design is such that if you are amplifying a misrepresentation of people, you may do them significant damage.

EMPATHY AND HUMILITY

Designers sometimes forget about the fundamental relevance of humility. People engaged in inherently creative professions like design or architecture often possess certain romantic notions about artistic genius. Often this blinds graphic designers to their own hubris, in terms of what it is they know and what it is they do not.

What is it to be human? Graphic designers too often assume they understand. "Even as a professionally trained anthropologist I could never make that statement," says Dori Tunstall. "There is a certain aspect of the graphic design community that feels comfortable making that statement and then making design judgments based on it—without any desire to test it, because they fear it may disprove their artistic genius. Design intuition can only be acquired through training, grounding and experience—gained over several years. Intuition is useful, but it can become problematic when used as a way to avoid accountability."

Ethnography has been used for years by social scientists to understand life from the point of view of the people they are researching. By spending time with groups of people and taking copious notes, ethnographers are able to capture valuable information about the way people live. By applying the same methods of observation and questioning, ethnography is becoming a valuable tool for understanding consumers. By watching consumers in their own environment, or even joining their subjects, ethnographers broaden their understanding.

Applied ethnography focuses on understanding the audience's perspective and applying it to design. The process is exploratory and relies on open-ended questions and observation. It's most useful at the beginning of the design process, when understanding audience needs and perspectives are an invaluable component of concept development. This technique also brings to light what audiences actually do, as opposed to what they say they do. Routinely, this has proved to be a deficiency of traditional qualitative methods, such as focus groups.

Companies now employ ethnographers to conduct design research, thereby giving them a better understanding of audience needs, and in the long run, giving them a competitive edge. The process employs interviews and examination to observe behaviors and understand relationships, as well as to see how a product or service is used in the context of a subject's daily life.

For most design firms, full-blown ethnographic research is both cost and time prohibitive. But even as casual observers, designers can learn a lot from an audience. Once a qualitative exercise like a focus group session has been conducted, designers can dig deeper, conducting one-on-one interviews along with ethnographic observation.

IN CONCLUSION

Research is a valuable tool for gaining insight into the organizational needs of clients and their perspective audiences. A designer who takes the time to understand a client's business needs and the needs of audiences is in position to bridge the gap between the two. In this way, a designer can motivate an audience to engage the process as well as the product, in a manner that hopefully meets or even surpasses the goal of design.

In a 2007 *Financial Times* interview, Joel Podolny, former dean of the Yale School of Management, and head of Apple University, says, "If you talk to the CEOs, what they are obsessed about is how you get a handle on what customers want." Without an understanding of the audience that the organization serves there can be no relationship, financial or otherwise.

Through research, designers gain an understanding of what motivates audiences. By reaching out, designers learn not only about their basic needs, but also about what is meaningful to them. The information gathered allows designers (and clients) to better satisfy their audience's needs and desires.

Research does not, however, exonerate designers and clients from making design decisions. Many aspects of our understanding are beyond measure and depend on intuition and inference. These thoughts must be weighed equally with research. While both are flawed, each is an important tool for decision-making. One thing is for certain: Design is not an exact science. It relies heavily on interpretations and insights gained from close observation of a subject and an environment. Ultimately, it is a professional estimate that most accurately reflects the ephemeral demands of the marketplace.

chapter 7
WHAT'S THE BIG IDEA?

MANAGING THE COMPLEXITY
OF CONCEPT DEVELOPMENT

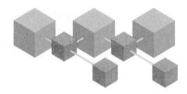

With business and audience research captured, designers are prepared to develop concepts. Concept development is part art and part science, mixing intuitive powers with various creative thinking frameworks to arrive at unexpected destinations. Every designer has a unique approach to developing concepts. Consider the following.

THINK WRONG

John Bielenberg is the principal of the San Francisco design firm C2 and the winner of over 150 design awards from organizations like the AIGA, *Print* and *Communication Arts*. For Bielenberg, "thinking wrong" is the key to the design process.

In the mid-1990s, Bielenberg was working with an investment-banking client who had hired a behavioral psychologist from Cornell to look at how investment managers make decisions. In particular, decisions like overweighting information and other irrational thoughts. This was an inspiration for Bielenberg. He realized that designers might well act in a similar way.

"Heuristics are pathways in the brain," explains Bielenberg. "Language and speaking are examples of these pathways. When you talk, you're not thinking about talking, you just do it. This allows us to function in the world. But I also started thinking about how it might limit the creative process. In design, you might get a project like an annual report, and you sit down at your computer and you're laying out 8½ × 11-inch page spreads, which would be a heuristic bias for what an annual report should be."

Bielenberg started thinking about how designers could break out of these conventions and generate multiple alternatives before deciding on a "final" direction. Bielenberg describes his process as "trying to disrupt the ortho-doxies—both in our clients and ourselves—and the way we solve problems." Bielenberg calls his method "Thinking Wrong." Based on nonlinear thinking principles similar to those that best-selling author and creative thinking guru Dr. Edward de Bono explored, "Thinking Wrong" is built into Bielenberg's process, occurring at regular intervals throughout a project, acting as a kind of "Thinking Wrong" gate. This helps prevent designers from slipping back into a conventional approach. The checks occur after the design brief is cemented and design prototypes are constructed.

"The human brain tends to think along predetermined linear pathways," says Bielenberg. "Such thinking can inhibit true innovation and creative exploration." An example of an exercise used to break out of conventional thinking involves having the creative team choose random numbers, then using those numbers to locate pages in an encyclopedia. For instance, the group might pick the number 153, and then turn to page 153 in the diction-ary. There, they would look for the first entry for that page. The word is then used as a jumping off point for thinking about the problem at hand. "If we are trying to develop a creative concept for an annual report, the team has to use their word as a starting point," Bielenberg explains. "This definitely sends you in a direction you would not have gone in otherwise."

In today's world, design assignments have a tendency toward sameness. The client's and designer's understanding of what is good is typically based on what they've seen previously. Breaking from a conventional approach is critical to creating work that will differentiate a client from their competition. Says Bielenberg, "What people pay attention to is what is different."

MAGIC

In his *Design Observer* article, "This Is My Process," Pentagram partner Michael Beirut describes his creative process in looser terms. "Somewhere along the way an idea for the design pops into my head, from out of the blue," he says. "I really can't explain that part; it's like magic." Beirut's approach depends more on iteration and intuition than structured organization. In his article Beirut points to a link between his work and that of a theater company, as they both must deliver a production within a strict time frame, yet avoid being so rigorous as to preclude innovation. Calling on the book *Artful Making* by Harvard School of Business professor Robert Austin and Swarthmore theater professor Lee Devin, Beirut points out the change in work, from a production mode to a knowledge mode, elevating collaboration and iteration as key parts of the design process. Like a theater production, design requires that innovative ideas be developed on tight deadlines, while the final product is unknown. A strictly linear process will not work, whereas an "emergent" approach makes sense.

COLLABORATION

Roy Spence, CEO of the Austin, Texas-based advertising agency GSD&M, stresses what he calls "dynamic collaboration," as a cornerstone of his creative process. The process is collaborative, engaging as many "smart people" as possible. Spence says the first step is to admit that you don't have the corner on "smarts." Once you come to grips with your limitations, you can begin to look outside of your organization for partners who can raise the level of thinking. Such collaboration is critical to letting ideas break the boundaries of organizational thinking.

Spence believes in ideation, not brainstorming. Through GSD&M's ideation lab, an online discussion board with several moderators, a question is posed to a large group of participants. All responses are anonymous—which means they all carry the same weight. An idea "top ten" list is quickly distilled. The ideas are voted on, then handed over to a creative team. Spence believes that client involvement creates ownership in both the process and the final outcome. "We ask people not to create our advertising, but to help create the strategy and ideas behind it," he says.

Each concept development method applies a certain set of rules to unravel a problem. Some apply nonlinear thinking, like John Bielenberg. Others, like Michael Beirut, let ideas build upon each other until an answer emerges. Still others use collaboration as a means for uncovering the best ideas. Each approach has its value.

Concept development is one of the most challenging phases of the design process. The ability to harness research and think in nonlinear ways is essential to developing new and meaningful concepts. Concept development and ideation tools fall into several categories, including lateral thinking, vertical thinking, and parallel thinking. Each method is different, yet all consist of a similar structure—reflecting the overall design process of problem definition, information gathering, information sorting, incubation, and evaluation.

CREATIVE AND DIVERGENT THINKING

With businesses embracing innovation as a key driver of their success, the focus on sustained creativity is now being looked at as an important core capability. As we move from a knowledge economy, where left-brain analytical skills are being outsourced and right-brain creative skills are now coveted, creativity is being recognized as an important driver of the economy.

As designers strive to think beyond the ordinary, creativity techniques offer a framework for developing ideas on a consistent basis. Some techniques are intuitive, but structured, heuristic methods can also trigger free association and reveal unexpected connections and opportunities. Though there are many methods for arriving at new ideas, much of creative thinking follows a basic structure of problem definition, ideation, and concept selection. The definition phase, also known as the fuzzy front end, takes raw ideas to the development stage that yields a concept. The concept is then verified to ascertain its ability to produce a product that works and can be delivered on time. Divergent thinking considers customers and their unmet needs. This can lead to opportunities for new ideas, as data is gathered and reviewed. Convergent thinking takes the data and prioritizes it based on customer needs. This leads into concept development, where ideas are formulated and mock-ups produced. Concepts are then selected through a process that considers business goals and audience needs.

This chapter explores various techniques for developing new ideas and enhancing the process of concept development. Ideas rarely come from a single source. The romantic notion of a lone creative genius struggling mightily with a problem, then suddenly birthing a fully formed solution is outdated mythology. Idea development is more typically the product of any number of individuals who collaborate to solve a problem. Accordingly, most of the creative exercises discussed in this book involve clients and audiences. Further, it is recommended that participants reflect a diversity of disciplines and represent cross-departmental units. The intention is to mix together as broad a range of concepts, experiences, and perceptions as possible—in order to drive and strengthen the creative process.

THE FUZZY FRONT END

The preceding phases of business and audience research play a key role in concept development. Without knowledge of the client's business goals, the competitive forces with which it must contend, and its audience's needs, values, beliefs, and motivations, there is little hope for a creative, targeted solution. The information discovered in these earlier two phases will become the basis for concept development solutions. In the words of Louis Pasteur, "Chance favors the prepared mind."

PROBLEM DEFINITION

Understanding and defining the problem to be solved is the first step in concept development. Although the problem may seem obvious at first glance, deeper explorations can help get past assumptions. When design problems are not clearly defined, they can appear to have too many options. Too many options creates a "too big" scenario, where the project goal is so nebulous and design options seem limitless that designers can easily become paralyzed, as if looking into a great abyss. So where do you start?

Two simple tools for discovering problems include the Five Whys and the What, Where, and How approaches.

FIVE WHYS

The first step is to simply write a problem statement. This can be a simple declarative sentence that describes the problem, such as "The house is on fire." The next step is to ask "why" in successive levels until the root cause of the problem is clarified. The approach gets participants beyond assumptions that might stand in the way of the actual problem that needs to be solved.

WHAT, WHERE, HOW

Another approach for clarifying a problem uses three simple questions to root out the causes of the problem: What is happening currently? Where do we need to go? How will we get there? These questions help create a reference for problem definition and are directly related to the business and audience research conducted in the earlier phases.

What is happening currently? Designers can start by looking at what is currently going on with the organization or audiences. By synthesizing information from the business and audience research phase, a general picture of what is happening internally and externally can be drawn.

Where do we need to go? This question is based on the project goals. By looking at the organization's strategy for moving forward, designers can narrow the focus of their efforts.

How will we get there? This question outlines the project objectives. Again, by referring back to the business strategy or audience needs, specific objectives can be identified.

Clearly identifying and articulating the problem to be solved provides a common focus for project stakeholders and ensures that efforts are not wasted.

BREAKING CONVENTIONS

Much of creative thinking is about changing assumptions and using techniques that fall into the four general categories of metaphor, changing perspective, random stimulus, and creating combinations. No discussion of creative thinking can occur without mentioning Dr. Edward de Bono. Famous for his work unraveling the nuances of human creativity, de Bono wanted to dispel the myth that creativity comes from our childlike innocence and our ability to hold the right side of the brain in check when addressing problems. Instead, he believed that creativity is hard work and requires a level of discipline that anyone can achieve, not only designers or inventors.

De Bono developed a number of creative approaches, many of which are used by such noted designers as Stefan Sagmeister and John Bielenberg. In contrast to vertical thinking, which is sequential and more related to logic or mathematics, de Bono developed lateral thinking, which uses information as a jumping off point, but not as a hard and fast parameter. For instance, the vertical thinker says, "I know what I'm looking for," while the lateral thinker says, "I'm looking, but I won't know what it is until I've found it."

An example of lateral thinking is using random words as jumping off points in a search for new perspectives. By pulling random words from a dictionary, participants can free-associate with the word to see where it will take them. Random words force participants to look at a problem from a completely different perspective, guaranteeing to break them out of conventional thoughts.

Another one of de Bono's more popular lateral thinking techniques is called "Six Hats Thinking." For this exercise, participants assume the thinking of various attitudes; for instance, black hats are judgmental, white hats are data driven, red hats are emotional, and so on. By taking on the role of the various hats, participants change their usual perspectives and think in new ways about a problem.

Both techniques provide users with new points of entry for thinking about familiar subjects, giving them the opportunity to break free from heuristics and make associations that do not fit within their normal sense of order.

INCUBATION AND THE CREATIVE PROCESS

When asked, "Where do you get your best ideas?" a remarkable number of people answer, "In the shower." The shower, apparently, constitutes a perfect environment for developing new ideas. As such, it provides a readily accessible and pleasant experience that discourages conscious problem solving while enabling the mind to relax. A period for setting the problem aside allows for incubation, a term developed by English social psychologist Graham Wallas. Wallas is most noted for his work outlining the five stages of the creative process: preparation, incubation, intimation, illumination, and verification. Wallas believed that the essential contribution of incubation was to allow all unimportant or misleading information to simply fall away.

Consider the "tip of the tongue" phenomenon. Most of us have experienced the inability to retrieve a word at a given moment. No matter how hard you try, you are unable to locate the word in your mind. This phenomenon occurs when your mind conjures an inappropriate, or similar answer, blocking the correct one. Only after disengaging from the search is your mind able to produce a correct answer. Studies indicate that taking a break (incubation) during problem solving or memory retrieval increases the chance for better retrieval at a later date.

In an incubation study conducted by C.A. Kaplan in 1989, two groups of participants were asked to work on a problem for four minutes. One group was asked to work on the problem until they produced a solution. The second group was asked to work for two minutes, then take a thirty-minute incubation break, during which time they were given an unrelated problem to work on. They were then asked to use a final two minutes to work on the initial problem. Results showed that the group that took an incubation break came up with an equal number of ideas in each two-minute session, whereas the first group produced fewer ideas during the second two-minute period.

Although research into incubation has yet to provide a definitive explanation of how it works, studies to date indicate that periods of time spent away from problem solving can improve the speed and quality of solutions.

Many creative techniques involve the suspension of conventional thought processes and the linking of seemingly unrelated ideas. Says de Bono, "Creativity involves breaking out of established patterns in order to look at things in a different way." The following section presents established methods for developing creative ideas.

IDEATION

All the methods described in this chapter are meant to be participatory, and to include designers, clients, and audiences. By including these key stakeholders, designers are able to capture firsthand responses from clients and audiences. Many of the projective research techniques discussed in the previous chapter are also valuable ideation tools that can be used for both gathering audience insights and developing new concepts.

BRAINSTORMING

The creative process can take many forms. Frequently, it starts with a simple brainstorming exercise, then progresses into more elaborate (and often less rational) exercises. Alex Osborn, a principal at BBDO advertising agency during the 1930s, is credited with developing the classic brainstorming technique.

Brainstorming is an ideation technique where groups of people attempt to solve a problem by collecting as many ideas as possible. Osborn coined the term "brainstorming" at BBDO, but acknowledged that the technique had its origins with Hindu teachers in India.

From an early age we are taught to make judgments when making decisions about the people we meet and the situations we are in. Without a doubt this is an important survival skill. However, when it comes to creative thinking, judgment can be a hindrance. Classic brainstorming works on the credo of "deferred judgment." All ideas are considered and criticism is not allowed. The reasoning? An "off-the-wall" idea is easier to tear down than build up. All fears put aside, brainstorming spawns spontaneous conversation—the key to its success.

In the brainstorming process one idea builds on another until a unique solution emerges. Ideas generated in this fashion are then evaluated by a group of up to six people consisting of project participants. Because of its ability to bring diverse ideas together, consensus, rather than voting, should be employed to make any formal decisions. Ideas are then sorted into categories and ranked, based on their potential for solving the design problem, as initially defined.

The primary objective is quantity, rather than quality. If participants think they need to develop "The Idea," their thinking will stagnate and the flow of ideas will slow or stop. The more ideas developed, the better. Participants should be reminded not to worry about arriving at a final concept. Rather, their objective is to generate building blocks and possibilities, which can in turn be mixed and mashed together to create even more possibilities.

NECESSITIES

- Whiteboard or flip chart, big enough for everyone to see
- Pens for every participant, different colors work best
- Comfortable space, so people can get up and walk around
- Food

A moderator or facilitator plays a key role in making a session successful. The moderator sets ground rules and keeps the session on track; she also makes sure momentum stays consistent. It's not unusual for a session to start slowly, then peak early. After members have eagerly contributed initial thoughts and ideas, the session may die down and stagnate, as individuals search within themselves for "better" ideas. At this point, the moderator needs to be prepared with questions to get the group to bounce ideas off one another. Comments like, "Good idea, Joe. How would that idea work with Mary's?" or "How would we do this if we were _____?"

STEPS FOR BRAINSTORMING

Step 1: Assemble the group. Gather a group of four to six people in a comfortable space.

Step 2: Start with an exercise. Lead the group through a brief warm-up exercise, like storytelling. One person starts a story with a leadoff sentence. The person next to them must build on the story, then pass it on to the next person, and so on.

Step 3: Define the problem. Test it against the group objectives. Clearly state the problem in writing, so that everyone can see it.

Step 4: Review the ground rules.

- Avoid all criticism
- Don't edit or censor ideas
- Focus on quantity, not quality
- Build on the ideas of others
- Number all ideas
- Avoid discussing or questioning ideas
- Have fun

Step 5: Choose a facilitator. Appoint a facilitator to manage the session and maintain ground rules.

Step 6: Appoint someone to record ideas as they are created. Collect ideas on a whiteboard or a flip chart with tear-off pages, so you can walk away with the collected information for future reference.

Step 7: Conclude the session.

Step 8: Collect ideas. Prioritize, combine, and collect the ideas that have the most potential to address the problem.

Step 9: Refine ideas. Take the final ideas and refine them using another ideation technique.

BRAIN WRITING VARIATION

Several variations of brainstorming use a passing or piggyback technique. The passing technique allows participants to work on their own for a short period. Then, at a designated time, they pass or share their idea with the group and receive a new idea to develop. In brain writing, a moderator gives everyone a problem to solve. The group works individually on the problem, writing down possible solutions on a sheet of paper. After a determined period of time (say, two minutes), the participants stop writing. Each person passes his paper to the person sitting on the left. They then have an additional two minutes to build off the idea handed to them. Alternatively, they can develop an entirely new solution. Once all of the sheets have been returned to their original owners, all the ideas are reviewed, and final selections are made.

PICTURES AND IMAGES

Designers have always understood the power of images to communicate, and now businesspeople are getting into the act. Dan Roam, business consultant and author of the book *The Back of the Napkin*, has been using visual thinking as a method for quickly communicating ideas in a way that engages participants and brings them into the problem-solving process. As Roam and others have pointed out, audiences are often reluctant to express their true feelings for fear of being "wrong" or "inappropriate" in front of their peers. This makes collecting reliable feedback difficult. Through the use of images, audiences are freed from their self-censorship and can express themselves without risk. Because of this, images are great tools for developing concepts. They can act as a resource for making analogies and triggering new concepts. Image-sparking techniques include visual brainstorming, mood boards, brain writing, drawing, and totemics.

Images can be pulled from many sources, including magazines, newspapers, and the Internet. The images selected should not be directly related to the problem being addressed—this would inhibit divergent thinking. Images should also be fairly neutral in tone, to avoid being overly negative.

A standard method for working with images includes defining the problem in a statement and discussing it with the participants until it is clearly understood. Then, using a standard brainstorming technique, begin the session. Once ideas dwindle, pictures may be used to ignite new ideas. Images are useful for free association or as part of a "passing" technique in which participants share and build upon each othe'rs ideas by passing them around the table.

Some techniques that use images as a starting point follow.

MOOD BOARDS

Many designers start their explorations with mood boards, which combine images, words, and general palettes that reflect the look, feel, or idea of what a client wants to evoke. Market researchers have used mood boards since the early 1990s to uncover the attitudes, beliefs, and feelings of consumers. The technique is useful because it does not require design or drawing skill, yet it creates visually rich images in a short period of time. Mood boards allow participants to express their feelings and experiences in nonverbal ways. Some participants find this liberating. Similarly, designers can use mood boards as a way to develop new ideas and spark new approaches.

Mood board sessions can be held with any number of people. They require minimal moderation. Materials may include magazines, newspapers, and images from the Internet, along with pens, large sheets of paper, and glue. The more diverse the materials, the more likely participants will express themselves in meaningful ways.

A typical mood board session, as a participative activity to gain audience insight, might include the following steps.

Step 1: Provide a topic. Give participants a topic to explore. The mood board session begins by clearly defining the topic to be explored. The topic will be directly related to the design problem that is being solved. A mood board session might ask participants to explore a keyword associated with a product or service.

Step 2: Create collages. Ask participants to work with materials of their choice and to develop one or more collages. Images from the web, magazines, or photos are provided to the participants. Basic tools like tape, glue, and poster board are also supplied. Participants can bring their own images if they know the topic ahead of time.

Step 3: Describe mood boards. Ask participants to describe their mood boards. Once the mood boards are finished, participants describe their collages to each other and discuss the significance of the imagery they created. This exercise is often revealing as it provides a new way for people to talk about ideas. The boards can be reviewed with an eye toward finding similar patterns, themes, or content categories.

TOTEMICS

Another image-based method that combines both words and images is called *totemics*. Developed by Dr. Angela Dumas, a research fellow in design management at the London Business School, totemics is a metaphor-based technique whereby participants define concepts that need to be conveyed—for instance, speed, technology, simple, and work—using images of existing objects such as a car, chair, textile, hammer. Totemics takes the team through a metaphor-based process in which they determine benchmarks, define in words the characteristics they are looking for, find complementary images that correspond to the words, and creative a visual metaphor, or totem. The totem acts as means of coordinating the design team, aligning them around a common visual language, and clarifying the "fuzzy front end."

A typical totemic exercise would proceed as follows:

Step 1: Build a context. Customers are asked to present ideas or examples of brochures, images, or styles they like and don't like. This provides a reference point for the designer.

Step 2: Define the context. Team members narrow a customer's selections and develop a list of ten descriptive words to describe the piece. Next, they draw a depiction of the piece and write descriptive words below it.

Step 3: Build a vocabulary. Images showing furniture, interiors, textiles, consumer products, and industrial products are collected. (Each category shows a range of styles and approaches.)

Step 4: Select images. The team selects one image from each category to match the ten descriptors from step 2. Plus, each team member draws separate pictures to represent the objects shown in the slides, based on a selection of the ten words. A "what if" drawing is then created. Each team member also draws a picture of the slide as if it were the piece being developed. For example, if the image on the slide is the Eames Lounge Chair No. 670, the designer would translate the visual language of the chair to the design project at hand (brochure, website, packaging, etc.).

Step 5: Refine perceptions. The original ten words are reviewed. New words are added, as needed. The word list is then narrowed down to six or eight. The perceptual and physical qualities of the slides are discussed. The dominant qualities of the slides and the piece under consideration are established.

Step 6: Distill the totem. The drawings and slides are reviewed. Five or six are selected. The least powerful slides, words, and drawings are rejected. The remaining words, slides, and drawings represent the totem.

ZMET

One of the many problems associated with audience research is that audiences are unable to truly tell you why they like or dislike something. Traditional marketers rely heavily on data that is easy to collect. By going after "low-hanging fruit," they miss important dimensions of the audience's experience. To uncover audience's true motivations, Gerald Zaltman, a Harvard professor of Business Administration, and Jerry Olson, a professor at Penn State, formed Olson Zaltman Associates, a research-consulting firm that provides tools to companies looking to connect to audiences on a deeper level.

The ZMET (Zaltman Metaphor Elicitation Technique) method for uncovering "deep insights" uses images as a jumping-off point of understanding audiences' attitudes and feelings about a client's product or service. Zaltman developed his technique after using an ethnographic self-reporting technique that had participants use cameras to document their lives. Zaltman refined this approach while at the Seeing the Voice of the Customer Lab at Harvard University, where he used a cross-disciplined approach of psychology, linguistics and neurobiology to understand audiences and their perceptions.

The process starts off by asking participants to collect images that express their feeling toward a product or service. The participants then meet with a trained ZMET analyst who helps them think about the meanings behind the image. The process uses psychological methods to uncover the hidden thoughts that lie beneath the participant's feelings.

DRAWING AND SKETCHING

Mark Dzerisk, industrial designer and vice president at Brandimage Desgrippes, uses drawing as an important tool for brainstorming. Dzerisk believes that the most effective ways designers can communicate is through visualizing, that it is indeed the key to a brainstorming session. The team building and cross function aspects of brainstorming are powerful, he says, but there is more value in a designer's ability to visualize an idea.

As design professor at Northwestern, Dzerisk helps left-brain graduate students use sketching as a problem-solving tool. He describes this as both "terrifying and liberating" for these students. He calls the method he uses "3×1 brainstorm." It requires about six people, a stack of drawing paper, and some drawing tools. If the problem to be solved centers around improving telephones for women, for example, Dzerisk would have the group develop a list of "female fast talkers." The group would brainstorm a list of anyone that would fit into the category. Next, Dzerisk would ask the group to make a list of things that the group might carry with them in their pockets or purses. Finally, Dzerisk would have the group create a list of things that communicate. Dzerisk believes that brainstorming requires nurturing, so throughout the list-making process, he keeps it light and encourages the group by giving them praise for their ideas. "You can chill an idea with a sneer," he says. "Ideas are fragile."

Afterward, Dzerisk circles one element from each of the lists—for instance, Oprah, change purse, radar—and asks the group to draw how Oprah would use her change purse to communicate like a radar. After ninety seconds, the group presents their individual drawings. After much praise is given to the group, Dzerisk then gives them another set from the lists to work from—Katie Couric, makeup compact, telegraph—only this time he gives them sixty seconds and follows with another round. By the end of the session, a plethora of ideas hang on the wall.

Dzerisk creates the framework and structure for thinking. By the fourth round, the group is thinking freely and the energy is infectious. The participants are feeling engaged and confident in their ability to not only problem solve, but to do it in a visual way.

Drawing allows participants the freedom to express their thoughts in a spontaneous way without having to use language. Many of our thoughts are held deep within our subconscious and rarely surface though conventional means. Drawing frees people from having to provide rational answers to questions and lets them express themselves on a deeper level. Types of drawing techniques include the following.

STORYBOARDS

Kevin Cheng, director of product strategy at Raptr and author of the book *See What I Mean*, believes that drawing offers a powerful storytelling tool for communicating everything from concepts to product development. Cheng points out that comics, or conceptual storyboards, are great at communicating ideas and stories in an engaging, entertaining, and concise manner and offer a powerful alternative to documentation that people are unlikely to read or understand. Consider how IKEA and LEGO understood the power of sequential images with their great assembly instructions. For Cheng, storyboards provide a tool for communicating complex ideas in story form, thereby making them more accessible. Just as wire frames abstract out the visual design elements, the storyboards abstract out the finer interactive details so you can focus on the product and whether it solves a user need.

Cheng believes that storyboards are most effective when used at the beginning of the design process. As a tool for aligning team members, storyboards help everyone involved get on the same page. During a project with Yahoo!, Cheng and his team found themselves in the middle of designing a product before they realized that their individual understanding of what the product ought to be differed greatly. "We had started work before we were properly aligned," says Cheng. To get the team back on track he created three storyboards that communicated the core ideas and use cases of the feature they were designing. These storyboards were short (six to eight panels each), and he distributed them to everyone on the team, as well as up the chain to senior VP management. Then he showed them to potential users to get their feedback. The storyboards were easy to digest, and the stakeholders quickly understood their meaning. In the end, they proved to be far more efficient than any requirements document could be, plus they brought about conversations that clarified the direction of the product.

Alternatively, the use of storyboards at the end of the design process is also extremely powerful, where they can be used as a marketing tool. Cheng sites Google and its use of storyboards for its Chrome web browser. Although the storyboard was thirty pages, it was a far more entertaining read than any document about a web browser could have been.

A typical drawing exercise uses the following steps:

Step 1: Define the problem. Write the problem in a place where all participants can see it clearly. Consider imagery that reflects the problem or is a potential solution to the problem.

Step 2: Draw. Using paper and colored pens, draw images as freely and as naturally as possible. Participants can use as much or as little detail as they choose. The goal is not to create a great work of art but to convey an idea.

Step 3: Write or discuss. Each participant can either write a short paragraph about the images she drew, or she can discuss her images with the group. The exercise provides an opportunity for participants to explore their motivations and perceptions about a topic.

BRAIN SKETCHING

Like storyboards, brain sketching involves sharing ideas through drawing. A session starts with the problem being defined to the satisfaction of the group. Participants are then asked to sketch a proposed solution within a determined period of time (no more than five minutes). When time is up, all drawings are passed to the left, and each person builds on the drawing he received. Once all papers have made their way around the entire group, they can be gathered and displayed for collective feedback.

Brain sketching takes elements of brain writing but uses images rather than words. This method involves a group of eight to ten people and starts with a brainstorming session on a specific problem, then proceeds as follows.

Step 1: Define the problem. The problem is defined and discussed by the group until clearly understood.

Step 2: Brainstorm. Use a standard brainstorming technique to begin the session, then switch to pictures when ideas begin to dwindle. This will spark new ideas.

Step 3: Sketching. Participants will have five minutes to draw their solution to the problem. Once time is up, participants then slide their papers to the person on the left. These sketches are then built upon by either adding to, or by developing, a new drawing based on the existing drawing.

Step 4: Collection and reflection. Once all the images have gone around the table, they are collected and discussed. These images are then used as jumping-off points for new ideas.

ANALOGY AND METAPHOR TECHNIQUES

METAPHORS

According to Dan Saffer, principle of the interaction and interface design firm Kicker Studio, design and metaphor are intricately, albeit subtly, linked. Says Saffer, "Human beings are wired for comparison and finding meaning. We take abstractions like 'time' and make metaphors out of them—often giving them a tangible, physical nature—in order to understand them: Time is money, for instance. This is a tool used all consistently in design."

Saffer remembers a time when he used metaphor as a concept development tool on a mobile device project. After a prolonged period of brainstorming, he took some time to clear his mind and visited the Musee Mecanique in San Francisco. The museum hosts a collection of coin-operated slot machines, music boxes, player pianos, games and orchestrations from the turn of the century to the present. Saffer recalls, "One of the games we played was an arcade game from the 1980s for reading biorhythms. Biorhythms are the pseudoscience of reading emotional, intellectual, and physiological cues for fortune-telling purposes, and in the case of the game, they are displayed on a chart. That chart, and the idea of cycles through time, became a metaphor we used in creating the concept for our project. The end result doesn't look like a biorhythm chart by any means, but by saying 'This project is like Biorhythm,' it gave us another direction to explore."

According to George Lakoff, professor of cognitive linguistics at the University of California, Berkeley, metaphor is central to human thought as it helps us understand and conceive of our world. Metaphors are figures of speech that make a comparison between two unlike things. A classic example cited in Lakoff's book, *Metaphors We Live By*, is that of debate as war. When we talk about an argument, we say things like, "He won the argument" or

"His criticisms were on target." More than just clever phrasing, metaphors reflect the way people think.

Lakoff identifies three types of metaphors: structural, orientational, and ontological. Structural metaphor is best exemplified in the "debate as war" example sited earlier, such that the language of one activity (war) is used to explain a completely different action (debate). Orientational metaphor deals with direction as meaning. An example would be, "I'm feeling up today." "Up," implying "good" or "happy." Finally, an ontological metaphor is similar to personification, when we project human activities onto nonhuman things. An example would be, "the car is guzzling gas," or "putting the computer to sleep." In many ways this is how people make connections to objects. By giving them the characteristics of humans, we are able to develop a relationship with them in a way we naturally understand.

At the heart of these metaphors are perceptions about meaning, which is why metaphors are an important part of design. When audiences see a communication, whether it is a brochure, website, or retail environment, they react to the visual meaning of the letterforms, images, and marks—all of which express ideas, creating relationships to actual experiences or things. Consider how image and form describe how the communication should be used, like a thumb-notch on a brochure or a button on a website. We know that buttons are to be pushed to cause something to happen, so we understand when we see a graphic button on a website that we are invited to push it (or, more specifically, click it), and something will happen.

For designers, metaphor provides a way to break out of conventional thoughts and cliché ideas. "Like putting an addition onto your house, metaphors expand the conceptual territory and alter the thinking environment," says Kim Erwin, associate professor at the IIT Institute of Design. "As a result, metaphors are not just oratory devices—colorful or memorable or interesting. They are *instructive*, because they push new information into the center of our vision and create future states that we test and explore."

Erwin identifies five types of metaphor that designers can use to help connect themselves, their clients, and the users with the value of a design offering.

1. **Behavioral metaphors:** These metaphors explain how a product, service, or experience might work. Consider the natural language search engine Ask Jeeves.com (now simply Ask.com). The site used the metaphor of a butler who would cater to all of our online search needs.

2. **Surface metaphors:** A surface metaphor implies how something might work. This is best exemplified by the computer interface.

3. **Adoption metaphors:** How do we learn how to perform new tasks? Adoption metaphors provide a way of understanding new tasks. Examples include automatic teller machines and wireless phones helped us transition and "adopt" unfamiliar products by invoking a familiar conceptual frame.

4. **Functional metaphors:** How might we use metaphors to suggest features and functions? Dashboard software is an entire category of applications that allow executives to monitor and track various indices of corporate performance, functioning much the way a car dashboard allows drivers to monitor the car's various systems.

5. **Construct metaphors:** How might we leverage well-understood constructs like stories, ideas, and characters that permeate the culture to explain new and unfamiliar concepts? *Grocery Store Wars* was a promotional sensation and current YouTube staple: It explains the organic food movement (the so-called "organic rebellion") using the characters and iconic scenes from *Star Wars* to explain the contrasting ideologies of conventional versus organic food movements.

Erwin recalls using metaphor to explain a retail concept for a rental car company. Using the idea of a "vacation mall," as a way to convey the concept of providing sundry items like sunglasses, drinks, disposable cameras, and snacks to tourists who are renting cars. Through the vacation mall metaphor, Erwin was not only able to frame the conversation with the rental car company, she was also able to imply the actions associated with the metaphor, that is, making small vacation purchases. Erwin believes that conversation-changing power is what strategists and designers need to learn to leverage effectively in everyday work.

Erwin uses metaphor at three phases of the design process: during analysis, to summarize and anchor user research findings; during synthesis, to create and describe new solutions spaces; during client engagement, to portray a future state that is clear and compelling and exert leadership that gets people engaged and enrolled in making that future state come to life.

But the power of metaphor comes in its clarity, coherence and internal logic that is extended to reveal new insights. Erwin offers the example of Al Gore's phrase Information Superhighway. "Al Gore sketched out a complicated but cognitively accessible future state that persuaded the entire U.S. congress, most of whom had never touched a computer—never mind sent an e-mail—to pass his High-Performance Computing Act. His vision laid the groundwork for the next twenty-five years of U.S. competitiveness. His metaphor made it happen."

As designers look for new ways of communicating ideas, the metaphor has become an important tool for making connections with audiences. By combining pictures and words, designers can create new levels of understanding for products and services, and help reveal deeper meanings beyond basic functionality.

Metaphor can lead to creating differentiation with audiences, too. By using metaphor during the concept stage, designers have a fresh way of developing a design solution. Metaphor techniques, like building totems, allow designers and clients to visually express what they are trying to convey without having to invest a lot of time creating detailed designs. Again, this method offers a way to clarify the design direction and align designer and client—before a direction has been determined. Additionally, as designers strive to embed more meaning in their designs, metaphor offers a way for them to connect to people on a cognitive level.

ANALOGIES

Analogies allow designers to take ideas about one subject and apply them to another. They are an important part of concept development, as they provide a means of "thinking different" about a problem by presenting a real experience to evaluate. Such comparisons can make abstractions easier to understand.

Step 1: Define the problem to be solved. The problem to be solved is clearly written so that all participants can see it. An example might be "car safety."

Step 2: Develop a verb-based sentence. Participants come up with a verb-based sentence that articulates the problem. For the above example this might be, "How do we make cars safer?"

Step 3: Alternate words. For each sentence, participants create a list of alternate concepts that is similar to the verb-based sentence. In the above case an example might be, "How do we make airplanes safer, or how do we make bicycles safer?" Alternatively, random nouns can be chosen and switched out to create a broader exploration. An example of this approach might be, "How do we make houses, dogs, cities, children, safer?"

Step 4: Selection. An analogy is chosen. The best analogy is one that offers suitable contrast but is not so close to the original problem that new insights will be hard to uncover.

Step 5: Discussion. Participants discuss the similarities between the analogy and the actual problem. Use the description to make a connection to the original problem.

Analogies can take several forms. Fantasy analogies give people an opportunity to make projections that are not based on rational thinking but on an "If you could do anything…" condition. Other analogies are more direct, calling on comparative descriptions such as "she swims like a fish." Personal analogies provide the opportunity for participants to envision themselves as part of the analogy. One example: Participants are asked to see themselves as if they were wheelbarrows to better understand potential improvements in wheelbarrow design.

SYNECTICS: MAKING THE FAMILIAR STRANGE

Synectics is an analogy-based ideation technique developed by William J.J. Gordon in the early 1960s. Meaning to bring together unrelated elements,

Synectics is a "problem stating, problem-solving" group technique that brings together people of various disciplines and perspectives with the goal of making the strange familiar and making the familiar strange. Synectics provides a mechanism for participants to break out of mental ruts and includes techniques such as personal analogies, direct analogies, symbolic analogies, and fantasy analogies.

Step 1: Understanding the problem. The process begins by making the strange familiar. This is done by fitting the problem into an acceptable pattern. While this is a standard step in all problem-solving activities, Gordon warns that one should not focus too much on the analysis but instead create a new way of looking at the problem.

Step 2: Making the familiar strange. Once the problem has been defined, the next step is to look at the problem from another perspective. An example of how this works is illustrated in the simple drawing technique of turning the object that is to be rendered upside down. Doing so instantly removes several preconceived notions concerning what something looks like. By changing the perspective and looking at a problem anew, the mind can break out of its heuristic tendencies. Gordon uses four areas of analogy to "make the familiar strange." These include personal analogy, direct analog, symbolic analogy, and fantasy analogy, described below.

PERSONAL ANALOGY

By looking at a problem from the perspective of the elements involved, new perspectives can be gained. For example, to understand how tires actually interact with a road, think of yourself as a tire. For this technique to work, participants need to break from rational thinking and become more playful, using role-playing as a means to gain perspective. The subject can be any animate or inanimate object or concept. By placing themselves in this role, participants can identify with the subject and thereby gain an understanding of the context in which the subject exists. These ideas can then be expressed to the other team members through writing, images, or role-playing.

DIRECT ANALOGY

Direct analogies call on existing examples of similar solutions for a problem. Nature provides a rich resource for analogies. It's important, however, to have some distance between the subject and the analog. If the comparison is too similar (comparing chair legs with human legs, for instance), there is not enough of a leap to generate innovative ideas.

Step 1: Problem solving. Like all problem-solving activities, direct analogy begins with defining the problem. An example might be how to motivate donors to give to an organization.

Step 2: Create the analogy. Once the problem is identified, analogies can be created. For this example, it might be milking a cow.

Step 3: Describe the analogy. Outline the characteristics of the analogy. In this case you could say that milking happens at regular intervals, that the cows are led to and prepared for milking, that the milking is automated, and that pampered cows produce more milk then those that are neglected.

Step 4: Apply the analogy to the subject. Make extensions from the analogy to the subject. For the analogy of cows and donors, the following extensions apply:

- Milking happens at regular intervals.
- Donors should be contacted regularly so they expect future contact.
- The cows are lead to and prepared for milking.
- Make the process for donating easy.
- The milking is automated.
- Make the experience process driven for greater returns.
- Pampered cows produce more milk then those neglected.
- Provide donors encouragement and rewards.

SYMBOLIC ANALOGY

Symbolic analogy uses objective and personal images as a means of describing a problem. If the problem is to show how people find products at an online store, you could make a connection to *Where's Waldo*.

FANTASY ANALOGY

Fantasy analogy asks the question, "How in our wildest fantasies does X work?" By deferring judgment, participants can think without the constraints of practicality or logic. Says Gordon, "When a problem is presented to the mind, it is most useful to imagine the best of all possible worlds, a helpful universe permitting the most satisfying possible viewpoint leading to the most elegant of all possible solutions." By breaking free of the "givens" and reaching a newfound freedom of thought, new ideas can come to the surface.

CONCEPT SELECTION

Concept selection is the third and final stage in concept development. Once ideas have been generated, they need to be vetted by internal stakeholders and audiences alike. There are varying degrees of selection process. Some are more involved, like the matrix method, and others are less intensive, like dot voting. The right method depends on the complexity of the problem and concept, as well as the level of risk associated with making the choice.

DESIGN REVIEWS

Many designers face the challenge of having their work reviewed by various levels of stakeholders. Often that conversation helps further define the direction of the design solution. Designers can share ideas with users and executive-level staff to get feedback at this early stage. Together, they should agree to the direction before they move forward so that they are efficient in the more labor-intensive phases of development.

"We are really serious about approvals," says AOL's Allison Bucchere. "Every Monday and every Wednesday we have half an hour in everyone's calendar for a design review. This is on everyone's calendar, so it doesn't slow our process down by having to herd all of those people."

Once concepts have been developed, it's time to decide which ones hold the most promise. Having multiple directions to choose from is good when you are exploring a range of options, and (ideally) pushing boundaries. Clients may experience some anxiety if only one concept is available for presentation—it might imply a lack of creativity.

Choosing the "best" concepts can be a challenge. Designers will always have a favorite in mind, but they need to consider the objectives of the client and the audience. Often, it's best to give the concepts time to incubate before making a selection.

When a choice is made, the rationale should be documented so the designer will feel competent to defend the decision. This also helps prevent two unfortunate things from happening:

1. Choosing a concept based on the designer's personal likes and dislikes.
2. Choosing a concept simply because a boss or a client loves it.

There are several approaches to selecting concepts. They range from casual voting to an elaborate matrix. Each has its proper use, depending on the time frame, the information available, and the importance of the decision.

MATRIX METHOD

This method uses a prioritized matrix made up of possible design options and criteria. It is helpful for comparing alternative design approaches and provides for an evolution of concepts. It can also become quite complex depending on the levels of consideration. Designers can benefit from a simplified version of this methodology.

To start the selection process, a set of criteria needs to be established. The criteria enables all concepts to be judged on the same scale. It should be based on how the design solves the problem, and how well it meets the client's requirements. As with all things visual, there will be some subjectivity in how people react to aesthetics, and this subjectivity should be given some weight in making the decision. Moreover, the concepts presented need to be similar in size, completion status, and execution. Presenting a half-developed idea next to one that is more fully formed will produce biased results, as participants will be drawn to ideas that are the most "finished."

The matrix method works as follows:

Step 1. Determine criteria for evaluating designs.

Step 2. Rank criteria in descending order.

Step 3. Select concepts to be compared.

Step 4. Select the favorite design. All other options will be measured against this one.

Step 5. Rate the concepts based on these criteria.

At this point, you should have established which design concepts have value based on the criteria established. This method helps keep designers focused on specific problem-solving criteria and keeps subjectivity in check.

VOTING

Simpler methods of concept selection include voting and critique. These methods can be employed when time is not a major concern or when a decision is not of critical importance.

DOT VOTING

This is a quick method for rating concepts. Give each participant an equal amount of red and green sticky dots. Ask them to place the green dots on concepts they like and the red dots on concepts they would reject.

QUICK VOTING

If a deadline is fast approaching, and you need to decide on a concept, another quick method is to have participants join in a round robin. Each person in turn makes a choice, then explains why she thinks it best solves the problem. This democratic process is great for screening initial ideas; however, it's a poor choice for arriving at a final decision.

ANONYMOUS VOTING

For occasions when there may be tension within the group, anonymous voting allows participants to give their opinions freely without fear of reprisal. The session facilitator gives participants a list of numbered ideas to choose from. Participants select their favorite ideas from the list and assign a rating (A, B,

C, D) to each. After writing their selections on a card, participants hand the cards back to the facilitator, who mixes the cards up, and tallies the outcome on a whiteboard or flip chart.

CRITIQUE

Design critiques are a staple of design education. Students routinely post their work before classmates, who are asked to comment on the various solutions. In professional organizations, such feedback is not only a critical component of the design process, it's also an important organization tool to motivate staff and spur growth. By soliciting different perspectives from their peers, designers are able to take a more objective view of their own work, while considering a variety of options for solving a problem.

Giving feedback can be difficult. Who wants to hear negative things about their work? Moreover, designers generally agree that critiques are particularly difficult because designers are often heavily invested in their work. Using a formal participative method, such as a critique, may take the edge off any disparagement—by allowing designers to explain their thinking and receive honest feedback within a "safe" environment.

FOCUS

For a critique to be useful, it must be focused. Both the designer and the critic must maintain a professional veneer. Both must avoid either making a critique personal or receiving feedback in a defensive way. Plus, those giving the critique should take the time required to make clear, understandable comments. Openness by all participants is a must if any value is to be derived.

Goals should be established at the beginning of a critique. For instance, when used in the early concept stages, critiques should focus on the primary design objectives as established in the design brief. By addressing these issues, early design concepts are ensured to be on target. As the concept evolves in later stages, and future critiques are conducted, more specific issues can be addressed.

The most productive critique group will be the one comprised of individuals within an organization who understand the goals of the design and appreciate the process. Keep the group small, two to five people, to retain focus and avoid distractions. Begin with a statement of design objectives as defined in the brief. Objectives should be written in plain view, such as on a whiteboard or presentation tablet. Keep criticism focused.

FEEDBACK

Comments and feedback must remain as objective and constructive as possible. A positive critique experience can help a designer expand his sense of possibility. Avoid pointedly judgmental questions—they stall a critique and yield poor dialogue. Focus discussion on how each concept addresses the problem, and how each style addresses it. Review branding and identity issues. Consider how a target audience might perceive each solution.

The creators of the work usually orchestrate the critique. It's important that they remain confident and avoid feeling defensive if others make negative comments. The critique should allow everyone a chance to give feedback. More input yields more ideas and options. A successful critique should prove emotionally supportive and intellectually stimulating for all involved.

IN CONCLUSION

Original ideas cannot be created solely by means of a method, but instead rely heavily on the experiences and knowledge of the people involved. With original ideas being the "stock and trade" for designers, having a quiver of techniques and methods that foster creative thinking can make the ideation process less frustrating and more efficient.

chapter 8

MAKING STRATEGY VISIBLE

DESIGN DEVELOPMENT

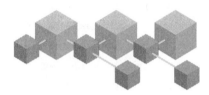

Launched in 1999, the fledgling DIY Network was to be a digital cable position holder for the bigger, better-funded HGTV. With just a million cable subscribers, DIY took hold and has been gaining traction ever since. With the goal of linking broadcast home project shows with online support (plans, specifications, instructions, etc.), DIY at the time of its launch was a mishmash of shows for both male and female audiences, and included everything from scrapbooking and knitting to motorcycle maintenance and home construction projects. The identities of the programming reflected a lack of focus as well, featuring myriad typographic approaches and design styles. According to Todd Decker, creative director for DIY networks, the original on-air identity was developed primarily with online technologies in mind. With the goal of making the on-air presence and the online presence cohesive, the style had a decidedly fun and inviting "Flash" look and feel.

In the last decade, DIY Network has evolved and now broadcasts to over 50 million homes. New network leadership developed a strategic plan to quietly relaunch the network with the goal of stepping out of the shadow of HGTV and differentiating itself from networks like Discovery, TLC and Bravo. The challenge, Decker recalls, was: "How do we grow our brand and gain new viewers without alienating the current audience? Who was our audience, and who do we want our audience to be?"

To help differentiate and focus the programming, two important decisions were made. The network, which had originally tried to be all things to all people, would focus primarily on a male audience. Additionally, they would position their on-air talent as the stars of the show. Decker says that the hosts weren't household names, but DIY felt that if they treated them as such, the hosts would in time take this position in the audience's mind. Prior to this direction, most of the focus was on the how-to as opposed to the presenter.

With this direction, Decker set out to develop a visual identity that would attract and retain its key audience, and differentiate its offerings from the competition.

PHOTOGRAPHY

This strategic change was reflected visually throughout the broadcast and online presence. Says Decker, "We sought a signature photographic style that would seamlessly integrate with the graphic aspects of the DIY Network identity. With the male-skewing audience also in the back of our minds, we looked for drama through contrast with the shadow density anchoring the image in the black-based environment. The goal is to create a striking, hyper-real image that is in harmony with the DIY Network environment."

A lot of thought went into how the photos of the program hosts would appear. They needed to be seen as authorities with confidence, but not arrogance. To achieve this, Decker made sure that the hosts made eye contact with the viewer, thus making a connection, and that the hosts struck poses that gave some indication of their unique character. Each held a unique but simple prop that implied a task or project. "The challenge is to capture the essence of the individual's personality while staging them as the skilled celebrity expert," says Decker.

TYPOGRAPHY

With a new photographic approach established, thoughts turned to the logos and typography for each individual show. After several attempts to link these disparate parts, Decker and his team decided a better strategy would be to lose the individual show logos and replace them with a common typographic approach, thereby linking the show during promotional titling and network navigation.

Berthold Akzidenz-Grotesk, a close relative to Helvetica and Univers, was the choice of typeface based on its strong but friendly looks, which Decker notes, "makes it the perfect no-nonsense promotional typographic signature for DIY Network." The font is versatile, providing numerous options including book, schoolbook, old face, rounded and next variations.

COLOR

The original DIY palette communicated ideas of fun and vibrancy via its high-key saturated colors. The goal was to cast learning as fun. With a new audience focus on men, the palette required a major overhaul. Decker conducted a visual audit of styles that would convey ideas of strength and masculinity, and arrived at the Russian Constructivist movement. With its bold graphics, use of strong blacks (and limited colors), and photomontage and geometric layouts, the constructivist style fit with the aesthetic needs of the audience. Explains Decker: "The Constructivists' bold use of color and kinetic elements were intended to create a reaction from the viewer on emotional and substantive levels, taking the audience out of the traditional setting and make them an active viewer of the artwork." Black is the key color in this equation. It conveys ideas of masculinity, sophistication, power and intensity, plus it makes the photographic and typographic elements "pop." The black is supported by shades of gray as well, which gives the palette some dimension.

The supporting colors were left intentionally unspecified, so that the designers had the flexibility to use colors that best fit the tone of their specific program. Decker says, "By using a bold, rich color grounded by black and supported by grays, a sophisticated muscular look is achieved." Going for a monochromatic effect, Decker developed subtle nuances to give the designs increased depth. By using gradients and lighting, Decker was able to achieve a more tactile sensibility for the viewers.

TEXTURE

If you observe the typical workshop, you find a wide array of textures—everything from steel to wood, plaster and PVC. By pulling from this rich palette of textures, Decker was able to convey ideas of something that is handmade—raw, imperfect, unique, tactile, gritty—thereby making the connection between the program and the audience. The textures used in the design needed to be carefully balanced so as to not create too much clutter, or a diffused focus. A "controlled chaos" approach was developed, which required a great deal of judgment on the part of the individual designers. Decker shared the successful design solution with the design team to help develop an intuitive sense of how much was too much.

MOVEMENT

Broadcast design has the added element of motion. This proved to be a critical element communicating the change from a general to a decidedly male audience. Moving from a softer, lighter motion, DIY embraced the energy and action associated with building projects—Decker describes it as "an intense 'rhythm of movement.' Quick, erratic pace, 'in your face' attention-demanding but not out of control."

STYLE AS STRATEGY

The DIY Network's redesign offers an example of how business, competitive, and audience needs can translate into a visual design strategy. Simply put, DIY's design is the visualization of the their business strategy, with the intent of influencing the audience's connections to the network, creating impressions and perceptions, and ultimately establishing drivers for interaction with the network. The goal was not to project the designer's sense of style on the client, but for the designer to be empathic and interpret the DIY's vision into a visible language that will resonate with the audience. In the words of legendary designer Ivan Chermayeff, "Good design, at least part of the time, includes the criteria of being direct in relation to the problem at hand—not obscure, trendy, or stylish."

Walk through your local mall and you immediately experience the importance of design in the marketplace. Every store conveys a unique message through its window displays, its interiors and the presentation of its products. The intent is to immerse the customer in the store's character and create a unique experience from the competitor two doors down. To win in the marketplace, you must stand out from the competition and express a unique value that others don't. Visual style is how that value is communicated.

Style permeates every aspect of our lives including what we wear, where we live, and ultimately how we express who we are. Style is about creating identity. It is prevalent in every aspect of our culture, from the politicians, whose crafted personalities strive to reflect the values of those they wish to gain support from, to high school students who hang on every celebrity and fashion trend as a means of fitting in and defining who they are. Even our choice of groceries is a reflection of style, as brands compete to be the most attractive, most socially conscientious, or most refined. All of these aspects of style are visual, and not necessarily based on content. Style as a means of conveying ideas (in particular, power) has been around for ages. Objects infused with style transcend their ordinariness, and become philosophical statements. A teapot designed by Michael Graves speaks volumes about the person using it. Design is never neutral; on the contrary, it is infused with meaning.

In relation to business, style is at the heart of economic growth, providing a key driver for need. In his book *All Consuming Images*, Stewart Ewan says that as society moved toward a mercantile economy, where goods and services were traded, artists, craftsmen, and merchants grew beyond the boundaries of their feudal roots using their business skills. As these merchants acquired wealth, they also acquired the trappings of the ruling classes. By mimicking the style of the elite, the middle class could project a sense of power and privilege. As it was true then, it is true now, that people have an intrinsic need to project their worth through the acquisition of rare and special items. As the ability to produce more items increased, the ability to purchase items became easier. As items become easier to acquire, they also become less valuable, thus a market for newer and rarer items developed. Through style, items are made "new." The common is transformed into the unique, and one's place in the social strata is established.

Style and value are articulated through the design elements of color, size, proportion, typography, imagery and experiences. The function of design development is to convert information about client and audience needs into form, message and symbols. Using these design elements, organizations convey who they are in a way they hope resonates with their key audiences. The elements of style are the foundation for identity and brand, and play a key strategic role by helping to create differentiation in the marketplace.

DEVELOPING A VISUAL STYLE

Linking visual design to business strategy is best demonstrated through the brand architecture development process. Based upon information drawn from the design research provided in the initial design process phases, designers make key style decisions. It is at this point in the process that a designer's skills, talents, knowledge and experience come into play. "The best designers are well fed," says Petrula Vrontikis, meaning that designers who have a broad range of interests and experiences in culture, travel, books and music, and who are constantly seeking information, ultimately bring more to the table when coming up with design solutions. The importance of the experience, intuition and emotion that individual designers bring to their problem solving cannot be underestimated.

The process for developing visual style calls on the familiar steps of business and audience research, competitive analysis, and a review of trends within the category, all of which have been accounted for in the earlier phases of the design process. With this information in hand, the designer can begin to analyze, internalize, and interpret, calling on their knowledge, skills, and experiences to develop a visualization of the client's strategy. What follows are the basic steps in developing a strategic visual solution.

PROJECT ALIGNMENT

The process for developing a visual style starts with a review of the research collected earlier. At this point, the designer should know key facts about the brand position, its character, its strengths and weaknesses, its competition, category trends, benchmarks, and audience needs. This information will have been collected in the design brief and used during the concept development phase.

Paul LaPlaca, creative director for Graco, uses the following steps when developing visual directions for products. A standard approach to kicking off the initial phase of the project is to hold a client review meeting in which the key project stakeholders review the goals of the project and discuss any last-minute business before design development. This client review meeting provides an opportunity for all the project stakeholders to voice opinions, develop consensus and define direction. By creating this opportunity for alignment, designers are able to mitigate common problems or redirection, or feedback from stakeholders later in the process when it becomes more time-consuming and costly to make changes. When stakeholders walk out of this meeting, they should know the following key aspects of the project.

What success looks like: Success can look like different things to different stakeholders. Management wants to stay on budget, marketing wants a deliverable that is effective, design wants a sophisticated visual approach, the client project lead wants a smooth process that stays on track and meets the needs of the organization. A determination of expectations for quality, budget and schedule should be established.

Scope definition: An agreement on the deliverables is another critical result of this meeting, as it allows the designer to allocate resources and determine time needed to complete the project.

Understanding the client brand: The client's brand position, architecture, target audience, character, and brand strengths and weaknesses should be defined so that a level of brand consistency is achieved. By creating alignment on these points, all of the project stakeholders can share a consistent idea of what the brand represents and how best to articulate its character.

An understanding of the business need: What are the strategic objectives and how does this project help the organization achieve its goals?

Understanding the audience: Key insights about who the audience is, and an understanding of their unmet needs should be defined at this time. This information is collected through research to gain an understanding of visual and other communication, helping to capture the "voice of the customer."

Understanding the competition: Competition drives strategy. In visual design, this means knowing what competitors in the category look like and making design decisions that provide a strategic advantage (not an aesthetic preference). Designers will need to see how the competition is using color, shape and typography to capture the audience's attention. This step helps define what design elements the client can and can't own.

DESIGN EXPLORATORY

Once this information is collected, design exploration can begin. It is at this point in the process that the research is brought to life. Up until now, no visuals have been developed. LaPlaca describes this phase as "all about the visual solutions that bring that brand to life." It's about the color palette. It's about the photo lens that is used when shooting photography. It's about the kind of photography that will be used. Is it soft photography? Is it hard photography? Is it just silhouettes? Design exploratory is about defining the parameters that you are designing against. Color, shape, typography and imagery are the primary visual elements that make up the design architecture.

COLOR AS STRATEGY

Color is one of the most important elements of design, as its effect on audiences is profound. Beyond psychological effects, color has been known to cause physical effects, such as the color red's power to raise heart rates, or pink's ability to lower them. No wonder it is one of the most important factors in identity. Consider Coca-Cola's red, UPS's brown, Dell's blue, and Apple's white. On their own, these colors could have any number of meanings for audiences. When they are associated with an organization, however, they take on a unique meaning and serve as key points of visual distinction. The key is to be consistent with color across all communications, so that awareness can take hold. More than images and words, colors tend to get remembered.

As more organizations standardize their identity colors, it's more of a challenge to be unique. With blue and red leading the pack as favorite identity colors, designers are looking for other options. Cingular Wireless's orange "Jack" logo and T-Mobile pink are examples of the trend toward hipper, happier, less-expected colors. Alternatively, UPS makes their brown color a central part of their identity and brand, going as far as to make it prominent visually and verbally in their advertising.

Nexium, the heartburn drug that brings in earnings of $6 billion a year for its creator AstraZeneca, is known as "Today's purple pill" in its advertising.

The color distinction is even reflected in the URL for its website, www. PurplePill.com.

In the competitive gin market, color plays a particular role in creating brand distinction. With Bombay Sapphire and Tanqueray owning the colors blue and green respectively, Beefeater entered into the fray with its premium offering (Crown Jewel) donning a distinctly regal purple glass bottle.

As a strategic tool, color can draw new interest in established products, create exclusivity, and inspire a level of sensory engagement on the part of the audience. According to the Color Marketing Group, the international association for color design professionals, color has a significant effect on the bottom line through its ability to increase brand recognition, improve readership, accelerate learning and comprehension, and convince consumers to buy.

SHAPE AS STRATEGY

Six thousand years ago, along what would be later known as the Silk Road, in the ancient trading post of Godin Tepe, Iran, Sumerians regularly lined up for their rations of beer and wine. The vessels containing the beer stood upright, while the wine vessel lay on its side. These two shapes were not only functional but also did the job of distinguishing the contents of the containers. Today, any number of products bring to mind distinctive shapes. Consider Quaker Oats's cylinder, which has an old-time association; the classic lines of a Coke bottle; or the sophisticated simplicity of the Absolut Vodka bottle. Like all visual elements, shape conveys meaning.

When the brewing giant Heineken decided to enhance its brand in order to reach out to upscale consumers, it looked to its packaging. The Heineken "H2" was the creation of Ora Ito, the French designer, who describes his style as "simplexity." The aluminum bottle, a streamlined shape similar to a shoulderless white wine bottle, features the trademark Heineken green with a subtle silver bottom that displays a subdued Heineken logo and miscellaneous product information. The fresh look of the bottle clearly differentiated it from other brands and increased sales for the company during its 2004 launch. Along with its new shape, the bottle also offers other benefits, including being unbreakable and keeping the contents colder longer. The versatility of impact-extruded aluminum opens the doors for design and marketers to push the limits of shape as a channel for unique brand expressions.

In the automotive design category, the Scion bbX was unlike any car when it entered the market in 2002. In the shape of a cube, the Scion reflected ideas of function, practicality, and probably had more in common with the design of a washing machine than Detroit's latest offerings. The shape was distinctive, deliberate, and the focus of a marketing effort that targeted entry-level drivers. The car, developed by Toyota, was created to get younger buyers into the Toyota brand, without them buying a brand that they associated with their parents. Cutting across the grain of sleek and sporty "fast" cars, Scion zigged when everyone else zagged. The shape spoke volumes about the drivers, who saw themselves as iconoclasts, rejecting the car culture of their parents.

TYPOGRAPHY AS A STRATEGY

Letterforms hold layers of information, conveying the actual meaning of words and at the same time lending inflection of meaning through their shape and form. There are as many theories and approaches to typography as there are designers: Jan Tschichold developed strict modernist typographic rules, which he later abandoned. Massimo Vignelli similarly maintains a strict philosophy around typography in which he only uses a small stable of fonts including Helvetica, Univers, Century, Bodoni and Garamond. Others, like Rudy VanderLans and David Carson, take a more liberal and expressive approach, breaking from the conventions of legibility and order. Regardless of approach, typographic forms provide a level of communication that audiences understand on an intuitive level.

Ultimately, typography gives voice to communication. It can be loud and in your face, or subtle, drawing you in by other means. The audience interprets the nuances of letterforms and imbues them with meaning. As the voice of the design, typography speaks volumes about the organization and its character. Consider the following.

Loud is the conventional approach of the commodity. Think of a car dealership and how it promotes itself. It's not uncommon to see gigantic type with hyperbolic headlines announcing the latest sale of the century. Nor is it uncommon for gimmicks like giant inflatable animals (gorillas seem to be particular to this industry) announcing sales or special promotions. Consider the work of Larry John Wright, the largest retail advertising agency in the nation, and producer of a significant amount of auto dealer advertising. Their mantra—Be twice as good, twice as fast, and half the price of the competition—speaks to their desire to get results for their clients, while putting an emphasis on process and efficiency. Their focus is not on beautiful design, but on design that grabs people and demands that they look. Typography plays a critical role. Just a glance at one of their ads for a car dealership and price leaps out at the viewer, via bold, sans serif fonts. People are naturally drawn to numbers, and they figure prominently in the designs of magazine covers as well as advertising. Often in vibrant reds, with borders, drop shadows, and gradations—every filter and design trick is used to make the typography leap off the page. The images of the cars are secondary, or even tertiary, falling behind a dominant call to action like, "24 Hour All Out Sell Out!" In contrast to the volume of type in these ads, there are government regulations defining a minimum point size for information: Any type that falls below 10 point is considered unreadable, and therefore unethical.

A softer voice emerges in the design of Thymes's Kimono Rose line of fragrances, soaps and lotions. Thymes, a homegrown personal care products company, grew from one woman's love of art and desire for beauty products made from natural ingredients. Designed by Duffy & Partners, the packaging echoes a timeless Japanese feel, with a "soft-spoken" palette of pastel shades and delicate flower and plant illustrations. The Kimono Rose brand name is discreetly placed in understated type. Much of the packaging has a handmade feel, using folded paper reminiscent of origami, and intentionally imperfect printing. The typography feels organic to the unique package design and does not compete for attention, though it stands out in spite of its simplicity.

In contrast, consider David Carson's designs for the popular surf culture/music magazine *Ray Gun*. Carson created a new and often chaotic design sensibility by breaking all of the rules of typography and photography. With his deconstructive approach, Carson went against convention, using the table of contents as a center spread and running the same photo twice—or upside down. Typographically, Carson took similar liberties, chopping and layering type, running small type on dark backgrounds, and whatever he wanted to do to devise new ways of evoking an emotional response. The overall effect was that of an artist who uses all media combined onto the page.

VISUALIZING CHARACTER

Color, shape, typography and image are the building blocks of visual design. Through these elements ideas of time, place, culture, and meaning find expression. The gestalt of these elements in relation to their competitive environment creates a strategic position in the minds of audiences, thereby creating the brand identity.

TIME

By deciding what timeframe the design needs to represent—past, present or future—designers can tap into a source of visual language. Style by its very nature is representative of the time in which it was created. It is ephemeral, changing not only from decade to decade, but in some cases minute to minute. This is reflected in myriad classifications of period/styles throughout history. By identifying the relevant associations of time, designers can answer questions like, "Does the organization have a rich heritage that is meaningful to the audience or should a more immediate contemporary approach be taken?"

Traditional representations call on design elements that evoke a timeless feeling. Universities are adept at expressing a sense of past through their elaborate ceremonies reminiscent of medieval rituals, their filigreed seals, and Latin mottoes. Though universities have a long and rich history (the oldest one in operation is the University of Al-Karaouine in Morocco, established in 859 A.D.), most modern institutions came about in the latter part of the nineteenth century. These institutions understood the need to link themselves to a rich educational history and often pattern themselves on the great universities of Europe. This "invention of tradition," as historian Eric Hobsbawm calls it, provides a sense of a historic past where none actually exists. Consider the American University of London, which displays a heraldic shield with medieval lion, eagle and flowing ribbon. From the looks of its identity, you could assume that the institution has been around for centuries. In reality, the university was established in 1984 and has been accused of being nothing more than a diploma mill. The institution has no campus and in fact has a mailing address in Houston, Texas. And yet, through its mark, it attempts to align itself with the rich heritage of other universities in the United Kingdom.

Contemporary style takes on a more up-to-the-minute timeframe, as styles change rapidly in the fast-moving modern world. Whereas styles of past decades are understood on more broad terms, contemporary style is at times just ahead of the curve. Consider how color trends change from year to year or how typographic styles shift with varying emphasis on modernism and classic, or combinations of both. Photographic styles change as well, shifting from journalistic casualness to self-aware studio compositions.

PLACE

The mythology surrounding Texas, Tuscany, or New York evoke vivid stories in our minds. The mere mention of any of these places conjures images of landscapes and people, attitudes, beliefs, and traditions. These powerful triggers are useful tools when connecting with audiences, offering many visual references for designers to pull from.

Consider the Hill Country Barbecue. New York is known for many things, but barbecue is not one of them. Hill Country Barbecue is a long way from the Texas hill country its name implies and is in fact located on West Twenty-Sixth Street and Broadway in Manhattan. Part of the charm of the place is its attempt to be the "real thing." The requisite rusticated signage featuring Rockwell fonts, the raw materials of the environment—cut limestone, bare wood, and brick—provide the makings of Texas, with the intent of transporting diners mentally to another place and a unique experience. A large rusted Texas star, a common site along the roadsides of central Texas, hangs above the stairwell.

CULTURE, SOCIETY AND STATUS

Design can connect to people on a very deep level, tapping into ideas of value and status. As social beings, people are tied together through beliefs and behaviors that rely on symbols as a reflection of their attitudes, values, and behaviors. Consider the following extremes.

Off the coast of Dubai, the Burj Al Arab Hotel cuts a striking figure. Inspired by the contours of a filled sail, the 321-meter-tall hotel stands on a man-made island that juts into the Arabian Gulf. Taller than the Eiffel tower and just sixty meters shorter than the Empire State Building, the Burj is the pinnacle of luxury and technology. With its cascading waterfalls and unique fire displays, the Burj offers more than just luxury accommodation—it offers a true experience. The hotel boasts thirty different marbles covering almost 50,000 square meters, along with 8,000 square meters of twenty-two–carat gold leaf throughout the building. The logo for the Burj Al Arab features stylized Arabic writing that conforms to the shape of a sail. Below, in refined serif face, the name of the hotel creates a base of the mark. Both elements appear in a dark gold color.

At the other end of the spectrum is Motel 6. Founded in the early sixties in California, the low-budget motel chain has evolved over the years in an effort to distinguish itself from competitors Econo Lodge and Red Roof Inn. The original $6 per night room rate has risen upwards to $40 over the years. In an attempt to keep costs down, rooms were designed for maximum functionality and ease of cleaning. Over the years, perks like free color cable television and allowing pets to stay have been added to the options. Motel 6 has always been aware of its position in the marketplace as the low-cost provider of no-frills accommodations. But as opposed to feeling low-rent, the chain has a self-awareness to it that makes it feel homey and even humorous. Through national radio and television advertising featuring spokesman Tom Bodett and his casual delivery and lighthearted slant, Motel 6 tells travelers, "We'll leave the light on for you." It remains one of the most successful chains in the nation. The Motel 6 logo features a large red number six with an intentionally rough white halftone screen outer glow. The word *motel* is set in a simple sans serif font. The company uses a palette of red, white, and various shades of blue, making for an "unfussy," homey feeling.

TESTING DESIGN SELECTIONS

Once design concepts and prototypes have been developed and internal design selections have been made, it may be necessary to test the selections further by presenting them to external audiences. Such tests can take the form of end-user focus groups, one-on-one interviews, design deconstruction exercises, forced choice attributes, and monadic ratings. Concept testing allows designers to gauge both how well they are addressing the needs of an audience and how well they are connecting with them in a meaningful way.

Scott Young is president of Perception Research Services (PRS), a company that conducts over six hundred consumer research studies annually to help companies develop, assess, and enhance their packaging and point-of-sale marketing efforts. Scott leads PRS's efforts in implementing qualitative, quantitative, store-based, and web-based research programs on behalf of Procter & Gamble, Kraft Foods and Staples, among many other clients. Young believes that smart designers are those who think about the goals of their work—not about making art or winning awards—and see research as a way to prove to their clients that their design work is effective and important.

At the very least, designers need to look at research as a valuable tool to justify what they do and do it better, as opposed to looking at it as a scorecard. Many designers have accepted this, but there is still tension, especially if findings don't line up with the designer's direction. For designers, concept and design testing is a critical step for ensuring their design work meets the needs of audiences and business. But, as Young notes, the goal is not to make audience into art directors. "It's wrong from every perspective to do that. Nor does it lead to better research."

NOT PICKING WINNERS

One of the traps that designers and clients often fall into is trying to pick the most aesthetically pleasing design or logo. Alternatively, designers should be thinking about which design option is most effective. This is a difficult stretch for many, as they believe and have been taught that "good design" is by its nature better for clients and their businesses. However, in some cases, the best-looking design is not always the most effective.

Young recalls a project with Gatorade. The packaging system was strong, and was widely understood as visually appealing, but it did not successfully express brand attributes like athletics and high performance, nor did it visually differentiate Gatorade from the competition on the shelf. Though the packaging was well executed, it looked a lot like the other sports drinks and did not break through the clutter on the shelf.

Unquestionably, visuals matter on a gut level. This is particularly true if it's a negative reaction. If a significant section of the audience agrees that something does not resonate, then that opinion is critical. However, a higher level of visual appeal, in and of itself, is not a driver of success and is only one of many things that contribute to success, including shelf visibility, shop ability, imagery, and communication and price value perception.

REVIEWING IN CONTEXT

The easiest thing to do is ask people what they like, usually in a comparative approach. This feels intuitive, and it yields a sense of likes and dislikes (for instance, if the designer can tell the client, "four out of five people liked the new design," everyone knows where it stands). Young warns, however, that getting reviews in a comparative context is not the same as the context in which they will be viewing the designs in real life, which will ultimately lead to a false positive on the test. "It's not about comparing options," says Young. "It's about simulating the introduction of new systems." To create this effect, Young introduces audiences to one approach and collects their feedback, then introduces another approach with a separate audience, then compares the responses of the two groups to see which resonated.

BENCHMARKING

As a first step in a design effort, benchmarking provides an opportunity for designers to establish a competitive baseline. It is necessary because often marketers make a judgment about the need for updating designs when no real need exists. They give the designers some basic feedback and rationale for the change—we have new competitors, we need it to pop off the shelf more, or something else—and the designer is left with little to work with.

Benchmarking is designed to give fundamental direction to designers at the outset of a project, by allowing the designer to focus her efforts on the real design issues, not the perceived issues. This is done by testing how the current design is working against the competition. One approach that Young uses requires two groups of audiences. With one group, he tests just the name against the competition. He tells them the name and asks them to draw the package from memory (as opposed to just having them describe the packaging which tends to produce generic responses). This gives him the opportunity to explore the "visual equities" of the packaging. The participants' drawings point out where visuals might not be resonating with audiences.

The name-only approach also provides a baseline for designers to judge whether the design is adding anything to the audience's perceptions of the client's offering. Does the design create excitement and a connection with audiences? If not, designers know that the designs need work to become stronger drivers for the audience.

Benchmarking provides an up-front means of testing design before investing a lot of time and effort into a direction. It answers the questions, "Is our design working? Are the elements of the design working? Are there elements that are working and can be built on?" By having specific information about what is and is not working, the designer can better focus his efforts. This does not take away the designer's creative freedom, but offers a better direction for what he wants to achieve.

"We recommend that research become part of the process of design, rather than a score sheet at the end of design," says Young.

THREE THINGS DESIGNERS NEED TO CONSIDER

1. **Context.** Designers need to think about the environment in which the designs will appear. If it's packaging design, they need to consider the realities of the shelf on which the design will appear. Visibility and shop ability is critical. How will the design break through the clutter? With one hundred products on the shelf, will the consumer be able to find what they are looking for?

2. **Competitive Context.** Designers need to think about their designs in relationship to the competition. Do the designs create a dimension that the brand owns? Is the company fun, inviting, innovative? Are these ideas coming across clearly?

3. **Time.** Most people merely glance at design, taking in only very basic information, like the brand name, the product name, the main visual,

and possibly one claim. Designers need to ask themselves if their designs are working within those tight time constraints. Is the design getting one or two key points of differentiation across? Many times, clients want to jam as much information as they can into a design, with the expectation that their audience will take the time to read everything they write. But in most circumstances, most notably packaging, design must communicate quickly and clearly to be effective.

In the early stages of the design process, when you might be considering multiple design options, a sequential monadic approach (see the next section) can be an effective way of testing ideas either within a focus group or online. Although not perfect, sequential monadic provides some logistical advantages, as doing multiple monadic studies might not be feasible. It's best to use this method when designs are in a filtering, refining stage, as it provides opportunities for people to discuss and explore options.

Never use a "beauty contest" (showing multiple design options and asking which stands out) to gauge success at the beginning of the process. An alternative approach is to offer four options in a sequential monadic approach, and to discuss each option individually, possibly against competitive designs. You can also bring in the current design to see what the audience perceptions are.

FEEDBACK FROM AUDIENCES

How do you stop audiences from becoming art directors? Designers can take a more holistic approach when soliciting feedback from their audiences by talking about the brand and the product first, before talking about design. When the conversation turns to the design, discussion leaders should ask about the design in its entirety, not about elements of the design. They can ask, "What words would you use to describe the entire design?" Listen for the answers, and then ask why. For instance, if participants say it looks old or dull, ask them why, and then you can talk about color or style.

Designers should not ask about design elements right off the bat, because that is not how audiences think. They will undoubtedly give answers, but they will tend to overstate design issues. Young's advice for designers: "Ask questions holistically, then listen for drivers rather than going for the temptation of asking about fonts, colors, or images."

MONADIC TESTING

The monadic method of testing ideas is considered the most reliable. Here's how it works: First, a single design idea is shown to one audience. Audiences are then asked to rate the design based on a set of criteria. By testing the design on its own, not only does the testing take on a real-life scenario, but designers are able to get an unbiased opinion from audiences about likes and dislikes. Seeing the design by itself helps an audience focus on the best individual design solution. Concurrently, other designs may be tested with other groups. After all tests are complete, including relative test responses, a determination can be made about which design best met the criteria.

SEQUENTIAL MONADIC

Sequential monadic methods are used as a cost-effective approach to design testing, providing both a monadic evaluation and a comparison evaluation. Two options are shown to audiences, one after the other. The use of this method tends to cause some variance in scores. If the first option is very strong, this may cause the second one to rate poorly—significantly lower than if it had been scored on its own.

DESIGN REVIEW

A design review is a set of activities used to evaluate how well the results of a design meet all quality requirements. During the review, specific problems must be identified and necessary actions proposed. Reviews usually happen at the end of each of the phases of the design process, allowing clients and designers an opportunity to check direction and ensure that all parties are aligned. Doing so helps mitigate misdirection and minimize costs for corrections.

EXPLORATORY TESTS

Once an understanding of audience needs has been established, exploratory tests can be conducted. Initial design concepts are critiqued to see how they might resonate with audiences. Questions are directed at audiences to determine what they think about the concepts, whether the design is appropriate, and if the design meets user needs. Testing concepts early in the design process helps designers challenge errors of assumption they might have made about an audience's needs or perceptions.

PRESENTING IDEAS TO CLIENTS

As designers, we understand about motivating people through communication. However, sometimes we forget when it comes to our own work. Great design poorly presented can kill an idea. To avoid this pitfall, designers must consider the psychology behind their client's decision making. When presenting ideas, designers usually have a solution they favor. Most designers can also tell you that their favorite idea usually does not get chosen. Sometimes it is overlooked because of legitimate concerns from the client, but more than likely, as Chip and Dan Heath argue in their book, *Made to Stick*, it has more to do with how the idea was presented. Was there a core idea (that provided shorthand for the client) behind the concept presented? Did the concept surprise the client? Was it credible? Was it emotive? Was there a story behind the idea?

HOW MANY TO SHOW?

If you carry the weight of a design legend, you can come to a meeting and present a single concept (instead of a group of them, like the rest of us). Most designers do not have that luxury, nor do our clients expect it. When clients hire a design legend, they are hiring the legend for his unique approach.

One of the truisms of design is that clients always seem to pick the designer's least favorite design option. Understandably, this makes designers uneasy about presenting multiple options. Cameron Foote, design business author and president of Creative Business, suggests using the standard practice of showing three ideas that cover a range of approaches: what the client asked for, what the designer thinks is best, and a happy medium. This represents added work as the designer is required to produce ideas that may not reflect their ideal solution, but it mitigates the possibility of bastardizing the preferred design later in the process, as the designer has control of the compromises they are willing to make.

Louis Gagnon, creative director at Paprika in Montreal, has perfected a presentation methodology that leads to very inventive work. "It is our philosophy to show three things," Gagnon explains. "First there is something safe. Of course it is good—not boring, but safe. It won't challenge the client too much. Then there is the more creative solution. And then there is, 'Get ready for this one!' We hope the client will fall in the middle, and usually they do. This middle might be pushing the limits for the average client, but it is just to the taste of those who have found Paprika."

As a general rule, you should never show work that you would not want to be associated with. Ellen Shapiro's advice: "Never, ever, show something you don't want the client to choose. If in doubt, take it out."

PRESENT IN CONTEXT

Scott Young of Perception Research Services suggests that designers do a disservice to themselves and their clients by presenting multiple design comps all at once. The trouble with this approach is that it turns the presentation into a "beauty contest" that pits design aesthetic against design aesthetic, as opposed to staying focused on design strategy. A better approach is to show work in relation to competitors, thereby switching the conversation from "which concept looks best," to "which concept provides us a competitive advantage." A monadic approach is preferred. Young also suggests that it's better to avoid conversations about the design aesthetic and rather focus on the brand and its meaning in a holistic way.

NAME THE CONCEPT

Rob Swan, vice president and executive creative director at BrandImage, has a firm rule in his studio: Every concept that is presented to a client has a name. "If you can't name a concept, then there is no idea there," explains Swan. "If you can't name the driving concept behind the design, then it's just pure aesthetics." The name provides a clear line of sight from what you are seeing in the design all the way back to the strategy. When Swan presents a concept, he focuses on how the design meets the need of the brand, how it competes in the category, how it meets the needs of the consumer, and last but not least, how it pays off in terms of the business strategy.

Along with naming concepts, Swan writes rationales. "The thing we are big believers in is leaving a trail of bread crumbs," says Swan. It used to be that great designers who built a cult of personality around themselves would come into the room and say great things about their design solution and then walk out. But if anyone else in the room had to go and present the work to someone else, they would not have the words to explain it. Swan provides his team a written rationale so that they can present the work to internal stakeholders, including their managers and other higher-ups. This creates investment and alignment amongst team members and clients. "Giving our clients the ability to 'manage up' and succeed within their own organizations makes them come back again," says Swan. "And driving repeat purchase for a consultancy is critically important. I love to see the final presentation, the final culmination of presenting the work for the first time. When we do it right and all the pieces fall into place I think it's like a work of art. To have the thinking sync up with the work, and the work pay off on the need, and have people getting and loving it—that's what it is all about."

The ability to present ideas clearly to the client is often the difference between success and failure. Regardless of how good the design solution is, it must be communicated in such a way that the client has a rationale for liking it. Depending on the design sophistication of the client, varying degrees of explanation will be required.

The first step in presenting is to show the client that you understand the problem that the design is intended to solve. By reviewing the criteria for success that was established at the beginning of the project, you align the client's thinking, so that you share a common mind-set.

As you show the work, focus on just a few key ideas that support the success criteria. Do not dwell on design elements, like typography or other design specifics, unless the client asks. What the client more likely wants to know is how the design meets his need. Discussing design is a trap that many designers fall into. They believe the client is as interested in the layout grid and typography as they are. Discussing such things invites the client to art direct the project, which is never desirable.

PRESENT IN PERSON

"I always present in person," says Petrula Vrontikis. "I hate to present in PDF form. It is the weakest way to put your work out into the world. You have no control over the way the client looks at the PDF and handles the PDF. It is completely out of your control. They show it to a bunch of people who haven't been involved and get scattered opinions."

Vrontikis presents comps and discusses them with the client, but usually takes the comps with her when she leaves the meeting. Her rationale for doing so is not one of distrust of her client, but that the purpose of the meeting is to review the comps in a professional atmosphere, where she can be present to answer questions. "It may sound controlling, but it is really strategic," says Vrontikis. "It keeps a clarity about what is being presented, how it is being presented, and what the feedback is."

Vrontikis says she feels sorry for many younger designers today, because they want to do their work at home on their computers. "They want to send it to clients via e-mail and have clients say 'Yeah, I want that one,' but it never works that way and it's very hard because they don't understand what went wrong. This is how they communicate and they don't realize that it interferes with the proper way that you are positioning yourself as an authority and a design expert."

Personality and interpersonal communication skills are important for presenters to master. The designer has ownership of the presentation, and it is an opportunity to move the client in a good direction. A designer who is too close to her work will not present it well. But a designer who maintains an objective stance and keeps the client's needs at the top of her mind will be able to negotiate a successful direction.

IN CONCLUSION

Through identity, color, typography, and experience, designers articulate their client's business, competitive, and audience needs into a visual design strategy with the intent of influencing audience connections to the network, creating impressions, perceptions, and ultimately establishing drivers for interaction with the network. Through research and analysis, the designer takes an empathic approach to develop an aesthetic that connects business goals with audience need.

chapter 9

DESIGN ACCOUNTABILITY

DESIGN IN THE LAND OF
THE BOTTOM LINE

Jacek Utko started his career as an architect; however, he soon grew disenchanted and moved into the field of newspaper design. A native of Poland, Utko became the design director for a series of Eastern European newspapers owned by the Swedish firm Bonnier Business Press. The newspaper industry was in decline, and many were predicting its demise within the decade. But Utko was not so quick to give up. With a background in architecture, design and engineering, he was at heart a problem solver, and so he looked at the issues newspapers were facing, and came up with a solution.

Utko went to work redesigning the paper. He is quick to point out that he did not collaborate or conduct research. He had a vision for what needed to happen, and he made it so. His process was simple—talk to the newspaper executives, understand their business goals, then design to meet those goals. It worked. After reviving Poland's Puls Biznesu, Utko went on to successfully work with newspapers in Russia and the Baltic States. He won several awards for newspaper design, and even more important, several of the newspapers began to increase in circulation. In Russia, circulation went up 25 percent; in Poland, 35 percent; and in Bulgaria, 100 percent. Without a doubt, design was the key driver for much of this success. Utko says it was about improving the quality of the product by adjusting the content, then bringing in design. He also believes, as he has proven, that design can change a company.

Or consider the classic 1964 consumer research experiment, in which Ralph Allison and Kenneth Uhl set out to see what impact the visual design of packaging played in consumer's understanding and experience of beer. Participants were presented with five unidentified glasses of beer, including the participant's preferred brand. Participants sampled the beers and were asked which one tasted best. Overall, they rated the beers equally, without preference to their preferred brand.

In the second phase of the test, participants were asked to sample the same beers, only this time the cans for the beers were present so that each brand could be identified. With the can present, the participants rated their preferred brand highest.

This test indicates that knowledge and experience don't always agree, and that design stimulus, like packaging, influences preferences. Louis Cheskin coined this term to describe this effect as "sensation transference."

The beer drinkers had obviously connected to their brand in some way other than taste. The packaging was essential to their enjoyment of the product and was the primary way in which they defined their relationship to it. The design of the package was the driver for their decision to purchase the product.

However, even with demonstrations like this one, public acknowledgment of design's ability to motivate and create audience experiences and its impact on audience decision-making had been foggy at best. Within the last decade, advances in the psychology of consumer buying behavior and the development of new techniques for understanding and measuring design impact have emerged.

For decades, design has been asking for a seat at the decision-making table, but that seat is attained only through accountability. Design's impact, which was once implied, must now be quantified. Organizations that embrace design as a strategic business tool expect that design will yield a return. Because of this, design—like other functional areas of organizations—will have to validate its effectiveness. To do this, design process must incorporate metrics and tools for measuring business success.

Design measurement has been the Holy Grail for designers who want to prove their value beyond aesthetics. In the past few years, several design competitions have emerged that, unlike most visually based competition, are driven by design's return on investment. The two most notable are Britain's Design Business Association's Design Effectiveness Awards and the Effies, sponsored by the American Marketing Association. In these competitions aesthetics take a back seat to the design's contribution to business success.

So what does success look like? Deborah Dawton, chief executive officer of the Design Business Association, describes one way they measure success: "[We] look at the original goals, decide whether they were significant in a business context, and whether or not they were achieved or exceeded." Says Dawton, "It is also crucial that the entrants show evidence that other influencing factors, such as reduction in price or a major advertising campaign, did not cause the results claimed by the design."

In the Effies, entrants submit case studies of their projects that detail the specifics of the design's contribution to meeting the client's goals. Judges rate the design's impact on results (30 percent) and how the design met the strategic goals and was articulated and implemented (70 percent).

But even with the criteria defined, many questions remain when it comes to measuring design effectiveness. The issue is even more complicated considering that every sector of the design industry has its own particular way of measuring success. Packaging measures return on packaging investment, web design measures traffic and conversion, communication design and branding measure perception and attitudes. Environmental design measures customer experiences. One thing is for certain: Good looks are meaningless if the final design does not contribute to the goal of the organization.

WHY IS DESIGN HARD TO MEASURE?

Design has several issues it must overcome if business is to accept it as a valuable tool. Part of the challenge lies in the fact that design does not exist in a vacuum, and it is very difficult to isolate it from other factors like production costs and industry trends. For this reason, the metrics for measuring design success must be identified early in the process. The best time to measure for success is when other factors, like price or promotions, are static and can be ruled out as contributing success factors.

On an aesthetic level, design becomes entangled in debates about art and beauty. Design in communication has a broader role than simply creating visually appealing images, but the design industry does have a fixation on the beautiful. Competitions that focus on looks rather than effects perpetuate this fixation. As Joe Duffy, chairman of the branding and design firm Duffy & Partners, says, "The design business continues to navel gaze. Designers are still designing for designers rather than working to convince the business world of the importance of design in our everyday lives." The design community has not fully embraced design success measurement primarily because it's afraid of being held accountable. It's also due to the lack of time and resources needed to quantify their work. However, as Rob Wallace, Managing Partner and Strategic Director of the brand strategy and design firm Wallace Church, says, "Without [design] accountability, [designers] have no autonomy. Once we embrace this, and put ourselves up against a financial model, and prove our value, will come the time and budget required to prove it time and time again."

Part of the reason for the undervaluation of design is that although we live in a visually complex society, we are not generally educated about images. Much of the emphasis is placed on the written word, the comprehension of meaning and grammar. Little instruction is given to interpreting visual images. It is assumed that because seeing is a sensory skill, that people have an inherent understanding. However, as any designer will tell you, the appreciation and understanding of visual cues and messages is not widely understood by the public, at least not to the degree where they can articulate the meaning behind what they are seeing. Those who are visually illiterate have no framework for explaining what they are seeing, which leads to classic comments like, "I know good design when I see it."

Another issue that makes design hard to measure is that there is not a concrete way of understanding how people receive and interpret visual messages. Any given image can have multiple meanings, depending on the experiences, attitudes, and beliefs of the person looking at it. Cultural context and the semantic content of the design all play a part in how the piece is interpreted. For the most part, this portion of the process is a black box, as we can never be sure exactly what goes on inside the audience's heads. Audiences go through many mental processes when decoding visual messages, viewing visual metaphors, and pulling out key messages from those that are irrelevant. Design relies heavily on cultural context and the archetypes that are commonly understood, but final design meanings are implied rather than a direct indication. Ultimately, there is no way to create a universal understanding of a design artifact. Because of this, businesses are looking at ways of reaching out to more people in increasingly personal ways, including customization and long-tail business models. As Virginia Postrel notes, "The world is becoming more and more pluralistic. There is more variety in the ways people express themselves both as individuals, as groups, and as corporations. There is no social consensus that there is just one best way. The question for business is: How much diversity can you profitably produce and distribute? The answer, increasingly, is 'more.'"

Design has never been at the top of business's items to measure. Again, the value of design has been seen, until recently, as aesthetic, with little contribution to the bottom line. This is understandable given the mind-set of those in charge of business organizations, who have more expertise in cost analysis than visual rhetoric. Traditionally, businesses measured only what they had the tools to measure and avoided the murky area of design. Without the tools to measure design, business made no effort to account for its impact. Additionally, design was seen as a "soft" discipline that gave added value to products and services but was not responsible for the heavy lifting that ultimately makes products or services successful.

RESEARCH INTO DESIGN VALUE

For design to be considered as a business tool, it had to be measured in a business context. By focusing on the bottom line, the discussion becomes simple. Starting in the late 1980s, research into the relationship between design and business started to be done, most prominently through the collaborative efforts of the UK's Department of Trade and Industry, the Design Council, and researchers Robin Roy, Vivien Walsh, Margaret Bruce, and Stephen Potter.

By the late 1990s, Americans Julie Hertenstein and Marjorie Platt conducted similar research with help from the Design Management Institute. Results from these surveys validated design's role in businesses bottom-line success, whether through improvements in features and product innovation or styling.

COMMERCIAL IMPACTS OF DESIGN (CID)

In 1987, Robin Roy, professor of Design and Environment and director of the Design Innovation Group, and his colleagues at the Open University in Britain, conducted the "Commercial Impacts of Design" (CID) project, the first significant study of design impact on business. The study looked at 221 small- to medium-sized organizations (sixty to one thousand employees) in the UK that had received government funding provided by the Department of Trade and Industry to employ design consultants. Projects included new product development, engineering, and graphic design, and represented a sample of British manufacturing.

The survey followed a simple three-stage methodology that reviewed design inputs, design process, and commercial outcomes. Design inputs included money invested in design and research as well as the cost of design management expertise. Outputs included costs, risks, effects on trade, and financial benefits. The implementation of the project was also considered. In-depth interviews and mailed questionnaires were used to solicit information from participants.

SIGNIFICANT FINDINGS

- 90 percent of the projects were profitable. Projects that were designed had an increase in sales of an average of 41 percent over projects that were less design savvy.

- 48 percent of projects recovered their investment in design within a year.

- 89 percent recovered their investment and made a profit.

- 41 percent of repackaging projects led to an increase in sales.

- Graphic and packaging design proved to have the highest return on investment.

- Of projects that failed, the losses were relatively small compared to the investment. One cause for failure was the lack of collaboration between the design consultant and the company's internal team. Other causes included several non-design-related factors, such as external financial reasons. Some participants whose projects "failed" still considered the project worthwhile, as it introduced them to design-management techniques they could use for future projects.

- 28 percent of the survey participants admitted having issues with the design consultants they hired, though only 10 percent indicated that the issues were "major." The problems were grouped into four categories: quality of work, poor design management, communication, and service-related issues.

QUALITY OF WORK

Of the 28 percent that had issues with the design consultants, 61 percent stated that the designs were of poor quality or failed to meet the requirements as stated in the brief. This lack of quality was deemed to be due to the inexperience or skill of the designer. The designer's lack of consideration for the design brief and desire to "do their own thing" was also a reoccurring issue.

DESIGN MANAGEMENT

The selection, briefing, and management of the designers caused issues for several of the firms. Poor briefings with the designers lead to misdirected designs or incomplete understanding of the design goals. Many of the design-management problems were linked to communication issues.

COMMUNICATION

At the heart of most failure was communication. Companies reported that the breakdown in communication often lead to misdirected design that did not meet their needs. Designers who were reportedly "hard to get a hold of" or committed to other projects caused a breakdown in communication. When designers underperformed, it tended to result in a reduced amount of communication as well.

SERVICE

The fewest issues were service related. In several cases, designers passed the project on to junior designers, who did not completely understand the specifications of the deliverable and were not present at the client meetings.

As a result of the survey, companies had an increased appreciation for the importance of design consultants, with half of the companies increasing their use of design consultants. Overall, companies felt that they had better understanding and attitude toward design consultants and design management.

MARKET DEMANDS THAT REWARD INVESTMENT IN DESIGN (MADRID)

In 1997, Roy and his colleagues conducted a follow-up survey in conjunction with Britain's Design Council. The study set out to understand how investments in design vary with the markets the company operates and how design can be used as a competitive strategy. The long-term benefits of design were also considered. The study was built upon the CID study, reanalyzing much of that material, then implementing a follow-up survey of forty-two CID businesses eight years after the initial CID project. This study confirmed that businesses that were successful tended to have the resources available to invest in design, and that business success and investments in design and product development are likely to be mutually reinforcing, while poor financial performance and a failure to invest can lead to a cycle of decline.

Where the CID study indicated that successful projects paid more attention to product performance, features, and quality than underperforming products, which focused on design style or cost reduction, the MADRID study indicated that companies had a new appreciation for design as more than just a "style" tool, and saw design as playing a significant role in the business. The CID survey indicated that a "broad, multidimensional approach" was employed by successful projects, while projects that were unsuccessful used design simply for style. The MADRID survey indicated that individuals were beginning to recognize design as a business tool and indeed gave an indication that design contributed to business success. And although it was not conclusive to support the premise of design's contribution to business, it did spark more detailed and encompassing studies.

SIGNIFICANT FINDINGS

- Successful projects had used design to help "up-market" products into more profitable markets.

- Successful projects used design as a way to make product improvements in features and quality as opposed to solely for style.

- Successful projects involved a "broad, multidimensional" approach to design that focused on product performance and quality, as opposed to a styling function or cost reduction.

WINNING BY DESIGN

By categorizing companies based on the number of design awards received, peer recognition, and inclusion in the Design Council's Design Index, Roy and his team determined that companies that invested in design received a higher rate of return than companies that were less design conscious. Good design was not a cure-all for bad business practices, however, but it was observed that companies that invested in design also were effective at managing their businesses. In the book *Winning by Design,* Roy, Walsh, Bruce, and Potter recount their research of over one hundred industry leaders worldwide.

Hertenstein and Platt

In 1996, while working with the Design Management Institute, Julie Hertenstein and Marjorie Platt, professors at the College of Business Administration at Northeastern University, developed a framework for measuring design as a contributor to business performance. By looking at companies who valued design, Hertenstein and Platt were able to show that companies that invest in design had greater returns.

In 2001, Hertenstein and Platt followed up their initial study with another that looked at design's impact on financial performance. They used a wider range of industries and examined fifty-one companies and twelve measures of performance over a five-year period.

Hertenstein and Platt's Methodology

The first step in measuring design impact was to establish criteria for design on financial performance. Design experts recruited from the Design Management Institute defined design performance, while standard measures of return on investment and net cash flow to sales were used to measure financial performance.

Firms were selected based on the industry they were in, the general public's awareness of their products, and the design experts, who would be familiar with the companies and have a sense of their design skill. The four industries selected were furniture, automotive, consumer appliances, and computers. Only publicly traded companies were used so that financial information was available for review through Standard & Poor's.

The design experts ranked the companies based on their commitment to good design. They judged good design by the number of design awards won, peer recognition, the firm's emphasis on design investment, and the quality of the designed artifacts the firm produces. In total, there were fifty-one companies ranked; the top half designated " effective design groups," and the lower half design rated "less effective design groups."

Four areas of financial performance were used as measures: growth rates, returns related to sales, returns related to assets, and total stock market returns. Comparisons were made over a five-year period between the effective and less effective design groups. A total of forty-eight comparisons were made.

Forty-five of the forty-eight comparisons indicated that the companies with more "effective design" outperformed companies with "less effective" design.

SIGNIFICANT FINDINGS

- Companies that valued design made financial gains averaging 32 percent higher than the industry norm. Those companies that did not value design averaged 13 percent below the industry average.

- Returns on sales was 23 percent higher for the companies that valued design, while companies that did not value design had averaged 36 percent below the industry average.

- Although the findings give a strong indication of the relationship between good design and good business, Hertenstein and Platt offer several caveats regarding the findings: First, a reminder that design alone does not determine the success of a company but is the culmination of multiple factors. Next, they point out that companies that are savvy about design are probably equally as savvy about business matters. And finally, they remind us that the limited nature of the survey, which only reviewed fifty-one companies, is in no way all-inclusive.

DESIGN COUNCIL 2004–2005 REPORT

The Design Council of Britain was established to communicate design's role in making businesses competitive. The Design Council provides design support for managers, promotes the strategic use of design, and shows how design can address the economic and social challenges of the day.

The Design in Britain National survey is based on 1,500 telephone interviews with business leaders of companies ranging in size from small (50 people and under) to large (over 250 people), and heads of design in the UK. These interviews were augmented by financial research conducted by Public and Corporate Economic Consultants (PACEC).

Sampled companies fell into four overall categories: utilities and construction; manufacturing; professional business services; and retail, wholesale, and leisure services. Results were "reweighted" to correct for any bias so that the data gave a representation equivalent to a census of all companies in the UK.

Not surprisingly, the survey indicated that those companies that gave design a key role in the business performed financially better than those that did not. Seven out of ten companies indicated that design had increased the quality of their deliverables.

SIGNIFICANT FINDINGS

- **Quality:** 24 percent of businesses in a state of upward growth reported that design was a contributing factor for its upward movement.

- **Competitiveness:** The survey indicated that companies that value design and make it part of their business processes had increased rates of innovation and were able to bring added value to their products. The most profitable companies use design as a competitive strategy. As a competitive strategy, design proved to be an effective alternative to competing on low cost. Forty-five percent of the companies surveyed that did not use design as a business tool were left to compete on a low-cost price strategy, while only 21 percent of design-savvy companies still used process as their competitive strategy.

- **Financial rewards:** Companies like British Airways, Unilever, and Marks & Spencer used design strategically and outperformed the London Stock Exchange's 100 most capitalized UK companies (FSTE 100) by 200 percent over a ten-year period. Companies like generic drug firm Almus were able to find a competitive advantage by changing their package design. The new design made them stand out in the minds of pharmacists by being easy to read, thereby minimizing dispensing errors. After the redesign of their packaging, Almus exceeded its first year's sales expectations by 300 percent.

APPROACHES TO MEASURING DESIGN IMPACT

The studies outlined provide an understanding of the challenges and possibilities related to measuring design's impact. They make a clear indication of the cause and effect of design on organizational outcomes. For individual designers, there are several means of showing ROI on projects. The following approaches illustrate ways for measuring both print and web communications.

FINANCIAL APPROACH

There are several well-known financial approaches to measuring brand impact. Most center around calculating the cost of investment in brand assets by asking questions like: What would it cost to build the brand from scratch to its current status? Or, more simply: What have we spent in the course of the brand's life on brand development (including design, logo and identity, colors, sounds, taglines, and trade dress). Another asks: What price would the brand yield if it were put up for sale?

A more specific example of a financial approach to measuring design can be seen in the work of Rob Wallace, managing partner of the Manhattan-based brand and package design firm Wallace Church. Wallace shared a methodology for calculating design value in a 2001 *Design Management Journal* article, "Proving Our Value: Measuring Package Design's Return on Investment." The article attempts to show not just a methodology, but that design can be the most cost-effective marketing tool available to organizations. Wallace believes that design is in a golden age in which it is recognized as a business tool and a profit driver for organizations. Wallace cites the development of titles like *Chief Design Officer* as an indication of design's elevation in the business world.

Organizations are making design a core competency and offering it as a unique value to customers.

As Wallace says, "We have to look to ourselves for allowing design to continue to be perceived as a marketing service. But I think that time is ending, and I think there is an opportunity to elevate what we do in an organization." How does design elevate itself? By being accountable, just like the other functions of an organization are accountable, like accounting, operations, or manufacturing.

But for many clients, the need to measure design is not a major consideration. Many firms do not have the time or resources to tackle such a project. "I'm often fighting an uphill battle, as our clients frequently don't have the time to do the entire process correctly," says Wallace. Most clients are indifferent. Already overburdened, clients are more concerned with getting the job done and moving onto the next project. Additionally, they are very sensitive to having their financial investments made public, making and therefore reluctant to share information even with their design consultants. Along these same lines, designers are reluctant to measure their work in a financial way, the fear being that, if they can prove their contribution to a profit, they are equally accountable for when the profits fall.

When calculating design ROI, Wallace uses an accounting methodology. First he establishes the business' base costs, and then identifies what would happen if nothing changed in the communications platform. This creates the baseline. The same measures are used again, plus cost for the new communications program, in this case, package design and advertising, are included. This gives a measurement of profit based on the original investment made by the organization.

Wallace maintains that he is basing his findings on only has a small representation of design projects. Until he has a deeper pool of research to pull from, he cannot suggest that the results he is presenting are statistically projectionable, but that they do imply the value of design on the bottom line.

Wallace sites a recent redesign project for a nationally known brand. At the time of the redesign, the company was a billion dollar brand. Within eighteen months of the redesign, the brand had risen to $1.3 billion. Though the advertising and merchandising changed, the products themselves remained the same. The amount of advertising stayed the same, but the design aesthetic of the advertising changed, influenced by the change in the packaging design.

To understand how design influenced the profits, Wallace tries to identify the impact of each of those communication elements. What is the percentage of the total number of shoppers that would have seen the advertising? Wallace uses the number of 7 percent, which he believes is a fair assessment based on his experience. He then considers that 100 percent of shoppers who had the opportunity to purchase the product and see the package in the store.

Weighing those two tools, the cost of advertising with a 7 percent reach versus the cost of packaging with a 100 percent reach, advertising generated $7.21 in value for every dollar invested. Design, however, resulted in $415 on average in value.

ATTITUDINAL APPROACHES

Attitudes are a common metric for measuring brand equity. Attitudinal approaches ask: What is the level of loyalty to a brand? What is the level of satisfaction? And how do competitors measure up to the brand? How do audiences rate the quality of the brand and how prominent are the brands in their minds?

Measuring marketing and brand communications has always been a challenge. When seen in a vacuum, the formula appears to be simple: Establish a benchmark prior to launching a new product, place a product in the marketplace, create communications that promote the product, and measure after a period of time to track the sales. The reality is that markets are very complicated, and the difficulty of tracking results makes communications measurement a low priority for most companies. Adding to the complexity, organizations are no longer the sole provider of information that customers receive. It is now just as likely that audience attitudes will be affected by information created by someone outside of the organization via website, blogs, and chat rooms. Yet, as organizations attempt to reach out to audiences, both internal and external, the ability to measure the effectiveness of brand and communication becomes more important. From an organization accountability perspective, communications departments are expected to prove their contributions to the organizational success and need to develop reliable methods of measuring their effectiveness.

Because the affect of communications on audiences is not always immediate, most of what gets measured is not behavior, but attitudes. By focusing on audience perception, association, awareness, and beliefs about the organization or its offerings, communicators can "predict" what their future actions might be. Some fairly reliable tools make these measurements, which makes this method attractive.

Consider the work of the UK-based market research firm Millward Brown, thought by many to be the leader in brand and advertising tracking. With clients in areas as diverse as automotive, food and beverage, and pharmaceuticals, Millward Brown uses several proprietary tools to track brand attitudes, which they believe are directly related to financial performance. Their tool, BrandDynamics, allows clients to track the impact of their brands across several attitudinal stages, including its presence in audience minds, the relevance of the offering, its ability to perform, its value above competitor's offerings, and finally achieving customer loyalty. This method allows organizations to track their client's "journey to loyalty," and provides a framework for showing what messages need to be developed to move the audience ahead in the relationship.

Once there is an understanding of where their most-valued audiences fall on the scale, the organization's strengths and weaknesses are analyzed using a metric that compares the organization's brand to competitors at each stage of the "BrandDynamic pyramid." The pyramid has at its base awareness, then the next step up is relevance, then performance, then advantage, and finally bonding resides at the top of the pyramid. By comparing what issues exist at what level of the journey, organizations can make a determination about where to focus their attention.

The next step looks at the brand's potential for future success. By identifying how well the organization's brand attracts and retains audiences, a projection is made about how the brand can grow over time. This information is then used to compare the organization with competitors. By creating a matrix with the axes of presence (awareness) and growth potential, the organization's position in the market can be established. From there, qualitative work is conducted to better understand areas of interest. The results of the analysis are then used to develop and refine the brand strategy of the organization, with the intent of increasing the return on investment of the brand.

Although attitudinal research provides information about audience perceptions and competitive relevance, it does not give a clear link to financial success. If the goal is to measure actual return on investment, a methodology that offers a quantifiable measure must be developed. Behaviors are the most direct indication of communications ROI.

BEHAVIORAL APPROACHES

With the ability to jump from one online offer to another in a matter of seconds, a dissatisfied customer can instantly change his purchasing decision. Organizations that conduct business online have one single challenge; convert visitors into users and one-time users into loyal customers. To do this, they must ensure that they are providing the products and services audiences want, and also that they are making the experience easy. The only way to ensure that the engagement process is working is to test it with real people. This approach is commonly known as "user experience" or "customer experience management."

The web offers organizations a uninque opportunity to track audience behavior. Through techniques like behavioral targeting, Google can track typed entries and respond with ads that are related to the user's query. So if you did a search for "sailboats," you would see ads related to sailboat manufacturers, sailing vacations, or charters. If you were to search again for "weather," you would receive ads for area wind reports or wind-tracking devices. With this ability to track user behavior, online advertisers have better understanding of how users are interacting with the site. The ability to identify and quantify user behaviors offers a valuable measurement alternative. The ability to observe what users do offers organizations the opportunity to better understand what they value.

Experience offers another area of measurement. By making websites easy to understand, allowing users to perform their tasks quickly, and providing a pleasing experience, organizations are able to gain loyalty from customers and audiences, which over time can equal increased profits. Usability is directly related to design decisions that are made when creating the site. Usability testing is a standard part of any web design process and is a key strategic design tool for aligning the design team with the user and establishing organizational needs early on in the process, as opposed to later, when it becomes more costly to make changes. By maximizing the user experience, organizations can potentially increase sales by making it easy for audiences to collect information or make a purchase.

Peter Merholz, president and cofounder of Adaptive Path, a leader in user experience design, advises organizations on user experience strategies to realize the maximum value from their product design and development investments. Adaptive Path's mission is to show that user experience is related to business ROI. "I would argue that good design is design that has the desired impact," says Merholz. "If designers aren't willing to step up for such accountability, we will continue to be paper-hat-wearing order-takers for other parts of the business."

For Merholz, the method of measuring is straightforward: Find out what is important to the client and focus the design on meeting those needs. In an example given on his blog (a term that Merholz is credited for coining), Merholz considers a project for a financial services client. The client's needs were not unusual: add more accounts that will increase in value over time and increase the amount of assets held. With these primary goals in mind, Merholz developed a range of measurements that design could impact. These were then focused even more, so that only four areas would be addressed. With these measurements in place, Merholz was able to focus their talents, energy, and resources on solving a specific business goal for their client.

CONVERSION ANALYSIS AND DESIGN IMPACT

More directly related to communication design is conversion analysis, where an understanding of a target audience's need and personality are used as a foundation for developing design and content. Brian Massey, principal of the Austin-based conversion firm Conversion Sciences, says that, "Each time a visitor to your website takes another step toward solving their problem, they receive a gentle increase in confidence and satisfaction. It may be that they've found that critical piece of information they were looking for, or they see they're on the right track. When you create a series of these experiences for your visitor, you move them closer to taking action."

As Massey points out, the ultimate goal of design is to create action, whether it's getting someone to participate in an event, make a purchase, or simply connect with another person. Some websites take a shotgun approach and try to appeal to everyone in the market. Usually this strategy ends up failing because the messages were too broad for anyone to feel that their values or needs are being reflected back to them. Conversion takes the opposite approach. By developing a deep understanding of a company's most valued customers and building communication around their needs, websites can become powerful tools for turning viewers into engagers.

A key step in Conversion Sciences' approach is the development of personas. By collecting detailed information about the most valuable customers (MVC) characteristics and personality traits, a profile can be developed that will help define a marketing strategy based on the unique needs of that group. Content providers and designers can then project, based on the profile, what type of information the MVC needs, how they would like it delivered, and how to create an experience where MVCs feel comfortable.

Massey starts by conducting a "conversion interview" in which he helps clients organize their existing information about their customers. This information is then put into a "conversion profile" that describes their decision-making process and their motivation for going to the site. The interview focuses on several questions that help clients determine their most valued customer. By understanding who spends the most money at their site on an ongoing basis (long-term repeat customers), organizations can focus their messaging and information to suit this audience's needs.

Once this data is collected, customers can be grouped according to their interactions with the company. The data can then be used to determine what customer behaviors should be influenced, which customers will return the most profit, what new customers should be acquired, and which customers should be moved to the next level of offerings.

Once MVCs have been determined, Massey creates the "conversion profile." The profile is given a name and photo so that the persona feels like a real person, even thought it is in actuality a composite of MVC traits and characteristics—a brief description of the persona's position within the organization, their age, and some basic information about the organization he works for. The persona is also assigned a personality type, such as meticulous, spontaneous, panicked, or careful.

A customer commentary is developed in which the persona outlines how they see their business and how they would like to interact with the website. The commentary asks, "What type of information do they need? How do they need it delivered? How do they make buying decisions? What do they need to understand about the company to make them feel comfortable enough to work with them?"

Next the persona's "points of resolution" are developed into a list. The list acts as a map for pages that answer the persona's specific needs. Before a customer feels comfortable to buy, she must have her questions answered. Points of resolution offer opportunities for customers to resolve questions they might have about the product, while always providing an opportunity to buy.

Once the visitor has had her questions answered and is ready to engage, Massey considers what types of "conversion beacons" are needed to take the visitor toward the conversion point. Conversion beacons are actions that the persona might want to take once on the site. For example, if the persona is interested in information about the service or product, they might be able to download a brochure or a white paper. The final phase is the conversion point. This is where the visitor chooses to engage the website and take the desired action.

With a strategy developed, the next step is to reflect the strategy in the design of the website. Massey is able to give advice on the development of the site's information architecture so that it leads the MVC toward answers to their questions. The visual language of the site is developed so that the MVC is drawn to key messages that are of interest to them. Navigation is made intuitive, again, taking MVCs quickly to the information they need. The copy reflects the language and voice of the MVC so that they not only understand but relate to the site. The design of the entire site reflects the MVC's personality and the personality of the company.

The profile acts as a touchstone for everyone involved in the development process. Copywriters can write in a voice that is familiar to the MVC, designers can create a visual language and environment that reflects the character of the MVC, and relevant information can be organized and delivered in a way that appeals to the MVC.

Conversion rates, or metrics, tells the company how well its website is motivating visitors to take a "desired action." Conversion can take many

forms. For retailers, it can be about the number of visitors that made purchases online. It can also be the number of visitors that have downloaded a
newsletter or filled out a registration form or given you permission to contact
them. All of these can be considered a form of ROI. Each of these returns is
driven by design decisions regarding copy, visual design, content placement
and architecture.

IN CONCLUSION

The price for a seat at the decision-making table is accountability. For
designers, this means being able to communicate the value of design
in terms of a return that is valuable to their clients. Whether tracking
changing attitudes, behaviors, sales numbers, the return on investment
of design activities or customer satisfaction, designers elevate their work
by establishing metrics for their projects. Although design does not exist
in a vacuum, design metrics begin to illustrate the value of design and
provide a way to track the effectiveness of design activities.

chapter 10
PLANNING IN A
TURBULENT ENVIRONMENT

MANAGING THE DESIGN PROCESS

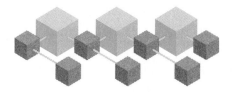

There is a set of well-known frustrations that designers face on a regular basis: poorly defined design goals; clients changing direction midproject; and late direction from stakeholders. All of these are notorious for knocking projects off track. Fortunately, the causes of all of these frustrations can be addressed during the project-planning phase, which offers designers a means for managing their projects so that good design does not get killed along the way.

Traditional project planning brings to mind a sequence of activities that are broken into specific phases. Linear method provides a logical flow of events that are predictable and easily understood by stakeholders. However, a hallmark of the linear method is that once a phase is completed, it is difficult to go back and make changes to preceding phases, as any change impacts all future phases, thereby creating a great deal of rework. Another constraint of the linear method is that rarely do projects unfold in well-defined sequential steps. This is particularly true for design projects. Given the iterative nature of design, it is more often the case that projects go back and forth between phases as design requirements change and discoveries are made. Design is also more collaborative and requires less top-down control and more inclusive methods of project management.

Alternatively, agile methods preplan for iteration and offer increased flexibility. The model is similar to the old swimming pool game of Marco Polo, in which the player that is "it," with eyes closed, tries to tag other players by calling out "Marco," to which the other players respond "Polo." By hearing the voices of the other players, the player that is "it" slowly closes in on the target. Similarly, the agile method uses rapid prototyping to quickly develop ideas, test them with stakeholders, then refine the work based on the feedback. This volley continues until the prototype meets the stakeholder's expectations.

Regardless of which method is used, both linear and agile methods share characteristics common to the discipline of project management, including defining a scope of work, planning and scheduling, execution, monitoring, and control and closure.

One caveat about design project management: Not all projects require strict project management. A judgment needs to be made at the outset of the project as to the level of management required. A rule of thumb is that if you are going to spend more time managing the project than actually doing the work of the project, it's probably not necessary.

The phases of project management run parallel with the phases of the design process. Strategy development and research are encompassed in the planning phases; concept and design development fall in the execution phase. Sign-offs, design briefs and change orders are part of the monitor and control function. The project management framework provides designers with: an opportunity to create alignment with clients on direction; a means of monitoring project status; a controlled way to react to changes in project requirements; project transparency; and project accountability for both clients and designers.

THE MAJOR AREAS OF DESIGN PROJECT MANAGEMENT:
- Project planning
- Planning and scheduling
- Monitoring and controls
- Closure

PROJECT PLANNING

Because of the complexity and collaborative nature of design projects, designers need a means for syncing the areas of scope, budget, schedule, staff, and stakeholders of any given project. Project stakeholders need to be informed, project resources need to be strategically allocated, and schedules need to be vetted to meet the client's delivery expectations. In addition, projects need a flexible framework to accommodate shifts in requirements, changes in goals, and busy stakeholder schedules.

THE MAJOR AREAS OF DESIGN PROJECT PLANNING
- Project initiation
- Defining the scope of the design project
- Developing the project proposal
- Developing the work breakdown structure

PROJECT INITIATION

Most design projects start out with a request to bid from a potential client. One of the first steps in response to the bid is to calculate the resources required to complete the project. Hours and staffing are determined, rates are calculated, and an initial proposal is submitted to the client.

Design specifications and the client's strategic plan are provided to the designer during this phase with the expectation that the final design or scope of the project may change due to findings during the business and audience research phase. The client's strategic plan is reviewed to see how the design project can support the overall goals of the organization. Another important consideration at this phase is whether or not the project is worth the client's time to take on. By reviewing the client's organizational goals and comparing them to the project goals, a determination can be made as to whether the project is worth pursuing.

As part of project initiation, design management consultant Emily Cohen believes in what she calls the "getting to know you phase." With most stakeholders's attention dedicated to the process, sometimes they forget that the relationship is equally as important. Strong relationships help the designer create internal advocates who trust and respect them. With the availability of project management software, there runs a risk of losing personal contact with clients. When real relationships are formed, clients are willing to provide more project-related information and become advocates for the designer. Designers that make the effort to meet with clients, ask questions, and engage with clients are more likely to increase their project win rate.

DEFINING PROJECT SCOPE

The first step is to define the goals of the project. Much of this is determined in the business and audience research phase. Once a clear goal has been determined, the next step is to define what actions need to take place during the project. Like the action plan in strategy development, the scope of work planning allows the designer to consider all the tasks associated with a given project. The goal of determining project scope is to identify the specific areas of work you will be conducting so that clients and the designer are clear on what is and what is not going to be done. Defining the work at the outset of a project is critical to getting the client-designer relationship off to a good start. By setting, in no uncertain terms, the expectations for the project, both client and designer become aligned.

To clarify, project scope is different from design scope. Project scope is concerned with defining the work that is required to produce the design. Design scope is concerned with the features, function and character of the design that is being created.

PROJECT PROPOSAL

It is recommended that every project begin with a project proposal that responds to client needs not with any strategic input or creative direction, but simply an outline of the scope of work and the costs involved and what the objectives and value of the engagement are. The proposal discusses the parameters of the project, outlines the scope of work, describes the process, and outlines particulars like how many concepts will be presented, how many type revisions, layout revisions, and concept revisions are included in the price. Specific project objectives are not addressed at this stage, as this information will be uncovered later in the process. Once the client accepts the proposal, a contract is signed and work begins.

PROJECT BRIEF

Once vetted, the project proposal becomes a project brief that acts as marching orders for the design team and client to move forward. It's also a reference point throughout the project to ensure the team is hitting its marks. The project brief outlines the justification for the project, including outlining the business and audience need, project specifications, a list of deliverables, and project objectives. The design team and clients constantly check this document during the course of the project. The core team stays with the project from beginning to end, and they know the goals and parameters. The core team then introduces their additional staff to those goals and parameters.

Design Brief

For more strategic or complex projects, it is suggested that a design brief be developed. Different from a proposal, the design brief provides more design-specific information. The design brief is developed collaboratively between the design team and the client. Having the design team actively participate in the development of the design brief creates a sense of ownership and understanding that would not develop if they were simply handed the document. The brief aligns both the client's business and creative objectives and defines the success criteria.

PLANNING AND SCHEDULING

Developing a project plan and schedule requires several considerations, including the list of activities and tasks, determining the dependencies of activities, estimating time to complete the various activities or phases, determining who will do the work, and then developing a fully fleshed out schedule.

IDENTIFY THE DELIVERABLE

The first step in establishing the schedule is defining the deliverable. No planning can take place without a clear understanding of the client's expectation. Once the design deliverable has been established, the project can be broken into its component parts. By doing this, the designer and client have a clear understanding of how the project will get done. It also provides an opportunity to think about and discuss the various aspects of the final design. Tools like Gantt charts help everyone visualize the process and see the relationship of the various phases and activities. The breakdown also provides a framework for tracking project status.

WORK BREAKDOWN STRUCTURE

Most design projects are made up of several deliverables. A branding project can consist of brand research and design development, which includes identity, color palette, typography, templates, production and testing. Each individual element requires specific steps to complete. To manage these steps, a work breakdown structure that outlines activities, tasks, and subtasks for creating each project deliverables can be created. The work breakdown structure, or WBS, is a valuable tool for identifying the project deliverables and the dependencies of project elements to each other (you can't design the visual layout of a website until the navigation and site architecture are developed), and makes a large unwieldy task like a website redesign more manageable by breaking it into groups of smaller activities.

The WBS acts as a coordinating guide for almost all project activities, in particular scheduling and staffing. As a tool for monitoring project progress, the WBS delineates each project task in order of its need for completion. This provides an easy way to "check off" project activities and see the status of the project. For the project stakeholders, the WBS provides a shared understanding of how the project will unfold, its various parts, and their roles and responsibilities.

The best way to break down a project is to work with all the participants that are involved in the project, including the client. Together, the project team—writers, photographers, designers, traffic coordinators and clients—can discuss the steps in detail. The advantage of doing this activity as a group is that it brings together team members of all the disciplines involved and provides an opportunity to understand the project from multiple points of view. This also allows the team to understand the dependencies of project activities, allowing for more realistic scheduling. Additionally, since the team is present at the meeting, everyone is "in the loop" with the overall project plan, and understands their roles and responsibilities.

To start a WBS, designers can state the top-level activity. (For the purposes of demonstration, we'll use the development of a brand identity as a model.) Subsequent phases and activities are then determined—tasks and subtasks. As a general rule, no task should be shorter than eight hours or longer than eighty hours. Each activity needs to have a deliverable with a specific delivery date. A deliverable could be anything that can be seen as proof of the completed activity, whether it is a document or a design comp. Once the deliverable is received and approved, the designer can proceed to the next activity or phase.

Most visual design projects have a standard approach, so the general phases and activities are familiar: the creation of a brief, the development of an idea, the development of rounds of comps, finalization, production and delivery. However, at the task level there can be many variations. Some design projects may require multiple client meetings or coordination with photographers or writers. All of these activities need to be considered at the outset.

EXAMPLE:

1.0 Develop brand for Amalgamated Wiffleball

    1.1 Define mission and vision

        1.1.1 Data collection

            1.1.1.1 Review executive reports

            1.1.1.2 Review mission and vision statements

    1.2 Define goals

        1.2.1 Review mission and vision

        1.2.2 Conduct feasibility analysis

        1.2.3 Develop action plan

    1.3 Understand the business

        1.3.1 Conduct SWOT analysis

    1.4 Understand the competition

        1.4.1 Conduct differentiation analysis

        1.4.2 Conduct benchmarking study

        1.4.3 Conduct PEST analysis

    1.5 Understand the audience

        1.5.1 Conduct quantitative

            1.5.1.1 Issue survey

1.5.1.2 Issue questionnaire

1.5.1.3 Develop report

1.5.2 Conduct qualitative

1.5.2.1 Host focus groups

1.5.2.2 Conduct interviews

1.5.2.3 Hold projective technique workshops

1.5.2.4 Conduct ethnographic study

1.5.2.5 Develop report

1.6 Develop concepts

1.6.1 Analyze fuzzy front end

1.6.2 Conduct ideation workshops

1.6.3 Select final concepts

1.7 Create designs

1.7.1 Identity development

1.7.1.1 Conduct design explorations

1.7.1.2 Make client revisions

1.7.1.3 Refine designs

1.7.1.4 Produce final designs

1.7.2 Color palette development

1.7.2.1 Conduct design explorations

1.7.2.2 Make client revisions

1.7.2.3 Refine designs

1.7.2.4 Produce final designs

1.7.3 Typographic study

1.7.3.1 Conduct design explorations

1.7.3.2 Make client revisions

1.7.3.3 Refine designs

1.7.3.4 Produce final designs

1.7.4 Style guide

1.7.4.1 Conduct design explorations

1.7.4.2 Make client revisions

1.7.4.3 Refine designs

1.7.4.4 Produce final designs

1.8 Test designs

1.8.1 Conduct monadic testing

1.8.2 Hold focus groups

1.8.3 Conduct interviews

1.9 Measure outcomes

1.9.1 Balanced scorecard

1.10 Refine

Developing the WBS is an iterative and collaborative process. Once all project stakeholders have approved the WBS, the next step is to develop a project schedule.

CREATING WORK PACKAGES

Starting with the WBS, each activity and task should now be broken out into distinct activities. The next step is to determine if the activities, or "work packages," are in the right order. For instance, if we look at our WBS for developing the brand for Amalgamated Wiffleball, you will need to conduct the activities of "define the mission and vision," and "define the goals" before you can start the activity of developing concepts. Understanding and organizing the WBS based on these dependencies is critical in the scheduling process.

DETERMINING TIME AND STAFFING

Next, each work package needs to be estimated for time, resources, and staffing. If we look at the work package for "Understanding the competition," there are three activities that need to be conducted. If we look at the task "Conduct differentiation analysis," we know that someone will need to be assigned to do that activity, and a timeframe for conducting the activity will need to be determined, and resources will need to be allocated.

Estimating Hours

A common trap designers fall into is underestimating the amount of time needed to complete a task. Some try to give the client the fastest time possible in an attempt to seem efficient. The downside is that when projects go over, the designer ends up looking bad. A better plan is to provide an estimate that considers additional time of staff availability (vacation or sickness), technical problems (computer or software malfunctions), changes in scope, and general circumstances. By building in some additional time for these considerations, designers set a reasonable expectation with clients and provide themselves a cushion should anything out of the ordinary occur.

Time planning starts with the WBS. By looking at each individual activity, designers can ensure that they account for every task that needs to take place, thereby providing an accurate time estimation. The WBS also provides an opportunity to identify activities that can happen concurrently. Most projects do not happen in a linear fashion, with one activity taking place at a time. Many activities can be done at the same time, as long as they are not dependant on one another. For instance, in the Wiffleball example, the activities of understanding the business, the competition, and the audience can all happen concurrently.

The easiest means of charting a project is through a Gantt chart. The Gantt chart shows the start and finish for each activity in the WBS. The Gantt chart provides an at-a-glance overview of the overall project timeline, the timeline for each individual work package, work package dependencies, concurrent work packages, and project milestones. Most project management software packages will automatically create Gantt charts by determining the earliest start time and an estimated time of completion for each activity. The resulting chart shows each activity in sequence, clearly showing concurrent activities and those with dependencies.

Smaller projects naturally require less scheduling. If a project can be completed in a day or two, a detailed schedule is not necessary. Simple checklists can be used to keep projects on track and team members updated.

STAFFING

After an estimate of hours needed to complete the project are defined, it's time to assemble the project team. Although it sounds cliché, people make a difference in the success or failure of a project. Interpersonal skills, like communication and the ability to form bonds with co-workers can make or break a project. Assembling a cohesive, collaborative team is of the utmost importance for project success.

Consider the work of Diane Klein, the former managing director at ESI Design, an interactive design company in New York known as much for its work with Sony, Time Warner, the Kennedy Center, Ellis Island and Best

Buy as it is for its owner Edwin Schlossberg, one of the pioneers of interactive experience design. In her career, Klein has engaged in all sizes and scopes of projects, from the Shanghai Corporate Pavilion developed for World Expo 2010 to developing compelling exhibits for the Children's Museum of Los Angeles. In her role as managing director, she managed project teams, schedules, budgets and communication, ensuring that designs were executed on time and to her clients' exacting specifications. With a staff of about sixty, ESI had a range of skilled employees it could call on. Working in groups based on availability and skill sets, Klein coordinated teams made up of environmental designers, graphic designers, interaction designers, systems designers, and production managers, in addition to a project manager and a project executive. Most of these teams start off smaller in the goals and parameters phase and grow as the project progresses and becomes more complicated.

Project management plays a key role in maintaining team collaboration. As a project lead, the designer is responsible for determining the proper skill sets needed to complete the job, and recruiting the appropriate talent. Aligning the team requires leadership, coaching and mentoring skills as well as the ability to negotiate and motivate team members. Team members should be experienced in the area that they are assigned, have a vested interest in working on the project and be able to work collaboratively with other team members. Ultimately, the project will succeed not because of one or two superstars, but because all individuals were able to contribute in their respective capacities.

THE ROLE OF THE DESIGNER AS PROJECT LEAD

- Team builder
- Communicator
- Motivator
- Problem solver
- Leader

DEVELOPING THE SCHEDULE

Once you know what you will be doing, the order you will be doing it in, and who will be doing the work, you can then begin to develop a schedule. Identifying the individual steps and the time it will take to complete them are the foundation of project planning. For clients who have to answer to bosses and hit drop-dead dates, the schedule is their lifeline to the project and a key factor for success.

Scheduling requires that client and designer agree on dates for delivery of content and final product. Schedules are great motivators for both clients and designers, who have shared responsibilities in a design project. To be effective, schedules also need to be public so that both parties can see what's happening and when. There are several online tools available that allow for public display of schedules and other project-critical information including Aquent's RoboHead and Basecamp.

PROJECT COMMUNICATION

On any given project, a designer makes numerous calls to clients; sends countless e-mails confirming estimates, schedules, and changes; and tries to document all of this information in a centralized place. Managing this flood of communication can be difficult, and it definitely can detract from the designer's time for developing ideas, but designers should realize that from a client's perspective, this communication is critical to growing the relationship. Design management consultant Emily Cohen believes that effective project management is not based on systems, but on the personal relationships that are developed between designers and clients. "People put so much focus on process that they forget about relationships," says Cohen. "If you have a good relationship with your client, you have an internal advocate, and people that defend you and love you, and want you to work with them. And if you make a mistake, they forgive you." Cohen advises that before you start to document, you should spend time building the relationship. "Most firms spend a lot time on systems that, say, initiate a project through technology, but there is no personal contact. Many times, I go back to teams and tell them that they need to reinitiate personal contact, because that's really important. Once you build a relationship with somebody, you get a lot more information, you build advocacy and it is much stronger."

MONITORING AND CONTROLS

Throughout the design process, there are many opportunities for projects to get off track. When expectations become misaligned or communication is poor, projects can turn from portfolio pieces to those that are quickly filed away, never to be seen again. Design process offers a structure for mitigating these risks in several ways, including through a clearly understood framework for working, and through a series of control documents that provide "stage gates" at critical points in the process. Typically, these documents include a work order, design brief, change order and schedule. These documents help the project stay on course, offer an opportunity to check project status, and catch any variations from the original work order. More importantly, these documents can alert designers of potential problems before they become major issues.

BALANCING PROJECT DOCUMENTATION

Having tools to manage design risk helps alleviate common frustrations like schedule overruns, multiple revisions, and off-target directions. But for most designers, documenting their work activities can be a burden. Designers want to concentrate on design, not paperwork, but it must be understood that quality design does not happen by accident and is the result of planning and project control. The goal is to find a balance between the amount of risk you are willing to take with the number of controls you are willing to put into place. High-risk projects require more controls. Low-risk projects require fewer. Each project should be assessed at the beginning to determine the probability of something going wrong. If you have a finicky or indecisive client, you might consider taking extra time to document the scope of the project. If you have a client who has a flexible deadline, you might focus on the schedule so as to not get caught in the trap of going from no deadline to immediate deadline. Making theses assessments at the outset can help align expectations, and thereby make for a smoother-run project.

The ability to control and document projects is an accepted aspect of project management—but you don't want to go overboard. In-house design management expert Andy Epstein remembers a time when the paperwork got to be too much. "We had a lot of forms to keep the project moving along and as a precaution to see where project breakdowns might have occurred," he says. "We actually got to the point where we had fourteen forms that had to be filled out to move a project through. That was just unworkable." The key to project documentation is finding balance. By looking at the complexity of the project and the complexity of the designer's relationship with the client, the right amount of documentation can be determined. As important as it is to manage project risk, it is possible to have too much process and too many forms. Projects that are quick and dirty, where the client is low-budget, require a lot less documentation than projects that are highly strategic and complex.

CONTROL DOCUMENTS

All design projects require a direction, a schedule and a budget. When projects are initiated, these are the things that will ensure the project unfolds according to plan. Various control documents, discussed below, keep designers and clients informed every step of the way.

> **The design brief:** The brief aligns the client and designer so that they share a common understanding of the direction of the design.

> **Change orders:** Change orders are a critical part of the design process. Because of the iterative nature of design projects, change is not only expected, but in most cases, is a requirement for producing meaningful work. Change orders allow the designer and client to track iterations and revisions during the course of the project.

> **Schedule:** Time is often the biggest determining factor in how design projects are executed.

> **Budget:** Cost affects every aspect of the project, influencing the look and feel of the design and the resources that can be brought to bear.

THE DESIGN BRIEF

Satellite Design is a San Francisco graphic design firm specializing in brand identity and print communications. Amy Gustincic, its principal, is an award-winning designer who has more than fifteen years of experience in design and strategic communications. Like many designers, the design brief plays an important role in her overall design process.

Here Gustincic describes the value of the brief: "The document is sent to the client to make sure we are all on the same page and that our research findings are in-line with their knowledge, the client is the expert in their business. We make assumptions and then we use the brief as a benchmark for evaluating our design... so when we come back and the design is pink, and the client says, 'I don't know why your design is pink,' we can say because we looked at our design brief and we had agreed that the audience is twelve-year-old girls, and twelve-year-old girls like pink."

Design Illustrator Von Glitschka uses his creative brief as an opportunity for clients to give him whatever creative direction they see fit. This often includes examples of logos they like or colors they don't like. Glitschka always asks them why they like something or don't like something. "Sometimes," he says, "even though they might not like a color, that doesn't mean that I won't use it. Especially if their rationale is a personal preference. Sometimes the most appropriate color for them might be the color they don't like. Part of my job is getting them to a point where they realize that the logo is not for them. Agencies understand that, but it can be hard to explain to a small business owner without sounding like an elitist."

THE VALUE OF THE DESIGN BRIEF

Once information has been gathered it must be put into some format that all of the stakeholders can share and review. The creative brief is a document that acts as a guide for the direction of the project. The brief outlines information about the firm, its audience, its business strategy, its competition, its objectives and the scope of the project. It works as both a project management tool and a design directive. Possibly the most important function of the brief is that it aligns all of the stakeholders involved in the project, thereby minimizing the chances of going down dead ends.

The brief is created by the design team in cooperation with the client. By working together on the brief, the clients and the designer have an early opportunity to work out issues and clarify misunderstandings regarding direction.

The design brief answers all the strategic questions a designer needs to know to do meaningful work. What is the objective of the firm? Who is its target audience? Who is its competition? How does the client perceive itself? What are the audience's perceptions of the client? What are the design parameters that define the client? How will project success be measured? In addition to answering these important questions, the brief outlines schedules, budgets and the process involved in the project.

The brief also answers many of the subjective questions and provides an opportunity for designers to hone in on the client's visual expectations. Often clients will describe what they want, but verbal instructions about creative elements can be widely interpreted. *Contemporary* can mean many things to many people. The brief provides an opportunity for designers to coach clients in expressing what they are looking for with the goal of avoiding miscommunications down the road.

The brief is developed after the initial client meeting and at the close of the information-gathering stage. The designer and the client should work on the brief together. At a minimum, the designer should prepare the brief, then allow the client to review and edit as they see fit. Client participation ensures that the direction is accurate, the business goals are clear, and the stakeholders are aligned, This step goes a long way toward establishing a smooth design process and helps mitigate issues like abrupt changes in direction, politics, and design micromanaging.

The brief is also a way to get "buy-in" with the client. The more explicit the brief, the better your chances of getting quick approval on a project. The brief also gives the client and designer an opportunity to collaborate, allowing both parties to participate in defining the parameters of the project. By including the client in these initial steps, they may find it less necessary to micromanage the design aspects of the project.

Once the brief is developed, it is critical that all stakeholders approve it. This is one of the most important functions of the brief. Often stakeholders will have different levels of involvement in the project, different ideas of how things should be expressed, and different ideas of what points need to be made. When this happens, designers become caught in the middle, and the chances of heading in the wrong direction, or having a false start or a split concept increase. "The one common fallibility is if someone comes along in the process that wasn't there at the start," says Tim Bruce of the Chicago design firm LOWERCASE, INC. "Usually we try to define who's going to make the decision pretty clearly. And usually if we run into trouble, it's because other people weigh in later on. We work pretty hard to know who is making all the decisions so we can bring them along, especially on the big projects." By getting signed approval from the top decision makers, designers defend themselves against these speed bumps. This forces the client to arrive at a consensus and hash out any internal disagreements before concepts and designs are developed.

THE PARTS OF THE BRIEF

The brief is composed of several sections that reflect data collected in the design research phase. Answering the questions outlined below will effectively build the skeleton for your creative brief. The information gathered in the research process (business, audience, competition) will provide you with the answers.

Project Summary

The project summary states the general project information, goals and relevant background information for the project. The project summary defines the project, stating what is to be done, why it is being done, and the value that it brings to the client. This overview acts as an executive summary of the project. The summary answers three basic questions about the project.

- What is the single purpose of the new communication?
- What are the long-term goals?
- How will we know if the project is successful?

I. **Define the problem.** It's easy to begin a project with assumptions. For example, assuming the client needs a new logo or a new brochure. Before making an assumption about what the client needs, the problem must be defined. This is the first step in establishing the direction of the project. By clarifying the problem and getting everyone to agree, designers are able to address the need, as opposed to jumping ahead to an off-the-shelf solution.

2. **Define objectives.** Objectives are the tasks that must be accomplished to achieve the goal. When defining the objectives and outcome, a timeframe and metrics for how the goal will be achieved need to be defined.

3. **Determine success criteria.** How will success be defined? In most cases, there is a measurable business outcome associated with the project.

Business Analysis

The design is being created to fill a business need. Business analysis answers questions like:

- What is the client's business strategy?

- What assumptions about the company's relative position, strengths and weaknesses, competitors, and industry trends must be made for the current strategy to make sense?

- What is happening in the business environment?

- What are the key factors for competitive success?

For designers to be effective business partners, they must understand the firms they are serving. Design without information is pointless. It does not serve the firm, and it marginalizes the role of the designer.

Audience Profile

An audience's ability to accept messages depends on how well the message fits with their beliefs, attitudes and values. People hold any number of beliefs, a few attitudes and a small number of core values. With a thorough understanding of these traits, a designer can develop an effective design that is appropriate to the audience. The audience profile should provide enough detail to enhance everyone's understanding of who the audience is. This section answers the following questions:

DEMOGRAPHICS
- Who is your target audience?
- What age are they?
- Where do they live?

- What is their economic status?
- What is their level of education?
- What is their marital status?

PSYCHOGRAPHIC
- What is their social status?
- What type of lifestyle do they lead?
- What beliefs do they have?
- What values do they have?
- What do they read, watch, subscribe to?

BEHAVIOR
- What does the target audience do when they engage with our communications?
- What do we want the target audience to do when they engage with the communication?

Perception/Tone/Guidelines

This section gives the foundation for how the firm will be represented visually. The perception and tone section answers the following questions:

- How do you define the organization's style?

- How does the client organization see itself?

- How do their clients perceive them?

- What does the target audience currently think and feel about your organization and the current communication?

- What do we want them to think and feel?

- How will this new communication help achieve this goal?

- What adjectives describe the way the communication and organization should be perceived?

- What are some specific visual goals the communication should convey?

Communication Strategy

What is the overall message you are trying to convey to your target audience? Is it that your company is cost-effective, secure, reliable, efficient? Communication strategy asks the question: How will we convince them? Communication strategy answers the questions:

- What is the overall message we are trying to convey to the target audience?

- How will you convey the overall message?

- What are the supporting messages that need to be communicated?

Competitive Positioning

Business is competitive. For firms to exist and prosper they must develop an explicit strategy that helps them navigate their business environment. Firms look at social, competitive, industry, and internal strengths and weaknesses to formulate strategy that moves them toward their business goals. Success is often achieved through a strategy that considers the firm's relative position in the marketplace. Without competition there can be no strategy. Competitive positioning answers the following questions:

- How are you different from your competition, and what factors will make you a success?

- What unique value do you provide your customers that others don't?

- What areas of the current communication are successful and why?

Measuring Success

When measurement tools are applied to design projects to measure performance, the success level rises. Measuring design success has always been difficult because design does not exist in a vacuum and is often just one part of a business strategy. There are, however, two ways of looking at design success.

Project success looks at the speed at which the design was executed, the number of concepts developed, the amount of client and user input gathered, and the number of changes needed. In other words, project success looks at the quality of the final design. Success metrics answer the following questions:

- What metrics will be used to determine if the communications were effective?

- What are the criteria for the project's success?

CHANGE ORDERS

Change orders are a critical part of the design process. Because of the iterative nature of design projects, change is not only expected but in most cases is a requirement for producing meaningful work. Change orders allow the designer and client to initiate and track revisions during the course of the project, and provide an opportunity to discuss how the changes might affect schedules, cost, and overall project scope.

Without a clear definition of the project, it can be difficult to determine what constitutes a change and what was part of the original specification. Because of this, it is important to start every project with a clear definition, and that definition should be recorded in the work order and the creative brief. If requests from the client are made that change the scope of these documents, a change order is used to track the variation.

Changes often happen without notice and generally require quick action to keep the project moving forward. Before changes are made, however, they must be documented so the client can approve them. By doing this, the designer protects himself from spending time on changes the client may not approve. Documenting the change ensures the designer will be compensated for his additional work.

PROJECT CLOSING

Closing out the project represents the final step in the process. The goals of this step is to make sure the final product has been delivered and has met the expectations of the client, and also to collect information about possible process improvements. This phase also allows for housekeeping activities like collecting and archiving final files.

The project officially ends when the client accepts the final design. It is critical that the final deliverable be clearly defined at the outset of the project so that the project has a distinct ending. Projects with ill-defined deliverables can become costly as clients request various odds and ends. These small items quickly add up and strain the working relationship between the designer and the client. The end of the project also offers an opportunity for feedback from the client on the process and the design.

IN CONCLUSION

As designers look to mitigate common frustrations, project management offers a framework for making sure projects stay on track and that design ideas are brought to light.

chapter 11

REFINING YOUR PROCESS

IMPLEMENTING DESIGN PROCESS

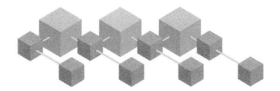

When pharmaceutical giant Bristol-Myers Squibb wanted to refine their in-house design processes, associate director of design Andy Epstein had his group engage in a classic process-improvement initiative. "What I found was that in the absence of any formalized process put in place, everybody was making it up as they went along," he says. "They were constantly reinventing the wheel by deciding who, when, and how projects got handed off to each other. It was like they were building a plane while they were in the air."

Epstein contacted Aquent Management Consultants to bring a formalized structure to their process-improvement initiative. Aquent first interviewed the different players in the creative process, gathering information about their roles and responsibilities. They then constructed a workflow chart that outlined the various steps projects went through.

Epstein and the consultants identified the existence of three different categories of work. Tier 1 projects were those where the creative team was working from scratch with a brief. Tier 2 projects were derivative and based on existing design work, for instance, turning an existing ad into an exhibition display. Tier 3 projects were production projects where an existing piece required a change, for instance, an image needed to be swapped out or type that had to be changed.

Because of the complexity of the processes required for each tier, unique workflow diagrams were developed, outlining who was included in the process, when they would be engaged, and what their role would be. Work instructions were developed for each of the steps, carefully outlining each staff member's role.

Says Epstein, "In project initiation, there might be three or four different people involved—the account management, senior designer, a print production person to bring up issues from a printing perspective. They would all have different roles at that particular step. Each step in the workflow had different work instructions associated with it."

This process helped standardize how all projects would be executed. Because of the complexity of the process, the documentation was very detailed. To make the document more accessible to the staff, it was refined so that staff would be able to understand and absorb the new process into their jobs quickly. To ensure that the staff was clear on the processes, they were given training so that the new processes would quickly become integrated into their workflow.

"It is critical that any group has their SOPs [standard operating procedures] documented," says Epstein. "In addition to being an important tool for their team, no matter how large or small, it ensures that the projects move in an orderly fashion."

Epstein also sees another advantage to refining and documenting process: "It is a great training tool for your clients, because it schools them in how they fit into the process and why certain things have to happen at certain times so that the project can be successful."

At some point in the project, a client will typically propose a one- or two-word revision and expect that it can be done in a matter of minutes. But even such a minor change requires a lot to manage quality control, to make sure what results are accurate. "It might take a half a day," says Epstein. "And the client is like, 'What the heck, I'm just asking you to change two words and you're telling me it's going to take four hours?' By having this process documented you can go back and say, 'Look, it may take the designer a matter of minutes to make the change, but we also have these other key steps involved that add extra time but that are there for your protection.'" The client may still be annoyed, but at least he sees that you're doing it for his benefit.

THE IMPORTANCE OF PROCESS

All designers use processes, whether implicit or explicit. From collecting project information to preparing design briefs and scheduling meetings, these tasks often are done with little consideration—except when something goes wrong.

As professionals, designers need to work efficiently and effectively, taking into consideration not only their own business operations but also the needs of their clients. Firms that regularly review their process and adopt a continuous process improvement philosophy will ultimately be more nimble when addressing issues with projects, staff, process, and organizational structure.

WHY CHANGE?

All organizations, whether they are a big design agency or a two-person design boutique, use processes. Process improvement is a natural step for firms as they look to refine their workflow and create more efficient work environments. By taking time to review the existing process and identify gaps in workflow, inefficient practices, or areas of frustration, designers can make changes that ultimately add to customer value. Such actions help foster long-term client relationships, which in turn improve the bottom line.

Most design firms begin with a single designer, then grow organically as clients are brought on board, the staff expanding and contracting as the situation dictates. The process that the founding designer establishes is usually based on her experiences and not necessarily planned or structured. Because of the intuitive nature of design work implicit processes are common in design firms—often its easier simply to do what you feel you need to do than it is to sit down and analyze the best way of getting something done. Additionally, design processes have not been well documented, so the ability for designers to look to others for models can be a challenge.

Once a design firm grows beyond one or two designers, the need for defined processes becomes more pressing. Design organizations of this size become collaborative environments, and they require a common understanding of "how things will get done" and a plan for managing quality, cutting waste, increasing response time and reducing costs.

SYMPTOMS OF A BROKEN PROCESS

All designers dread the client phone call that informs them of something that has gone wrong on a project. The printer misses the delivery date, a typo is discovered after the piece has been mailed, or the designer is accused of not being responsive enough. All of these can be chalked up to breakdowns in the process, and yet, when projects go astray the first thing people do is look for someone to blame. Blame seems to be hardwired into our heads. To a degree, blaming people seems like a reasonable reaction, as we expect those involved in mishaps to be accountable; however, most project-related problems are not people related but represent breakdowns in the process. Process improvement guru and author Dan Madison believes that only 15 percent of work issues are related to people, with the remaining 85 percent attributed to process.

Classic design problems include slow development times and rework, or having multiple rounds of revisions. These are easy to identify, as the client will usually let you know in no uncertain terms when these things aren't working out. But there are probably an equal number of problems that go unspoken, and as a result never get fixed. Though these issues may be small, they all result in wasted effort, which ultimately impacts your bottom line.

COMMON DESIGNER FRUSTRATIONS

- Slow concept development
- Resistance in getting concept buy-in from the client
- Changing course in the middle of a project
- An unacceptable amount of client revisions
- Getting top level sign-off
- Unclear client goals
- Marginalization of design value

COMMON CLIENT FRUSTRATIONS

- Slow or frustrating design process
- Incorrect work
- Unclear process
- No ownership of the process
- Inconsistent processes within the design firm

DESIGN PROCESS IMPROVEMENT PROCESS

Design process refinement includes seven steps.

1. Create the team
2. Create a process chart of the existing process
3. Review client needs
4. Create a best-practice process chart
5. Create a new process chart
6. Share the new process with the team
7. Test the new process

EVALUATING YOUR PROCESS

Process evaluation is made up of several basic steps. These include the creation of the team, defining the existing process, a review of client needs, developing a vision of the new process, and developing a strategy for implementation of the new process. These steps provide a format for evaluating process that considers staff, client, and management perspectives on process improvement.

STEP 1: CREATE THE TEAM

The old adage "people support what they help create" is particularly true when it comes to process improvement. For many years, workers acted as pawns for management who usually had little or no firsthand knowledge of their workers' activities. By the 1960s, quality management pioneer Kaoru Ishikawa had introduced the idea of quality circles, a system where managers looked to the people who actually did the work to make improvements in production, safety and design. This shift from a top-down management style is credited with creating a more engaged workforce and ultimately more efficient work environments.

The first step in creating the process improvement team is to identify the various people and roles that will be active in the process. The list will include people from both the design and the client sides. Anyone who has a role to play in the process should be included on the team, as their input and participation are critical for the success of the exercise.

Getting Buy-In

As it's been noted, the first step to getting buy-in from participants is to invite them into the process. Again, your mantra should be, "People support what they help create." But beyond just inviting them into the conversation, you must understand what motivates them. By connecting with them on a values basis, you inspire them to become active participants. Do they care about quality? If so, speak to them in terms of quality. Do they care about creativity? Then speak to them about creativity and how the new process accommodates their interest. People are emotional. They react to ideas that have meaning to them. They don't care about your agenda—only their own. To get them to actively participate, you must bring them into the process with the promise that they will get something out of it.

STEP 2: CREATE A CHART OF YOUR EXISTING DESIGN PROCESS

The next step in analyzing your design process is to chart out the specific activities that you engage in during your projects, and identify roles and responsibilities. A standard process flowchart will list project participants down the left-hand side and tasks listed out in a timeline across the page.

To create a chart of your design process, you'll need a large space that multiple people can view at the same time. Sticky notes and whiteboards work best, as they allow for easy correction. Outlining your process is not as easy as it sounds, and you will likely need to make changes along the way.

In step two, you begin to identify the various activities that make up the process. Working left to right, write out the various steps in your process, using the channels to assign specific steps to specific roles. The activities you identify must reflect what is actually happening in your process and should not be idealized. The activities should not go into too much detail, as your chart will get too big. Activities should easily break down into individual tasks.

Creating the Design Cross-Functional Flow Chart

Team members should then ask themselves what excellence looks like at each step in the process. Once the chart is complete, review it with your team to check for accuracy. If all are in agreement, the team can move onto the next step.

The Four Lenses of Process Analysis

In his book, *Process Mapping, Process Improvement, and Process Management,* Dan Madison identifies four lenses for analyzing process: frustration, time, cost, and quality. These lenses help pinpoint areas that are in need of refinement and act as a quick way to run diagnostics on a process.

Frustration

The frustration lens looks at the process from the perspective of the people directly involved. By bringing the team together and moving through the activities, everyone involved is given the chance to identify points of frustration. While the frustration lens is being used, participants should be reminded to focus on the process and not the people involved in it. People-related issues need to be handled separately with a manager. By identifying areas of frustration, designers and clients have the opportunity to discuss freely what isn't working and identify key problem areas and potential solutions. Discussing frustrations with team members and clients opens the door for improvements that come directly from the people doing the work and receiving the work.

Visually charting the process makes problem areas easy to identify. By having the process mapped out, areas of conflict can be identified and seen in relation to other activities. Additionally, you are able to see who owns the problem area, and whether problems are being created upstream or downstream.

Once areas of frustration have been identified, the team should brainstorm about possible fixes. Have each team member write a solution for the issue on a sticky note and hang them by the problem area on the chart. Hold off on any discussions about the solutions until all of the lenses have been employed.

STEP 3: TALK TO YOUR CLIENTS

After talking to several of your clients, you'll have a good sense of the strengths and weaknesses of your process, so you'll be prepared when examining these on a micro level. But before examining specific areas of your process, you'll need to look at your entire process as a whole. An understanding of what you're doing over the course of a project will help you to understand the dependencies that exist from phase to phase.

The first step is to ask clients what it is they need from the process. Ask them to list these in order of priority. They should then evaluate how well the current process meets those needs. By doing this, designers can get a better idea of what customers truly value. Often designers assume (or project) that clients are as interested in award-winning design, when in actuality they have other criteria for determining success. Once the list of criteria is created, designers should ask clients what the best performance for each of the areas looks like.

DETERMINING CLIENT NEEDS

- What do clients want from the design process?
- How well does the design team meet those needs?
- What does optimum performance look like for this criteria?

STEP 4: CREATING A BEST-PRACTICE FLOW CHART

Organizations regularly look to competitors to understand new and more efficient ways of operating. By reviewing the practices of others, designers can break out of process ruts and discover new methods for working. The team should look to competitors (who do similar types of projects), as well as organizations that may be outside of the design industry but have a reputation for outstanding process. Once identified, these processes should be mapped out in a similar way as the initial design process chart. The team should then compare their process with that of the competitors, identifying activities that are unique or that are not considered in their own chart, finding gaps between their current performance and what is considered excellent performance.

STEP 5: CREATE THE NEW PROCESS CHART

When developing the new process chart, it is important to remember the overarching goal, which is to provide added value to the client. By looking back at how clients described what was valuable to them, designers can focus on specific changes when creating the new process. The redesign needs to look at the process anew. Although there will probably be valuable elements in the old process, designers should strive to see the new process with a fresh perspective.

One way of developing the new process is to ask participants to do some blue-sky thinking. The ability to envision what does not exist is a skill that most designers are fairly comfortable with. In the redesign it can be helpful to think about what the optimum process would look like. A quick way to document the team's thoughts and get unique perspectives on how the process could be improved is through a simple brain-writing exercise. These exercises can be written from the team's perspective or even the client's, and can take on several formats including writing about a specific goal (create the best customer experience, create the best quality product, etc.), or just an overall perspective on optimizing the process.

Once the blue-sky process has been written, participants will need to outline it in a process flow chart, discussing what is doable and what needs to be discarded as they go. The group then refines the chart until consensus is reached.

STEP 6: SHARE THE NEW PROCESS WITH THE TEAM

Share the new process with clients and staff. By presenting the new process and asking for feedback, you build a collaborative spirit.

STEP 7: TEST THE NEW PROCESS

Once staff and clients define and approve the process, they need to test it to find any activities that might break in a real-life situation. The design team can run simulations of a mock project, where each person takes on the role of a project stakeholder. The goal in this exercise is to push the process to the limit to see where it will break.

When the team feels the process is workable, they should test it on a limited basis—starting with projects where the risks are low. Testing the process with one or two real projects does two things: It provides the team with a final opportunity to make adjustments and also gives them a chance to gain confidence in using the process.

IN CONCLUSION

Identifying the cause of problems is a challenging task. Many times, it appears that the staff are the cause of mishaps when it is in fact the lack—or the breakdown—of a process. Process provides a common understanding of "how things get done" and mitigates wasted efforts. The evolution of design studios from small boutiques to full-blown agencies often happens in an organic way. As firms mature and more participants become part of the process, a well-defined framework for working is useful and necessary.

ACKNOWLEDGMENTS

This book could not have been possible without generous support of the design community. Over the last three years I had the opportunity to speak with some of the best and brightest in the industry, all of whom graciously shared their experiences and knowledge with me. My thanks goes out to all of you.

Sean Adams, AdamsMorioka; American Institute of Graphic Arts; Mira Azarm, University of Maryland; David C. Baker, Recourses Inc.; Karen Beach, Red Clover Design; Audrey Bennett, Rensselaer Polytechnic Institute; John Bielenberg, C2; Tim Bruce, Lowercase, Inc.; Allison Bucchere, Creative Lift; Stefan Bucher, 344 Design; Alonzo Canada, Jump Associates; Emily Carr, Gensler; Justin Carroll, Hamagami/ Carroll, Inc.; Kevin Cheng, Off Panel Productions; Emily Cohen; Matt Cooke, Iron Creative Communication; Ricardo Crespo, Mattel; Jon Dalton, Philips; Heidi Dangelmaire, 3iying; Troy Dean, InvestorPlace Media; Pamela DeCaesar, Sterling Brands; Todd Decker, DIY Network; Design Management Institute; Mark Dziersk, BrandImage; Andy Epstein, Designer Greetings; Kim Erwin, IIT Design; Matt Fangman, Fangman Design; Henning Fischer, Adaptive Path; Luis Fitch, UNO; Rose Gardea Holston, Aviso Communications; Von Glitschka, Glitschka Studios; Evan Graner, Wells Fargo; Amy Gustincic, Satellite Design; Tim Hale, Fossil; Gil Hanson, Hanson Design; Brain Haven, Forrester Research; Mike Joosse, AIGA; Diane Klein, Hipbone Design; Paul LaPlaca, Graco; Tim Larsen, Larsen Interactive; Dan Madison, Value Creation Partners; Dave Mason, smbolic; Brian Massey, Conversion Sciences; Scott Matthews, Xplane; Shawn McKinney, Savannah College of Art and Design; Jose Nieto, Square Zero; Paul Nini, The Ohio State University; Dmitry Paperny, Time Inc. Interactive; Carla Peay, The Creative Group; Shel

Perkins, Shel Perkins Associates; Joel Poldony, Apple University, Yale University School of Management; Kerry Polite, The University of the Arts; Darrell Rhea, Cheskin Added Value; Ben Roth, George P. Johnson; Dan Saffer, Kicker Studio; Liz Sanders, MakeTools; RitaSue Siegel, Siegel Resources; Ellen Shapiro, Shapiro Design Associates; Nathan Shedroff, California College of the Arts; Daniel Schutzsmith, School of the Visual Arts; Rob Swann, BrandImage; Dori Tunstal, University of Illinois at Chicago; Petrula Vrontikis, Vrontikis Design; Rob Wallace, Wallace Church; Todd Wilkens, Adaptive Path; Brad Wilkerson, 68 Comeback; Scott Young, Perception Research Services.

Special thanks to Megan Lane Patrick for helping getting this project moving in the right direction, Amy Owen for her guidance throughout the process, Grace Ring for her outstanding design, and Shawn McKinney for his contributions and insights.

INDEX

Absolut Vodka, 214

Adams, Sean, 99–101

AdamsMorioka, 99–101

Adaptive Path, 13, 82, 122, 146, 168, 247

Agile methods, 23, 252

All Consuming Images, 210

Allison, Ralph, 231

Amazon, 9, 135

American Marketing Association, 232

analogies, 36, 197–201

Anthem!, 49

AOL Living Network, 142

Apple, 58, 120, 137, 213

Aqua Teen Hunger Force, 132–133

Aquent Management Consultants, 273

Armstrong, Neil, 119

Artful Making, 178

AstraZeneca, 213

AT&T, 49

audiences, 32, 145, 154–159, 268–269.
   See also consumers; design research user
   experience approach
   collaboration with, 45–49
   feedback from, 142, 223–225
   needs of, 35, 101, 104, 107–110
   perspective of, 53–57
   understanding, 140–175

Austin, Robert, 178

Ayling, Bob, 110

Back of the Napkin, The, 187

Baker, David C., 72

Balanced Scorecard measurement tool, 138–139

Basecamp, 262

BBDO advertising agency, 184

Beefeater, 214

Beirut, Michael, 178–179

Bell Labs, 50

benchmarking, 129–131, 189, 221-223

Bennett, Audrey, 145

Bennis, Warren, 44

Beyond Reason, 90

Bielenberg, John, 53, 176, 179, 182

Blyth Industries, 104–106

Boatwright, Peter, 97

Body Shop, The, 58, 135

brainstorming, 36, 184–188, 190–191

BrandDynamics, 245

BrandImage Desgrippes & Laga,
   46–47, 190, 226

Bristol-Myers Squibb, 273

British Airways, 108–110

Bruce, Margaret, 234, 238

Bruce, Tim, 70, 267

Bucchere, Allison, 142–143, 201

Bucher, Stefan, 77, 83

*Built to Last: Successful Habits of Visionary
   Companies*, 118

Burdick, Anne , 3

Burj Al Arab Hotel, 219

BusinessWeek, 3

Byrne, John, 7

C2, 53, 176

Cagan, Jonathan, 97

Canada, Alonzo, 112–113, 139

Carr, Emily, 28, 78

Carson, David, 215–217

Carucci, Ron, 84

Casey, Jim, 17

change orders, 264, 271

Changemakers, 122–123

Cheaper by the Dozen, 41

Cheng, Kevin, 192

Chermayeff, Ivan, 209

Cheskin, Louis, 56, 102, 231

Cheskin Added Value, 7, 36, 56, 102

Chevrolet, 45–46

Choice Hotels International, 150
Chrome web browser, 192
Chuck Taylor sneakers, 45
CIGNA corporate headquarters, 44
Cingular Wireless, 213
Ciravolo, Tish, 151
Clients for Life, 68
clients, 29, 65–96
  client review meeting, 211–213
  client sign-off, 33–34, 52
  presenting ideas to, 225–228
  relationship with, 28-30, 65-96
  talking to, 53, 279–280
Cluetrain Manifesto, 146
Coca-Cola, 66, 146–147, 213-214
Cohen, Emily, 253, 262
collaboration, 2, 4–7, 11–13, 22, 24, 27, 42-49,
  65–96, 144–146, 178-179, 261
Collins, James, 117–118
Color Marketing Group, 214
Colour Juice, 45
Commercial Impacts of Design, 235–238
communication, 33, 78, 112–113, 136,
  237, 262, 270
competition, 32–33, 57, 125–127,
  211-213, 222, 270
  competitive strategies, 94–95, 127–128
Competitive Strategy, 126, 133
concepts, development of, 6, 18-19, 36-37, 41,
  176–205, 226–227
Converse, 11, 45
conversion analysis, 247–250
Conversion Sciences, 247–248
Cooke, Matt, 157–158
Cooper, Rachel, 4
Costco, 128
Cottam, Hilary, 148
Coupland, Douglas, 152
Covey, Stephen, 91
Cox, Tim, 130
"Creating the Identity for a $20 Billion
  Start-Up", 50
Creative Business, 225
creativity, 24-25, 41, 46–47, 179–183
  creative tension, managing, 86-87
crowdSPRING, 1
Crystal Clear, 22
Cullen, Moira, 66

customer management, 136, 246–247
Customer Scenario Mapping, 147
CVS, 55
Daisy Rock, 151
Dangelmaier, Heidi, 151
de Bono, Edward, 177, 181–183
de Mozota, Brigitte Borja, 62
DeCesare, Pamela, 39
Decker, Todd, 206–209
DeHart, Jacob, 11
Dell, 213
Deloitte Consulting, 112
Deming, W. Edwards, 13
Democratizing Innovation, 53–54
demographic studies, 34, 149–154
design, 2–5, 11–13. *See also* process
  and accountabililty, 6–7, 230–250
  design briefs, 30–33, 40, 52, 255, 264–271
  design exploratory, 213–217
  design research, 5–6, 34-36, 59,
    97-101, 106–107
  design reviews, 56, 123–124, 201–202,
    221–222, 224
  development of, 6, 19, 37, 41, 145, 206–229
  evaluation of, 37–38, 204–205, 219–221
  measuring, 232–234, 242–250
Design Experience, The, 4
Design Index, 238
Design Innovation Group, 235
Design Management Institute, 235, 239
Design Management Journal, 70
Design Methods, 24-25
"Designer's Guide to Consumer Research, A", 55
Devin, Lee, 178
Dichter, Ernest, 167
differentiation, 29, 93-95, 104–106, 128
Digital Equipment, 30
DIY Network, 206–209
Doblin, 172
documents, control, 264–271
drawing, 36, 168–170, 190–191
Drenttel, William, 60
Dreyfuss, Henry, 4, 103
Duffy, Joe, 98–99, 233
Duffy & Partners, 98, 216, 233
Dumas, Angela, 188
Dutch Boy, 151
Dzerisk, Mark, 190–191

Eames, Charles, 97
eBay, 135
Ecofont, 135
Effies, 232
e-loyalty, 155
emotion, managing, 70–71, 81, 90–91
empathy, 76–78, 104–106, 173–174,
Epstein, Andy, 66, 79, 263, 273–274
Erwin, Kim, 195–197
ESI Design, 260
Eskew, Mike, 18
ethnography, 5, 34, 36, 59, 171–174
Ewan, Stewart, 210
Extreme Programming, 22
Fast Company, 7
Fast Food Nation, 132
feedback, 22, 83–86, 187, 204–205
   from audience, 142, 223–225
   feedback loops, 37
Fifer, Julian, 12
Fifth Discipline, The, 86
Filtros, 141
Fischer, Henning, 122–123, 168–169
Fisher, Roger, 90–91
Fitch, 128
Fitch, Luis, 98, 140–141
Fitch, Rodney, 128
focus groups, 5, 11, 35–36, 161–166
Foote, Cameron, 225
Fossil Design, 48
Fountainhead, The, 43
Four Seasons Hotels and Resorts, 34
Friedman, Thomas L., 136
Funcom, 65
Future of Competition, The, 45
FutureBrand, 18
FutureNow, 157
Gagnon, Louis, 226
Gatorade, 220
General Mills, 55
Generation X, 152
Generations, 151
Gensler, 28, 78
Getty Museum, 100
Gilbreth, Frank and Lillian, 40–41
Gillette, 30
Glitschka, Von, 117, 265
goals, 31, 117–121

of business, 35, 37, 62–63, 101, 104,
   121, 138–139, 143, 180
   for critiques, 204
   of projects, 253–254
Godage, Gaute, 65
Goldstein, Robin, 156
Google, 192
Gordon, William J. J., 198–201
Gore, Al, 197
Graco, 102, 141, 211
"Graduate Education: Preparing Designers
   for Jobs That Don't Exist (Yet)", 3
Graves, Michael, 106, 210
Greenspan, Alan, 2
Greiman, April, 102
Gropius, Walter, 23, 44
GSD&M, 178
Gustincic, Amy, 264–265
Hale, Tim, 48
Hallmark, 143–144
Hammer, Emmanuel, 168
Hanson Associates, 161–163
Harley-Davidson, 105–106
HCI, 99
Heath, Chip, 225
Heath, Dan, 225
Heckler & Associates, 8
Heineken, 214–215
Heller, Steven, 3
Hertenstein, Julie, 38, 235, 239
Hill Country Barbecue, 218
Hobsbawm, Eric, 217
Howe, 151
IBM, 55
IdeaBounty.com, 1
ideation, 36–37, 145, 178, 184
IDEO, 172
images, working with, 168, 187–194
innovation, 9–10, 41, 52–53, 179
Interbrand, 37
interviews, 5, 11, 34–36, 79, 148
   one-on-one, 166–167, 174
iPod, 137
Ireland, Christopher, 36
Iron Creative Communication, 157
iStock, 1
Ito, Ora, 214
Jaworski, Janice, 49

Jones, John Chris, 23–27
Jones, Simon, 109
Jump Associates, 112, 172
Kaizen, 41
Kaplan, C. A., 183
Kathman, Jerry, 144
Kavanaugh, Patrice, 50
Kennedy, John F., 118–119
Kicker Studio, 194
Kim, W. Chan, 129
Kimono Rose, 216
Klein, Diane, 260–261
Kotler, Philip, 61
Kraft Foods, 9, 12, 39, 41, 132, 220
L'Oreal Paris, 45
Lakoff, George, 194–195
Landor & Associates, 49–51
LaPlaca, Paul, 102, 141–142, 211, 213
Larsen, Tim, 69–70
Larsen Interactive, 69
Laurel, Brenda, 99
Lean, 13, 41
LEGO, 11
Lextant, 98
Libby Perszyk Kathman, 143–144
listening, value of, 78–81
LogoTournament, 1
Logoworks, 1
Lombardi, Victor, 114
LOWERCASE, INC., 70, 267
Lucent Technologies, 49–51
Ma, Yo-Yo, 12
Made to Stick, 225
Madison, Dan, 279
MADRID study, 237–238
Mail Boxes Etc., 18
MakeTools, 4–5, 146
Making Meaning, 59
Martin, Roger, 8, 111
Maslow, Abraham, 154
Mason, Dave, 8
Massey, Brian, 247–249
matrix method, 202–203
Matthews, Scott, 169–170
Mau, Bruce, 13
Mauborgne, Renee, 129
McDougall, Alan, 135
McKinsey & Company, 137

Merholz, Peter, 247
metaphors, 189–190, 194–197
Metaphors We Live By, 194
MetLife building, 44
Microsoft, 55
Millenials, 151–152
Miller, Robert, 87–88
Miller-Williams, Inc., 87
Millward Brown, 37, 245
mission statements, 117–121
Moholy-Nagy, 23
monadic testing, 55–56, 224
mood boards, 187–188
Morgan, Christina, 168
Morioka, Noreen, 100
Motel 6, 219
Murray, Henry, 168
Mylius, Rodney, 109
"Need for Speed, The: Synchronization
     Ensures Brand Success", 49
negotiation strategies, 88–92
Netflix, 135
"New New Product Development Game, The", 22
Newell and Sorrell, 108–109
Nexium, 213–214
Nickell, Jake, 11
Nickelodeon, 100
Nieto, Jose, 52, 61
Nike, 135
Nini, Paul, 3, 13
Nonaka, Ikujiro, 22
Novartis, 12
Obopay, 133
Olins, Wally, 20
Olson Zaltman Associates, 190
Olson, Jerry, 190
Orpheus Chamber Orchestra, 112
Osborn, Alex, 184
Outside Innovation, 147
Pan American World Airways, 44
Paprika, 226
Pasteur, Louis, 180
Penn Maid, 161–163
Pentagram, 178
Pepsi, 163
Perception Research Services, 54–55, 220, 226
Perseco, 134
personas, 156–157, 248–249

Peters, Tom, 137
Phillips, Peter, 30
Pink, Daniel, 2, 171
Platt, Marjorie, 38, 235, 239
Podolny, Joel, 175
Porras, Jerry, 117–118
Porter, Michael, 104, 126–127, 133
Postrel, Virginia, 234
Potter, Stephen, 234, 238
Prahalad, C. K., 45, 137
Pratt Institute, 114
Press, Mike, 4
process, 8, 13–15, 18–23, 27–31,
    95, 236, 251–282
  management of, 40–57
*Process Mapping, Process Improvement, and
    Process Management,* 279
Procter & Gamble, 54, 220
projects, 6, 9–10, 30–34, 254–255
  alignment of, 211–213
  closing, 271–272
  monitoring, 263–271
  planning, 251–272
  summary of, 267
projective techniques, 167–171
prototyping, 5, 23, 37, 145
"Proving Our Value: Measuring Package
    Design's Return on Investment", 242
Psychology of Everyday Living, 167
Publix Super Markets, 130–131
Quaker Oats, 214
questioning, 82–86, 116, 164–166
questionnaires, 159–161. *See also* surveys
Rand, Ayn, 43–44
Rand, Paul, 17, 19, 100
Raptr, 192
Ray Gun, 216–217
rebranding, 17–20
Recker, John, 144
ReCourses, Inc., 72
Reid Smith, Ellen, 155
Reid Smith & Associates, 155
relationships, 77–92, 253–254, 262
research, 18, 36–37, 41, 50, 57, 79
  audience, 211, 220
  design, 2–4, 34–36
  market, 57–59, 142–143, 148
  participatory, 144–146

qualitative, 161–173
quantitative, 159–161
return on investment, 6, 37, 113–114, 242, 250
Rhea, Darrel, 7, 102–103
risk management, 9–10, 25–26,
    29–30, 41, 60, 93, 95
Roam, Dan, 187
RoboHead, 262
Rockwell, Chris, 98
Roy, Robin, 38, 234–235, 237–238
Royce, Winston, 22
Russo, Patricia, 50
Ryan, Claude, 17
Saffer, Dan, 194
Sagmeister, Stefan, 182
SamataMason, 8
Samsung, 7
Sanders, Elizabeth, 4–5, 146
Satellite Design, 264
Schlossberg, Edwin, 261
Schlosser, Eric, 132
Schultz, Don, 5
Schultz, Howard, 8
SCI-Arc, 100
Scion bbX, 215
Scrum, 22
See What I Mean, 192
segmentation, 34, 149–154
Senge, Peter, 86
7 Habits of Highly Effective People, 91
7–S Model, 137–139
Seybold, Patricia, 147
Shapiro, Daniel, 90
Shapiro, Ellen, 5, 72, 78
Sharp, Isadore, 34
Shedroff, Nathan, 59, 112–113, 115
Sheth, Jagdish, 68
Simon, Herbert, 23
Six Hats Thinking, 182
Six Moon Hill, 44–45
Six Sigma, 13, 41
Skype, 10
Slim-Fast, 55
smbolic, 8
Spence, Roy, 178
SPRANQ, 135
square zero, 52, 61
staffing, 259–261

Staples, 55, 220
Starbucks, 7–8, 58
Starck, Philippe, 106
Stern, Isaac, 12
Storch, Gerald, 106
storyboarding, 168–169, 192–193
storytelling, 171
strategy, 116, 137–138, 209–210
  "Strategy for Directing Innovation
    and Brand, A", 97
Strauss, 151
Stylelist.com, 143
Subject to Change, 82
surveys, 11, 79. *See also* questionnaires
Swan, Rob, 46–47, 226–227
SWOT chart, 35, 123–125
synectics, 198–199
Takeuchi, Hirotaka, 22
Tannen, Deborah, 150
Target, 7, 106
Taylor, Fredrick Winslow, 40
Tech Museum, 141
Tetenbaum, Toby, 84
Thematic Apperception Test, 168
Third Man, The, 86
Thirst, 65
"This Is My Process", 178
Threadless, 11
344 Design, 77, 83
3iying, 151
Thymes, 216
timeframe, 217–218, 222–223, 259
T-Mobile, 213
Total Quality Management, 13, 41
totemic, 188–190
Toyota, 215
transparency, need for, 13, 23, 63, 67, 72
trust, importance of, 29, 42–43, 65–67, 70, 75
Tschichold, Jan, 215
Tunstall, Dori, 171–173
Turner Broadcasting, 132–133
Twitter, 10
Tyneski, Frank, 3
typography, 109, 172, 207–208, 210,
  215–217, 227
Uhl, Kenneth, 231
unique selling proposition, 128–129
United Parcel Service, 17–18, 213

Universal Studios, 157
UNO Hispanic Branding, 98, 140–141
Upshaw, Dawn, 12
user experience approach, 246–247
Utko, Jacek, 230–231
Valicenti, Rick, 65
value, of design, 5–6, 8–15, 29–30, 32,
  45, 57, 62–63, 92–95, 234–235
Value-Creating Consultant, The, 84
values, 118, 128–129, 154
VanderLans, Rudy, 215
Varsity Media Group, 45
VH1, 100–101
Vignelli, Massimo, 215
Vinh, Khoi, 3
vision statements, 117, 119
visual communication, 36, 39, 57, 79,
  92, 94, 170, 187, 209, 211–217
visualization, 5, 37, 217–221
Vogel, Craig, 97
von Hippel, Eric, 53-54, 147–148
Vrontikis, Petrula, 79, 211, 228
Vrontikis Design Office, 79
Wallace, Rob, 9, 38, 233, 242–244
Wallace Church, 9, 233, 242
Wallas, Graham, 183
Walmart, 7–8, 106, 128, 133
Walsh, Vivien, 234, 238
Walton, Thomas, 70
Waterman, Robert, 137
Welles, Orson, 86
Whole New Mind, A, 2, 171
Wilkens, Todd, 13, 82, 146
Williams, Gary, 87–88
Wine Trials, The, 156
Winning by Design, 238
Winterhouse, 61
work breakdown structure, 138, 257–259
workflow diagrams, 273–274
World Is Flat 3.0, The, 136
Wright, Larry John, 216
XPLANE, 169
Yahoo!, 192
Young, Scott, 55, 220–221, 223, 226
Zaltman, Gerald, 147, 190
Zaltman Metaphor Elicitation Technique
  (ZMET), 147, 190

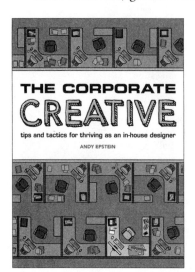